TELL ME ABOUT IT
2

A BOOK OF MEMORIES
COLLECTED BY

ST SUKIE DE LA CROIX

&

OWEN KEEHNEN

Rattling Good Yarns Press
33490 Date Palm Drive 3065
Cathedral City CA 92235
USA
www.rattlinggoodyarns.com

Cover Design by: Ian Henzel, LeatherLeaf Marketing & Design
Cover models Helen Macfarlane & Andre Chambers

Library of Congress Control Number: 2019952575
ISBN: 978-1-7341464-0-0

First Edition

For our long-suffering husbands

CONTENTS

PREFACE

Once Was Not Enough

We all have stories – sometimes poignant, sometimes entertaining, and usually very interesting. As two historians of the LGBTQ experience, we have been recording and collecting the memories, personal experiences, and anecdotes of queer folks for decades. *Tell Me About It* was a fitting extension of our ongoing work.

From the outset, the *Tell Me About It* series was intended to shed light on the lives and experiences of LGBTQ people by having them share personal anecdotes in response to a specific set of questions.

Great power resides in the sharing of our personal experiences. The process connects us and helps us to understand one another as well as ourselves. Who are we? What do we share? Where do I fit in?

Collecting the stories of LGBTQ is crucial. LGBTQ people have had their voices muted and their lives erased from the annals of history for centuries. This conspiracy of silence robbed us of something precious with repercussions that include widespread isolation, misunderstanding, secrecy, and shame. *Tell Me About It* was a way of helping to correct that legacy of suppression.

Response to the book was so overwhelming that we decided a second volume was in order. In *Tell Me About It 2* our goal was to represent a broader segment of the LGBTQ community as well as to expand the geographic scope of the entries. *Tell Me About It 2* includes stories from across the United States as well as England, Australia, Venezuela, Wales, Spain, Uruguay, the West Indies, Chile, New Zealand, and more.

Over the course of several months, we received dozens of honest, thoughtful, and funny answers from a great group of people. Choosing which responses were to be included in *Tell Me About It 2* was even more challenging than it had been for the first in the series.

Deep thanks to all the participants who shared a part of themselves. Your efforts have contributed to an insightful, entertaining, and rewarding exploration of our community, and helped us to decide that there will be a *Tell Me About It 3*.

– Owen Keehnen and St Sukie de la Croix

WHEN WAS THE FIRST TIME YOU REALIZED
YOU WERE DIFFERENT?

Washburn, IA (USA)

I think I recognized something was different about me around the age of six when I would watch *The Wild Wild West* on our black-and-white television with my father (his favorite show) and I thought Jim West (Robert Conrad) was beautiful. Even today, when I watch old episodes of the series, I still crush hard on him and his little toreador jacket. And then there are those episodes when he was shirtless in some scene, usually in peril, and I am still ogling the television screen. – Timothy Juhl

—————▽—————

London (UK)

Aged nine or ten, I liked my sister's dolls more than my action man. – Matt D

—————▽—————

Asbury Park, NJ (USA)

I think I always knew that I was different. I don't think I thought that I was a homosexual. Even when I was a homosexual, I didn't think I was a homosexual. I didn't think that my attraction was only to men. In today's terminology I would say that I'm pansexual. When I first came out, I thought I was bisexual to begin with. I think the culture we live in doesn't allow you to be bisexual. At least when I was a young man. I had to choose, and I chose men over women. I had been in a relationship with a woman for 20 years. She was the only woman I ever loved, the only woman I ever made love to. We have become friends again, so it's good. I used to say to people in the gay community all the time, "There's no difference where you put your dick, it's just as good one way or the other. The only difference is she has to strap one on to do you. And the issue is, if she was willing, it's not such a big deal." I never felt one negated the other, I always thought I could probably have sex with anybody, as long as there was a connection. As far as being different, I always felt I was different. I was very sensitive, the youngest child, the only boy, older parents, very touchy, very emotional. I was always made fun of as a child because I was emotional and very exacting about everything. Very anal retentive, as far as being OCD. It wasn't tolerated in the family I lived in. It was always a negative thing to be too emotional. It was always a negative thing to be too neat and orderly. My mother used to say to me as a child, "You're the only kid on the block, I could put you in a white suit and sit you on the porch and you'd be the only one clean after an hour, because every else would be covered in dirt and you wouldn't have a speck on you." I'd say, "Yes, because I didn't want anything to be dirty." I didn't want anything to be different in the way I looked. I wanted everything to be pure. I'm really a purist at heart. That's where my differences came in, I wasn't your typical dirty little boy, digging in dirt and playing sports. It wasn't my thing. I liked to draw pictures, I liked to dream, I was visual. It was always beaten down in me and the more they beat it down, the more I wanted to be that. It was very interesting. – Joseph S

―――――――∇―――――――

Temecula, CA (USA)

Probably since I was a little kid. I can remember praying to God and telling him, "We know that I'm a homosexual. We know that I'm gay. I know that I am." I couldn't have been more than 12 years old at the time. It's hard to be queer and religious. – Tim Barela

―――――――∇―――――――

Window Rock, AZ (USA)

I am from an immigrant family, first generation, foreign born. I lived a year on the Navajo Nation in elementary school, one of three white kids. I guess I always felt "different" because I was "different." I joke that I knew I was gay because me and a neighbor boy would go into the mountains of Window

Rock, Arizona and play *The Blue Lagoon.* He would take off his shirt and I would paint on my eyebrows with a sharpee (like Brooke Shields.) – Thomas Bottoms

————————∇————————

Chicago, IL (USA)

When I was in 6th grade and the only friends I truly wanted to hang out with were girls. They were the only people I felt comfortable with and the only people who didn't behave in a demeaning way. – Jim

————————∇————————

Montivideo (Uruguay)

It wasn't a specific moment. I realized slowly and I had sexual education in primary school, so it was normal when I was a teenager to meet men because they were my natural feelings. – Dr. Eduardo Levaggi Mendoza

————————∇————————

Chicago, IL (USA)

When my parents told me around the age of 12 to 14 ... but I really think I knew from the age of six or seven. – Don Strzepek

————————∇————————

South Bend, IN (USA)

Sometime around 12 or 13 I started noticing boys – boys in the locker room at school particularly. I remember telling myself, "This must be normal, all men look at other men's bodies." Sometime in Jr. High, I started fantasizing about kissing one of my teachers – he was this beautiful Italian man with a string mustache and wavy black hair. My conscious brain stopped me and kept insisting, "This is not right." I kept asking myself, "Why? Why am I doing this?" Gay – or even the idea of homosexuality – was something never discussed in my family, and in 1976 there was no media or Internet to simply say, "You're gay." I had no idea what this meant. I only knew, at that age, that I could never tell anyone about it ever. – Steve K

When Was the First Time You Realized You Were Different?

—————∇—————

Glendale Heights, IL (USA)

In 5th grade at Glen Hill school in Glendale Heights IL. I didn't understand this odd attraction I had to my male teacher, Mr. M_____, it wasn't sexual, just a strong attraction that I couldn't figure out. By 6th grade I had another male teacher, Mr. M_____, and though this might be "TMI" he must have worn boxers because daily you could see the outline of his very ample "appendage," though it was scary to me and I still didn't fully understand it, that is when I had a full on sexual attraction to men, I just couldn't keep my eyes off of his crotch. – Robert Hansen

—————∇—————

Detroit, MI (USA)

My earliest memories of anything, this is during the war [World War II], my uncle was too young to go into the military, but he was back at my grandmother's house. My grandmother and all my aunts who moved in. They were off working and so everyday my uncle would get up, get in the shower, and walk around naked. I was three or four years old and I was just fascinated with the male body, yet I had no idea why. It wasn't sexual, it was nothing like that. It was just this profound attraction to the male body. But I knew, and I don't know why I knew this, but I knew not to talk about it. There were never any questions. I just knew I was different. – Dan Brazill

—————∇—————

Chicago, IL (USA)

As a child I always knew I had feelings for other men. I actually organized a little "sex club" with other boys on the block. We would share any pornographic materials we could find. I loved to draw so I also drew pictures. – Kbro

—————∇—————

Milwaukee, WI (USA)

Probably around five years old, when I realized my sisters were treated differently than I was. I was envious then, but I know better now. – Louis Flint Ceci

4

When Was the First Time You Realized You Were Different?

———————∇———————

Chicago, IL (USA)

I would say during my high school years. During that time I had feelings, but did not know what they were. There was nothing as far as resources until I read a *Playboy* article that described cruising at Bug House Square. Of course, I had to investigate. – Gary Chichester

———————∇———————

(USA)

That's an easy one. My first memory, when I was standing in my back yard hugging a tree while talking to the wind. I remember saying out loud, "It's not supposed to be this way," meaning the world around me. Not long after I had a conversation with the wind, about the feelings I was having – in one specific case, an art teacher who was also the track coach for the middle schooler's always wore these short shorts, and no underwear. So I'd always be dropping my pencils to get a better view. Anyway, the gods and great goddess and spirits and all the others and I decided that because nothing in nature was a mistake, then my feelings were normal. Even if I was the only one. – Daniel Fisher aka Raid

———————∇———————

Buffalo, NY (USA)

When I was 10 years old, I knew I was attracted to men. My parents knew these people who had a boat and we went up to Lake Erie with the boat. The guy that had the boat, my dad's friend – we were jumping off the boat into the lake – the guy grabbed me, and he had this furry chest. I just knew that something was going on here. Something was happening. – Rory

———————∇———————

San Diego, CA (USA)

When I was a very, very young, if you remember '50's TV shows, even early on there was a variety of things that were different, but sexually what was special was there was a sixth sense about things. As far as being sexually different, I was sexually different but didn't realize it. I just assumed that everybody was like me. So when I liked a guy, I liked guys. Boys don't talk to girls, I had some friends who were girls, but when they were interested in me, I had no interest in them. The first guy I can remember who I can name, that I was in the point of tears over, was Chuck Conners in *The Rifleman*. He had this real daddyness to him. The clothes he was wearing were not clothes of the era, they went to New York and bought whatever, you know, but then the little armpit stains would show up and all the manliness, the super manliness was there, and I was just melting attracted to that. And then another one before that, a year or two before Chuck Connors, was a cousin that I had. We were living in San Diego and he came down from Fresno and visited. One sister who I was closest to, and boy, talk about competing for attention, and I wasn't knowing why at the time. He was wearing blue jeans, a black belt, white t-shirt, with a pack of cigarettes folded up under his sleeve, and I was almost crying in tears over that. I won't name him. – Dave

───────▽───────

Trinidad (West Indies)

I always knew I was different, the first time it sunk in I was probably 10 or 11. – Dale

───────▽───────

Long Island, NY (USA)

I was probably seven or eight years old. It was weird, I used to scope in on handsome men all the time. I would stare at them. I didn't know what it was until a year or two later when I heard about people being gay. But I knew what I wanted. – Ron

───────▽───────

San Diego, CA (USA)

To me, when I eventually understood that I was gay it was the end of a process of really understanding differentness. By the time I thought I was gay, I felt, "Oh yes, I am different and this is the expression of my differentness. I'm gay, how fitting. The feeling of being different was way, way, back. I remember one time in particular. I grew up in the Catholic church, God forgive me ... Goddess forgive me. There was one point where I was in 5th or 6th grade and I'd had enough of catechism and all that stuff. I was so angry at all the baloney. My mother was sending me off to catechism

6

class one day and I said, "I won't go. That's it." She was appalled because I was a good little boy. I was adamant. I said, "I'll never go back to that again." I knew that was so profound that I was different. I was not going to fit in to what people wanted of me. It was liberating and profound and scary. – Bill

———————∇———————

Los Angeles, CA (USA)

That was at three years old. I had a sister who has now died. We were a year and a month apart. My father treated me one way and he treated her another. With that, I always felt, "I want to be treated like he treats her. I don't want to be treated the way he's treating me, he never hugs me, he never kisses me." He wants me to go out and play ball. I'm afraid of those balls, they're coming so quick. Then he gets frustrated. Then if we are going to be punished, I really get it. With her, as soon as she starts crying, he's hugging her. I'm saying, "There's something wrong with this picture." – Kalvin

———————∇———————

Chicago, IL (USA)

In 4th grade, during a tornado drill, paired up with another boy, we played the hand slap dare game, and was turned on by his thick hands. – Martin Mulcahy

———————∇———————

Imlay City, MI (USA)

When I was younger. I felt alone at times but knew many people and was loved. When I started magic and was being a clown and performing it really set in stone that I was different and walking to the beat of a different drummer. – Greg R. Baird

———————∇———————

Chicago, IL (USA)

Probably in 8th grade. I always knew I was different. When my mother had to teach me how to kiss, I knew something wasn't right. I think it was high school prom and I said, "I don't know how to kiss." I wouldn't have known how to kiss a boy either. I always knew I was different. I never liked to do what the boys did, I liked to do what the girls did. My good friends have always been women. I have found throughout my life that they are more trustworthy than gay men. You can depend on women more than you can depend on gay men. I've had a few good friends and I can trust them, but in general I don't find gay men as trustworthy as women. – Laurie Cowall

—————∇—————

North Carolina (USA)

When I realized my parents didn't see the same etheric things that I saw – and I chose to shut down my third eye – I was probably three. But you're asking about queerness … hard to say. I remember a girlfriend's dad commenting on my playing Barbie with her, and my quick rebuttal that I was only playing with Ken! I was never not queer. – Gavin Geoffrey Dillard

—————∇—————

(USA)

You know what they say about hindsight being 20/20? Maybe age 15. I had a cousin my age, we were in love, we had sex. I always loved him. He did me. But life goes on and I went away to college. He went to a different school. Out of college I was drafted so I wound up, instead of going with the draft, I went to Navy flight training. You have to answer all the questions, "Do you have homosexual tendencies?" … "No!" I hardly knew what they were. I just knew that I liked men. – Hal

—————∇—————

New York, NY (USA)

I knew when I was a young child, really young. By kindergarten I knew I was not like other people. I didn't know what it was called. When I first started in kindergarten I remember because there was a play area that had blocks, and clothes, and shoes, and games. I was playing with a girl I was going to school with, I even remember her name, Beth ———. We were playing dress-up and I was taking all the high heel shoes and dresses. I knew that I was not like everybody else and that put the exclamation point at the end of it because a teacher came over. Other kids started to make fun of me – Beth ——— didn't make fun of me. She protected me from them. But I knew I was different then. – Keith Kollinicos aka Missa Distic

When Was the First Time You Realized You Were Different?

——————∇——————

New York, NY (USA)

At a young age. I knew that I liked boys at three years old. I say this because at the time I was growing up in a house in the South Bronx. It was a two-family house, there was another family that lived upstairs on the top floor. We had the two lower levels. They had a younger boy that lived up there and we would play together all the time because we were the same age. I can't remember who induced the "play," but we used to play in the closet in my sister's room. It was one of those things … I don't want to say it was the typical I'll show you mine, if you show me yours type of thing. It was more of a touch and feel each other's bodies kind of thing. I knew that I didn't do that with the girls and I didn't want to do that with the girls. I was only doing that with him. Now whether he did that with the other kids that we played with, I don't know. I only wanted to do that with him. Even when we were all together playing house, me and him would always sit on each other's lap. So, I knew then that I liked boys but I didn't know it was called being gay or homosexual. I found that out afterwards. I was probably about eight or nine years old before I realized what gay is. Through watching documentaries and listening to family conversations I realized how someone "different" is talked to and treated different. And you realize, "Oh, I'm just like that person they're talking to that way." It clicks in your head. – David Vega aka Lucifers Axe

——————∇——————

Windermere, Cumbria (UK)

I was always different because I was small and petite. I was kind of an observer all the time. I didn't fit in anyway. I always had absolute crushes on girls, even as young as five. There was also a gorgeous female teacher at school, and I would stalk her during playtime … if that is possible for an eight year old! I felt different because as a late developer I wasn't going through the same development as other children. – Helen Macfarlane

——————∇——————

Honolulu, Hawaii (USA)

I knew I was different as a little kid. I was maybe five and I used to dream about being in a Big Top tent. I was the ringleader. There's no reference for me to be dreaming something like that, but later on I became a dancer and produced shows, so I was a ringleader. I remember when I first felt that I was gay was in high school. There was a community center and I didn't really belong to it but I lived by it and I remember walking by and there was a guy who was teaching gymnastics after school to the kids. Of course, he had a gymnast's body and I think I had those inklings of, "Oh … tasty." – Simeon Den

—————▽—————

East Randolph, NY (USA)

I was arriving at my friend Scott's birthday party. We were in kindergarten at the time. His dad Marty was a soap opera perfect specimen – smooth, dark, handsome. As my parents were leading me around the side of the house to the kids in the backyard, Marty descended down a ladder from the roof – sweaty and shirtless. As he said hello and shook my hand, my whole body, inwardly, spasmed at his beauty. I think it was my first orgasm. I was sure that the whole world was different and that everyone had noticed my earth shifting response to his beauty, but nothing … It turned out to be just another normal day for everyone else. Granted, it took me a little while longer to figure out what exactly that initial reaction really meant, but I can tell you for sure, I never ever responded to my friends' moms that way! – Brian Kirst

—————▽—————

Maywood, NJ (USA)

When I was eight years old, at one of Aunt Rosalind's frequent summer pool parties, I walked into the living room to find eighteen-year-old Cousin Janet and her fiancé, Keith, laughing hysterically on the carpeted floor. In their bathing suits, Janet was holding a can of shaving cream and a razor while hairy-chested Keith said through snorting giggles, "Go ahead, shave it all off." I remember thinking at the time, "Oh no, don't shave off Keith's gorgeous chest hair!" But I stood there in silence, knowing enough by then not to object out loud. – Daniel M. Jaffe

—————▽—————

Maitland, NSW (Australia)

I think I always knew I was different, but I had no idea why. I came from a family that had very little normality or closeness, so there was no one to talk to about it. There were no gay role models at the time and the only time gay people were portrayed on television was as a joke to laugh at.

When Was the First Time You Realized You Were Different?

The moment that it all started to make sense to me was when I watched a program about the immoral people living in Kings Cross in Sydney. I was supposed to be horrified by the idea of men having sex with boys, but that was the moment I knew where I wanted to be and found my way there in a matter of weeks. – Ian Davies

———————∇———————

Manhattan Beach, CA (USA)

Grade school. I wasn't really a butch but I loved wearing my jeans. I hated it when my mom put me in a dress, never liked that. I loved to play baseball and skateboarding. I always hanging with the boys because the girls were playing with dolls. In the '60s, it was like, "What are you?" I just knew I liked girls. And I liked boys to hang out with because they were fun, like to do things and get dirty. Then I started getting crushes on my babysitters, if they were women and younger. Then I started getting crushes on girls in school. Then I got really angry because a lot of my good friends started getting boyfriends and they didn't want to hang with me anymore. So it was like they were with their boyfriend, and "So-and-so is with so-and-so." I didn't go to the prom, had no desire to go to any of these things. Then, as I got into high school, I saw the gap deepen, really, really deep. I hated school for that reason. – Siouxzan Perry

———————∇———————

South Bend, IN (USA)

The only thing I can recall is when I was seven or eight. My mother's side of the family always had family reunions and there was a second cousin, who was in his late-teens. I had a crush on him big time. I knew that I probably shouldn't, but I followed him around like a puppy dog. And then, when I went to high school, I wasn't interested in dating or anything like that. The only thing I liked in gym class was wrestling. – Marc

———————∇———————

Shannon, Northern Island (New Zealand)

That's a tough one because as a child I used to have spirit friends. They've been with me everywhere. I thought it was totally normal. They'd sit on my bed and I'd talk to them and my mom would say, "It's OK dear." I thought, "Am I normal or what?" But when it comes to being gay, I remember in our old farm homestead perving at my sister's boyfriend. I was checking him out. I remember when I met men with hairy forearms, I'd think, "I can't wait to be like that when I'm older." But then I grew up with seven sisters, but that's irrelevant. I would say I was probably eight when there was an attraction to my male school teachers, older guys … "I can't wait 'til I become a man." There was that sexual thing. I used to play with my friends too at 9 or 10. Even in that little country rural town there was probably a dozen gay guys there. – Gib Maudey

————————∇————————

Baltimore, MD (USA)

I was pretty young. I would guess by age 10 I knew something was different. I found men attractive, I would think about them. The biggest moment though was when I was 11 years old and I remember the centerfold of Burt Reynolds in *Cosmopolitan* magazine. I stared at that picture day after day after day. Just trying to peek under his arm, or whatever … – Cody

————————∇————————

Chicago IL (USA)

I always knew that I was "different" but there was no sexual label for it. From as far back as I can remember, I've always felt a particular connection with males. My first crush was for "the white boy" I shared a babysitter with. Even before any kind of sexual awakening, I remember liking his smell. – Chip H.

————————∇————————

Milwaukee, WI (USA)

I was very much a tomboy, growing up, so I was always different in that way, but I don't think I placed much importance on that difference until high school, when I was finding myself very much attracted to the girls at school. – Yvonne Zipter

————————∇————————

Baton Rouge, LA (USA)

I guess when I was in 2nd or 3rd grade in elementary school. I got picked on and cried a lot, so I knew based upon that, that there was something that made me different from other little boys. Now when did I realize I was gay? I was raised Southern Baptist, where homosexuals are perverts and child-molesters and they're going to hell or they're going to prison. And because of that I kept a lot of things really repressed and compartmentalized. When I'd think about it, I'd think, "Oh yeah I'm having certain feelings but that's not really who I am. This is who I am, I'm a good person. Good people don't have those feelings." I don't think it was until I saw my first gay porno mag at a bookstore on campus at LSU – I eventually went back and bought it – that I realized what these feelings truly meant. I was nineteen. – Michael Wayne

————————▽————————

Oxford (UK)

There are two types of different here, there's S&M top different and there's gay different. I realized I was S&M before gay, I think. Watching gladiator films. There's a film called *The Fixer*, quite a brutal prison type of film. I very much identified with the guys doing the brutalizing. Not the prisoners. So that's when I realized there was something S&M going on. Coming out as gay was part of me expressing my S&M side, just a pathway. For me, it wasn't as much of an issue coming out as gay, as it was for me realizing I was S&M. – Martin

————————▽————————

Southern California (USA)

I would probably say four because I always thought that girls were pretty, but I was always told, "Oh the boys are going to go crazy over you." I never identified with that. I didn't want that. I had this fascination toward girls. I remember when I first felt an attraction to women. I was maybe six and my mom took me to this company party and there were belly dancers. I was just mesmerized. I was doe-eyed and my jaw dropped watching this woman belly dance. Then my mom said, "Go belly dance with them." Of course, I was a shy little kid and said, "Oh no." Then one of the belly dancers came up behind me and hugged me and grabbed me by the arm and tried to make me dance with her. I was blushing and didn't know what to do, because there's a pretty girl, the belly dancer, and she's pretty. I don't know how to react, and I said, "Oh my god!" So that was the first time I knew as far as sexuality. And gender-wise I don't know if I had an awareness that I was different, but looking back I started acting different, I guess … something I loved doing as a kid, whenever my dad would get ready for work, he would shave. He would give me the shaving cream and I'd put it all over my face and I would take the butter knife and I would shave with my dad. I'd say, "I'm a boy too." – Bambi

———————▽———————

Fontana, CA (USA)

I was three or four. I had a sister who was a year older than me and it was her first day of school. I went with my mom to go drop her off. In the area that I grew up in, there weren't a lot of other kids around. It was just me and my sister. Up until that point I never really had friends. So when we went to this school, the kids play on the playground for a little bit, get comfortable. So I stayed there and played with my sister and that was the first time that I noticed gender because I had always played with the Barbies and never had any interest in playing with Hot Wheels or anything like that. I noticed all the boys were hanging out with the boys and I was in the group with the girls. For me, on the way home, I actually asked my mom if I was supposed to be a girl. So that's when I first noticed that something wasn't right. – Hayley

———————▽———————

Havana (Cuba)

I was a little kid. I remember I was still in Cuba and I would go for horsemanship, jumping, riding horses, equestrian. I would play the same games with the horses, the only thing is most of my riders had hooped skirts, I would make the skirts with Play-Doh. I started to notice that everybody's mom didn't allow the other kids to play with me because I would do Carnival or theater. There were always female characters everywhere, so I had to make female characters from my soldiers. The hair and the clothes and everything with Play-Doh. I must have been six. I didn't know anything about anything, but I figured later when I grew up that that's why I became a designer. – Juanmanuel Alonso.

———————▽———————

Riverside, CA (USA)

I was about five or six years old. A lot of interests weren't like boys growing up. I felt very uncomfortable dressing the way that I was told to dress. I had taken my best friend's sister's shirt and some shorts and at night I would literally hide them, then put them on under the covers to go to sleep because

I felt very relaxed and comfortable for the first time. Throughout the whole day, I didn't like doing boys things. It progressed and got a lot more intense after that. I remember being in the bathroom crying and praying that I'd wake up as a girl the next day. Thinking about it, thinking about things I could do to get there. – Chloe Decamp

——————▽——————

Vicksburg, MS (USA)

Probably very early around when I was five or six. I was in kindergarten and I always felt different. I like to play with the girls but I didn't like to play dolls and houses. I wanted to be the husband, I wanted her to be the wife. That was the beginning of it to me. That's when it started. Of course, I could see it but nobody in my family would recognize it. It was all dresses and pigtails. At 12 years-old I tried to tell my mother I was in love with my best friend. We were driving back from a swim meet and she said, "Of course you're in love with your best friend, that's your best friend." I remember saying, "No mom, you don't understand, I love her." Of course, I didn't understand what that meant either, but I remember my mom getting really, really, quiet. I was 12. That summer I entered finishing school and I had to go to finishing school every summer from 12 to 18. By the time I reached 18 my mother decided to tell me the reason she sent me to finishing school was so that I could become a lady. "And ladies don't like other ladies like that." So, if I'm a lady I'm not going to be gay. That was her reasoning. She wanted me to be either a doctor or a lawyer, or marry a doctor or a lawyer. I ended up marrying a redneck with a truck, a second-grade education and a multi-million-dollar business. – Jade

——————▽——————

Westmont, IL (USA)

I think I always realized that I was different in one way or another. Only because I can remember growing up in Illinois outside Chicago, 30 minutes outside Chicago. One of my parents was one of the biggest racists ever in the world. His entire family was. Mom's family was too. My mother didn't say anything one way or another about it. I always wanted to be everybody's friend. If they stood out, I wanted to be a part of that. I always wanted to be somebody who was different, someone who didn't fit in, a square peg. I remember there was an African-American family in our neighborhood. I thought, "Oh my god!" That was the first time I really experienced a friendship with a black girl. I was so happy. She had a great family, a good atmosphere, and I remember saying to my dad, "What if I married a black person?" And he said, "I'll kill him and then I'd kill you." I thought to myself, when he said that, "That just makes me want to go and be different." I mean, I love my father, but I remember thinking, "I'll risk it." I think that was probably 1972 that I realized that I was not like other kids in my neighborhood and that I was a little different. And it was around that time that I was first kissed by a girl and I didn't stop it. I can remember her name was Becky ———— and she had red hair – nobody I'd be attracted to now. But like I said I didn't stop it at all. – Cathy Melton

————————∇————————

Weymouth, MA (USA)

I think I was in 2nd grade. I was a good kid and a good student. I really enjoyed learning. I had a teacher in 2nd grade named Miss Lefferson – she was leaving after my 2nd grade was completed. I can't remember why, where, or what, but at the end of that last day of my 2nd grade I sat and cried because she was leaving. I think there weren't too many other girls sitting and crying because Miss Lefferson was leaving. I wouldn't say that I knew it then but, in retrospect, I'd definitely say that was one of my first inklings of what I should have recognized as difference. – Leslie Tisdale

————————∇————————

White Deer, Texas Panhandle (USA)

I grew up in the Texas Panhandle, White Deer is a little town of 1,000 people, out on a farm. I didn't have anyone to identify with. There were certain students who had the reputation of being gay but they were not taunted, they were not teased, or bullied. It's hard to be gay in a small town. Half the people in the town are my mom's relatives, half were my dad's. That's an exaggeration but it was back in that age when family was close to you. Then one day I crossed the county line. And that in itself can be the name of a book. Then I saw something I had not seen before. I think I can tell a story that a lot of men have. I never did quite feel like what I was expected to be as a kid. I was one of the last ones to be chosen for the baseball team. I wanted to play in the right field because there was less chance that I would be dealing with the ball. When I did, I wasn't very successful at throwing it. I did the boy things, I did the boy scouts, 4H, Club Calves, things that were masculine and was expected of boys on the farm. It might have been some guidance from my dad because he may have known that I was different and tried to channel my interest to these boy things. But it seemed like in Junior

High or even before, it seemed like I wasn't like Lewis _____ and I wasn't like Richard _____ . I thought they were the examples of what being a man or boy should be. They were classmates and one was always chosen as the team captain. I did play football in Junior High but I did not in High School. I gave it a shot, but it didn't fit me. I wasn't tough enough. – Don Rockwell Coffee

———————∇———————

Albuquerque, NM (USA)

Well, I knew in a nonchalant non-bothered way by 3rd grade; I was definitely a boy who was like the girls instead of being like the other boys, and I was proud of it and did things to underscore and emphasize it. The first time it really hit me that I was different in a way that was maybe going to cause everyone forever and ever to treat me awful was the summer after 5th grade when I was 11. Went to a summer camp where NO ONE knew me so I was starting fresh, and all the same horrible hateful behaviors reappeared almost immediately; prior to that, I had assumed that I had just had the random misfortune to be in the same school with some kids who hated me, and that they recruited other kids to torment me. – Allan Hunter

———————∇———————

Windsor, CT (USA)

1960? I always knew I was "different." It was how I knew what sex was. It was the thing I was bad at or wrong about. – David Pratt

———————∇———————

Seattle, WA (USA)

Probably in junior high to some degree, more definitely in high school. I didn't understand what gay was, so I just thought, 'Nice looking guy," and I had some insignificant things happen with guys at that point. But I remember when I was in elementary school, I would walk about five blocks down to play dolls with a girl that was in my class. I didn't really think anything of that, and my parents didn't seem to think anything of it, and her parents didn't think anything of it. So, it was not much of a problem. But looking back, that and my penchant for listening to Broadway musicals, not being interested in sports, being interested in the design of my room … all those little things, you look back and say, "Yes." – OT

When Was the First Time You Realized You Were Different?

————————∇————————

(Venezuela)

I was seven years old. I was playing with my cousin who was also seven years old. I realized something was going on and it was fun. We were touching each other, and we got caught. He got beaten by my aunt very hard. My mom said, "I'm going to tell your dad." I was so scared because I thought my dad was going to kill me. But nothing happened. I think my dad somehow didn't want to deal with that. – Carlos

————————∇————————

Detroit, MI (USA)

You know I'm an artist. I was always better than everyone else at that. Especially as a little kid. I realized I was gay around the age of 12. I couldn't differentiate between boys and girls, which one I liked better. But I prefer men, I like the way they smell. – Jack Farquhar Halbert

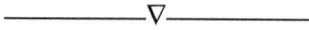

————————∇————————

(USA)

I think when I was 16. I do remember being in my room wondering what was wrong with me. I didn't connect it to being gay or anything sexual. I just had a problem with people and relating to them. I just thought, 'What's wrong with me, why can't I have friends." That may have been more than "gay" but "gay" was part of it. It changed when I was 21. I'm a late-bloomer. I had a gay experience and a straight experience. I spent four years mulling over that. Then, at 25, I decided I couldn't deny my gay side. So, let's just go with it for a while and see what happens. – Paul

————————∇————————

Canton Township, OH (USA)

When I was in the eighth grade I would cover my eyes with my arm in bed and fantasize about fooling around with other kids my age naked. I would flip it to a girl in my mind because I believed thinking about doing that with a guy was wrong. I would say to myself, "If I think about a guy for a little bit that is ok." – Mike Gifford

When Was the First Time You Realized You Were Different?

————————∇————————

London (UK)

You mean sexually attracted to men? I don't remember a date when I wasn't. When I was nine years-old I hadn't formed a concept of sexuality. I was highly attracted to men and highly indifferent to women. – Tess Tickles

————————∇————————

Milwaukee, WI (USA)

When I realized how much I loved dolls and how little interest I had in toys for boys. Whenever I flew a kite, I imagined myself Marlo Thomas on the opening credits of *That Girl*. I suppressed so much of me for years. No more. – Anonymous

————————∇————————

Juarez, Chihuahua (Mexico)

I'm from Mexico, so the first time I started having feelings for anybody was when I had a crush on this girl. This would have been when I was in 1st grade. I was in a Catholic school. Later in life I realized why I had a crush on her. It was because she looked like a boy. That's when I started feeling different. Then I started having a crush on the boy across the street. That's when I realized, "Well this is weird." I just didn't understand. I just knew that I liked being around him. He made me happy. – Felix

————————∇————————

Rugby (UK)

About seven years old. I didn't recognise it as desire, certainly not anything sexual, but I was aware of a sensibility that made me different. I wasn't particularly camp or effeminate as a boy, but sensitive, with an interest in aesthetics, popular culture, and an aversion to team sports. I didn't know I wanted to be with a guy, or what that meant, but somehow a part of me knew marriage and kids were not going to be my destiny. – Diesel Balaam

————————∇————————

When Was the First Time You Realized You Were Different?

Chicago, IL (USA)

I've always known, even before I knew what sex was, and knew to not talk about it. – Anonymous

———————∇———————

Chicago, IL (USA)

I realized I was different when I was in grammar school and found myself attracted to a P.E. teacher at the school. I can still picture his bushy mustache to this day but I won't embarrass him or me by disclosing his name but my friends who went to Goethe School will probably have a good idea who it is. – Robert Castillo

———————∇———————

(Chile)

I was 10, maybe earlier than that. I was in Chile at that time. I went to this beach and this beach has a lagoon on the side. I remember there were three or four guys in the middle of the water. I was swimming around them. Their wives were on land. I was looking at this guy and I noticed that something was going on. They take their swimming suits off. I really wanted to get close to them to see what was going on. I still remember the level of the water. There was not anything covering my eyes, but I was trying to keep my eyes open under water, because I wanted to see what was going on. My memory of seeing these guys, is that they were super-attractive to me at the time while the water was burning my eyes and they were waving to their wives. Now I can process what was going on, they were playing with each other" – Ives

———————∇———————

New York, NY (USA)

I was five years old in Mrs. Hollander's kindergarten class. I was with some kids playing house, and I was supposed to be the father. I remember thinking that I could never see myself doing that. I suppose the next time was when I was eight years old and had a crush on Billy Mumy in *Lost in Space*. – Ian H

———————∇———————

WHAT MOVIE, OR TV SHOW, WERE YOU OBSESSED WITH AS A CHILD, OR TEEN, AND WHAT CAUSED YOUR OBSESSION?

Temecula, CA (USA)

I was obsessed with TV in general. I can't remember a specific TV show I was obsessed with. I was the type of kid who had to watch television before I went to school in the morning. I knew what time it was to go to school because they had these little five and ten minute kid shows on, and when this show was over, and the next show was over, I knew that I had just enough time to get to school. I was just obsessed with TV and when September came and the new line-up of fall shows would be listed in the *TV Guide*, they'd have a grid. I would mark it, "We're going to watch this and that." – Tim Barela

———————▽———————

Window Rock, AZ (USA)
Indianapolis, IN (USA)
Chicago, IL (USA)

I saw the trailers in Window Rock, Arizona and the movie in Indianapolis Indiana, but an all-time favorite is *Looker* by Michael Crichton starring Albert Finney and Susan Dey. It deals with models becoming perfect, and an advertising agency that downloads them for commercials. The movie was viewed as ridiculous in the early '80s but has become shockingly prescient. "Hi, I'm Cindy, the perfect female type 18-25. How may I sell for you?" I mutter that to myself whenever I notice someone trying to convince me to buy something.

The movie was released on DVD. A friend bought me a copy when we lived together in Chicago, IL. Great movie. – Thomas Bottoms

———————▽———————

Chicago, IL (USA)

Little Gloria Happy at Last. I found the old money atmosphere and larger than life characters an incredibly appealing distraction from my own unhappiness at school. Spent hours upon hours at the library researching the Vanderbilts, Astors and other gilded era families. – Jim

———————▽———————

Montivideo (Uruguay)

The Seventh Seal by Ingmar Bergman. I was discovering cinema and death was an enigma when I was a teenager and I was scared. – Dr. Eduardo Levaggi Mendoza

———————▽———————

Chicago, IL (USA)
San Francisco, CA (USA)

All my life, well at least since the age of eight years old, I've had a love affair with San Francisco. It all started on a Sunday night when my parents reluctantly let me stay up late to watch the 1936 film *San Francisco* with Clark Gable and Jeanette MacDonald. I lay on the floor in front of the TV with my favorite pillow clutched to my little body and I was in love, with the opera, the drama, or the love triangle? Who knows? I only knew I wanted my own Blackie Norton, the role played by Clark Gable, a bad boy with a heart of gold. I wasn't Jeanette MacDonald, but I daydreamed that my own Blackie Norton fighting his way through fire, flood, and other acts of God to rescue me from the clutches of some villain or the humdrum of everyday life. That's one of my earliest memories of same sex attraction.

Perhaps even earlier than that when my parents were temporarily separated, and my mom was seeing a long-distance truck driver. He had a relief driver with him, I don't recall his name now, and mom brought me with her to the motel where they were staying, and this guy fixed a broken toy for me. I don't know why, but I liked him, maybe because he fixed my toy, maybe it was deeper than that, but I liked him and I can still see his face today if I close my eyes so I knew I was different than other boys. That and when I was in seventh grade there was a dance in school and the teacher made all the girls put their right shoes in the middle of the floor. She instructed the boys to grab a shoe and dance with the girl who belonged to that shoe. I remember watching all the guys diving for them, and I thought to myself they all kind of silly fighting over them that way. I would rather have taken a boy's shoe instead. – Jerry S

———∇———

Gainesville, FL (USA)

The Rocky Horror Picture Show – I started seeing it when I was 15 years old. It was an eye-opening experience for me to see a sexy transvestite, homosexuality being shown, and (since I was a budding show tune queen) great music. What's not to be obsessed with? (Plus, in Gainesville, if you weren't part of the college scene, there was NOTHING else to do!) It's also interesting to note that different cities have different traditional calls, so it makes a different experience wherever you go to see it. – Eric Andrews-Katz

———∇———

Greenwich, CT (USA)

I wanted to be the wicked witch from *The Wizard of Oz*. – Thomas Autumn

———∇———

Milwaukee, WI (USA)

I know *The Wizard of Oz* frightened me, and I would have nightmares about tornadoes well into my teens. – Louis Flint Ceci

———∇———

Madison, WI (USA)

42nd Street, or any Busby Berkeley movie, because they were so outrageous for their era, then *Star Wars*. I was a music freak and was really into the soundtracks for the series. – Vincent Rideout

———∇———

What Movie, or TV Show, Were You Obsessed with, as a Child or Teen?

Chicago, IL (USA)

Just about any Burt Reynolds movie, especially when shirtless with that hairy chest. – Robert Hansen

———————∇———————

St. Louis, MO (USA)

When I saw the TV ads for *The Poseidon Adventure* in 1972, I was immediately hooked. That big wave looming over the cruise ship, the people in the ballroom sliding as the room steeply tilted ... I HAD to see that movie! The weekend it opened there was a giant full-page ad in black and red ink in the newspaper. I bugged my parents to take me to see it, and even when they said they would, I kept at it to make sure they wouldn't forget. On a Friday night we went to the Mark Twain cinema in St. Louis and waited in a crowded lobby, with me gazing intently at the lobby cards on the wall showing scenes from the film. I wasn't disappointed that night. Whenever we'd visit my aunt, her house was down the road from Ronnie's Drive-In and I'd stand out on her front lawn and look way down the road to see if that capsizing scene was happening. If my family was leaving before that scene, I'd get my stepfather to pull over and we'd sit on the side of the road to watch that specific scene. I was in fourth grade at that time, and at recess I started a Poseidon Adventure of my own with a big group of friends. We'd start on the wooden cabin structure and sing *Auld Lang Syne* and then start screaming and "falling" down to the ground. From there we'd go all over the playground, climbing over structures and going down the slide, all as if we were making our way to the back of the ship. The group got bigger and bigger as the days went on, we never tired of it. I'm sure my parents thought it was a strange obsession, but for me it was a sense of adventure in which I knew I'd survive every time. I told my parents we got a lot of good exercise from the game, so it was a win-win. To this day I still love that film, and the other film that came close to this obsession for me (and friends) was the TV movie-of-the-week, *The Horror at 37,000 Feet*. – Todd Jaeger

———————∇———————

California (USA)

I Love Lucy or *The Jack Benny Show*, but these weren't sexual like *The Rifleman*. – Dave

What Movie, or TV Show, Were You Obsessed with, as a Child or Teen?

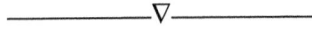

———————∇———————

Chicago, IL (USA)

Torch Song Trilogy and *My Beautiful Launderette* ... the champagne scene!!! – Don Strzepek

———————∇———————

California (USA)

Bewitched, my two favorite characters on it were Aunt Clara, the one that got lost and collected doorknobs, and Uncle Arthur. Of course, at that point, as a kid, I had no idea that Paul Lynde was gay. There was just something about him, that he said all the things that everybody else wanted to say but wouldn't. He was always getting into trouble but always came out fine in the end. It was cool, 30 years later, to meet him in person. – Art Healey

———————∇———————

Hoboken, NJ (USA)

Dark Shadows comes to my mind right away. I loved vampires. I loved that whole different artsy-fartsy kind of thing. People in costumes, drinking blood. I was into vampires, always have been. – Joseph S.

———————∇———————

Detroit, MI (USA)

Adventures in Paradise. It took place in the South Pacific. This guy owned a sailboat and he would sail between the southern islands, Fiji and so-on, taking people and delivering stuff. The dude was so fucking hot. He was amazing. – Dan Brazill

———————∇———————

Chicago, IL (USA)

The Poseidon Adventure. It was exciting and racy for a teenage boy and that capsizing! – Kbro

What Movie, or TV Show, Were You Obsessed with, as a Child or Teen?

——————∇——————

Chicago, IL (USA)

I saw *Mildred Pierce*, with Joan Crawford, one Sunday afternoon on TV when I was probably 12 and I thought it was the greatest movie ever made. Joan's suburban home was SO much the home I someday wanted, and the world she lived in was so urbane and glamorous. Zachary Scott was so svelte as the love interest, but I wanted to be the Jack Carson character; he was so big, so manly, so insanely self-assured. He was the only one who fucked Mildred and didn't care. If I couldn't BE him (and fuck Mildred), then I wanted him to fuck me. – R.M. Schultz

——————∇——————

Chicago, IL (USA)

The movie I was probably most obsessed with was the *Wizard of Oz*. The music and the magic took me "over the rainbow." I still love Rainbows. Other films would include *Auntie Mame, Singing in the Rain, The Women* and *Some Like it Hot.* – Gary Chichester

——————∇——————

(USA)

Lost in Space. I was a nerdy kid growing up. I didn't have many friends in school. *Lost in Space* was my obsession. I had posters on my bedroom wall. – Rory

——————∇——————

(USA)

The whole Saturday morning cartoon lineup from 1975-1982. After '82, cartoons went to shit. My obsession when I was five was the *Super Friends*. Especially after they added the *Challenge of the Super Friends*. More heroes, and more villains. I always wanted to see *Wonder Woman* and *Aquaman* get it on. It all changed in 1981. *Thundarr the Barbarian.* I was hooked. I wanted to be Ariel, but I wanted to make out with Ookla the Mock. He was so much cooler than some sword wielding hippie with a thirst for violence any day. – Daniel Fisher aka Raid

What Movie, or TV Show, Were You Obsessed with, as a Child or Teen?

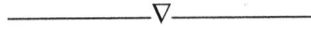

—————————∇—————————

Nashville, TN (USA)

Bewitched. I wanted magical powers. I wanted to be a witch, not a warlock. – Driveshaft

—————————∇—————————

(USA)

The Rocky Horror Picture Show. Need I say more? I do actually. In high school and college, I worked at a movie theater. That movie did so much for me as a young gay man. I see you shiver with anticipation. – Tripp

—————————∇—————————

San Diego, CA (USA)

The Rifleman. Chuck Connors was so macho. It's interesting, because as an adult that's not the type of guy I'm interested in. I'm more attracted to androgynous men. Connors was so commanding. I look back now and think, "What a severe guy." I remember there was one episode of *The Rifleman* where he was kidnapped, taken by the thugs, out in the desert and strapped up to a tree, his shirt off. He was sweating, and I was so thrilled I went and drew a cartoon, frame by frame of his ordeal. All the sweat coming off him, blood that was on him, and I took it to my father and said, "Look what I've drawn" … without realizing how homoerotic it was. My father looked at it, like, "Oh my God, what has my son done here." There were other TV shows. I was in love with Gene Barry in *Bat Masterson.* I got to meet him, got his autograph. The westerns of my childhood. – Bill

—————————∇—————————

Trinidad (West Indies)

The Sound of Music. The music, the scenery, the costumes. I realized there was opportunity to be whomever I wanted to be and falling in love was magical. – Dale

—————————∇—————————

What Movie, or TV Show, Were You Obsessed with, as a Child or Teen?

Los Angeles, CA (USA)

As a child it was Buster Crabbe as Flash Gordon. That sweaty body. Not really knowing what that was about. As a teenager I loved to go to the art houses and watch what would be considered porn films. There were several films that made an impact on me as a child, one was *The Wizard of Oz*. One that dealt with life and sexuality that would later mean something to me – when I got over the fantasy of love – was *The Umbrellas of Cherbourg*. The reason for that is the songs were just amazing. I can still cry over it. The practicality and love of that mother trying to tell her daughter that you don't know what life is going to bring. This was in those days when you had those fantasies you're going to get married, you'll be married forever. Here is this man who is wealthy and feels that she is an amazing person. He wasn't being pushy, he wasn't being arrogant, it's just that he was going to be there for her. Also, on the other end, the young lover she was so mad for was so caught up in the lust of things, that he really did not know that when life got hard, who was going to be there for you. That was the lesson I got from there. Who is that person who is going to be there? They may be there and taking them for granted. Especially that last closing scene where she and her boyfriend are parting and he's waiting for his wife and child to get back and she and her child are driving off to the husband. It was just so touching and real. – Kalvin

———————∇———————

Long Island, NY (USA)

I would say, as a child, *Rocky and His Friends*. It was fun. – Ron

———————∇———————

New York, NY (USA)

Now, Voyager with Bette Davis. I always related to the Aunt Charlotte character with the domineering parent. When I saw that movie, I just connected with it. But there's a second film, *Auntie Mame*, and when I saw that movie with Rosalind Russell, I connected with Mame. It was a freedom watching that one. It was a freedom that I wanted to go see the world, I wanted to do everything and everyone because I just wanted to live, live, live like the Agnes Gooch character. Those two films to this day, I'm still fixated with. – Keith Kollinicos aka Missa Distic

———————∇———————

What Movie, or TV Show, Were You Obsessed with, as a Child or Teen?

(USA)

Loved the TV show *Soap* as it was the first time that I saw a gay character on TV. It helped to know that there is potentially someone out there like me. – Greg R. Baird

—————▽—————

Amersham (UK)

Bambi, I absolutely adored *Bambi*, because it made me cry when Bambi's mother was shot. He was crying. I'll always remember, in the snow there was a red patch where her body had been before the hunter carried her off. I can even cry now thinking about it. – Bob Brown

—————▽—————

Pensacola, FL (USA)

I was raised in a very strict fundamentalist evangelical church. You didn't go to movies, that was sinful. You didn't smoke, or drink, or dance with girls who do. So, off I went to flight training never having seen a movie, then *Cat on a Hot Tin Roof* hit the movie theaters. I don't remember what year that was. I was starstruck with Paul Newman. – Hal

—————▽—————

Chicago, IL (USA)

American Bandstand … cute boys. It was a dance show. Dick Clark was the moderator. It was all these kids from Philadelphia dancing. And *Starsky and Hutch*, two handsome men. – Laurie Cowall

—————▽—————

New York, NY (USA)

There were a couple of TV shows I was obsessed with. The first one is *The Munsters*. I liked watching it because everyone was different and they all had their kooky ways about themselves. You could tell that when they introduced gay characters, or gay type of person – they never said it – but it was on the show. Like grandpa was always a little "different," you could see it in the way he talked. I picked up on that at a young age. – David Vega aka Lucifers Axe

29

What Movie, or TV Show, Were You Obsessed with, as a Child or Teen?

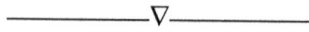

─────────▽─────────

Honolulu, Hawaii (USA)

I wasn't obsessed but every year at Thanksgiving they played *The Wizard of Oz*. I wasn't obsessed but I would always look forward to seeing it, even though I had seen it before. Back in the day you saw something once, it wasn't archived on youtube. So this was the one thing that was played every year. – Simeon Den

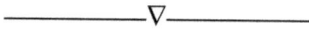

─────────▽─────────

East Randolph, NY (USA)

Friday the 13th, Part III seemed to play on a never-ending loop on HBO during the summer of 1983. As a major horror fan, it was definitely a dream come true. Whether it came on at three in the afternoon or one in the morning, I was always game to watch it. More than anything, though, I think I related to the film's heroine, Chris, played by an actress named Dana Kimmell. As a character, Chris was quiet and sensitive, very different from her louder and more rambunctious friends. I definitely felt a kinship with her because of that. I never quite felt like I bonded, fully, with my companions in high school. I always felt I was a bit of the odd man out, liked by everyone but not completely embraced. As a gay kid growing up in a small town, I also took an interest in the fact that Chris was the one who survived all the carnage inflicted by Jason, the story's unstoppable super villain. It seemed to me that if she survived, I would be able to, as well. She gave me hope that I would be able to escape my surroundings and build an existence more to my liking – far, far away from the unfriendly climes where I grew up. And I was able to! I settled in Chicago at the age of 18 and never really looked back. – Brian Kirst

─────────▽─────────

Calumet City, IL (USA)

In 1968, the Italian filmmaker, Franco Zeffirelli, released his version of *Romeo and Juliet*, starring the nubile British newcomers Leonard Whiting and Olivia Hussey as the star-crossed lovers. I remember it was playing at the River Oaks Cinemas in south suburban Calumet City. I remember seeing it over and over again because it was so radical to have actors who were actually teenagers playing the young lovers. And there was the (at the time) scandalous scene of the two of them waking from their wedding night and the camera's long, lingering shots of Romeo's bare buttocks. It certainly confirmed for me that I was on my path for a lifetime of homoerotic bliss. – David Cee

———————▽———————

Cherry Hill, NJ (USA)

Dark Shadows. In my early teens, I was completely obsessed with that gothic soap opera. I rushed home from school to watch it every day, bought teeny bopper magazines with photos of the male stars, read an entire series of novels based on the series. I could never get enough of it. All during this period, adults kept asking why I adored the show so much, but I truly couldn't explain. After all, the acting was mostly horrendous, the scripts were ridiculous, the pacing made oozing molasses look like a Nascar race. But I was nuts over it. Only years later, long after having come out, did I realize that the show's constantly repeating theme had echoed the deepest fears of my then-closeted self: if the true identities of the many secret vampires, witches, werewolves, etc. were ever discovered, they would be cast out from society, or destroyed. – Daniel M. Jaffe

———————▽———————

Manhattan Beach, CA (USA)

It has to be *Strangers When We Meet* with Kim Novak. I would fake illness and stay home from school if that was on TV. Back in the day, we didn't have VHS or anything, so we had to watch it when it was on. I would scour the TV guides and pick any Kim Novak movie that was gonna be on and then wake up in the morning, and "oh I feel horrible, I can't go to school." Then I'd stay home and watch it. That movie was probably, and still is, the sexiest thing I've ever seen. That and *Vertigo.* – Siouxzan Perry

———————▽———————

(UK)

One of my greatest obsessions was the TV adaptation of Alain Serraillier's *A Silver Sword* in the early '70s and would pretend to be Ruth, whilst my little sister (perhaps unbeknown to her) took on every other role during our playtime escapades! I was also into cowboys, we were always outdoors building dens and had the use of some willing ponies and donkeys, perfecting the fantasy of life on the range. I loved the show *Alias Smith and Jones* and also things like *Bewitched* came later and they had very pretty women with magical powers. – Helen Macfarlane

—————∇—————

(USA)

My obsession was *The Wild Wild West* because he had those short jackets with his nice butt sticking out. I used to think, "I'd like to get into that." – Marc

—————∇—————

Shannon, Northern Island (New Zealand)

As a child it would be *Lassie* because I used to show dogs, and I had rough-coated collies. And Lassie was a collie. *Black Beauty*, the horse, because I had horses. I was also obsessed with *The Partridge Family*. – Gib Maudey

—————∇—————

Baltimore, MD (USA)

There were a few TV shows that I enjoyed growing up, mostly the sitcoms. After I was a teen, but I thought *Cheers* was great. I had a crush on Woody Harrelson, that was a given. Before that all my other TV show favorites were sitcoms, *M.A.S.H.*, just because … I just like comedy a lot, it was a good escape. As a younger person I was on the edge of depression a lot. So, I liked watching comedies. – Cody

—————∇—————

(USA)

I would have to say *Xanadu* because all my brothers and sisters were older, so I was influenced by their music. I always got their cast-offs, 45s, once they were done listening to them. So I listened to Elton John, I listened to Partridge Family, you name it, whatever my sister had. I liked Olivia's records and then when I was 10 years old, I saw her on a concert for UNICEF. I saw that blond hair, and that eye-liner and that lip gloss. I said, "You know, she's everything I would want in a woman, but she's also the woman I'd like to be." I was 12 when that movie came out. That's when it grabbed me, I guess. It's just silly now because the movie is so … but to a 12 years-old it roller-skated. This is the thing about that movie's popularity today. It's the message.

What Movie, or TV Show, Were You Obsessed with, as a Child or Teen?

You can overlook the skates and the ridiculousness of opening a roller-disco, but it's the whole idea that somebody keeping tabs on you and can come down and help you fulfill your dreams. Maybe that's looking at the movie in an abstract way, seeing everything it isn't. – Bart

———————▽———————

Milwaukee, WI (USA)

When I was in junior high and high school, my mother and I would watch *Madame X* with Lana Turner whenever we could and cry and cry. I think it was the nobility of Lana Turner, protecting her son from the knowledge of her misdeeds, that got to us. – Yvonne Zipter

———————▽———————

Baton Rouge, LA (USA)

I could not get enough of *H.R. Pufnstuf.* I had to have everything about *H.R. Pufnstuf.* If there was a toy in a cereal box, I had to have that cereal. I collected magazine articles and clippings. I had a box of it. Piles of printed material about *H.R. Pufnstuf.* I don't know if it was because Jack Wild was cute or because he was an outsider in a magical world. I still have some DVDs. I saw the movie too. – Michael Wayne

———————▽———————

Chicago, IL (USA)

Star Trek: the original series, the only show on television to have a black person as something other than a cop, a crook, or kitchen staff. Since then, *Star Trek* has been one of the first television franchises to open discussions on non-heteronormative sexuality. This occurred, rather clumsily, and disappointingly, in *Star Trek: The Next Generation,* at a time when "gay" was still super-taboo, and not yet *Will-&-Grace-*Trendy. Trans issues were tackled (clumsily) by both, *Star Trek: the Next Generation* and *Star Trek: Deep Space Nine.* The franchise is carrying on the tradition now, with *Star Trek: Discovery,* which features an actively sexual gay male couple and an overt, duct-tape-wielding lesbian, with a snarky sense of humor and a pronounced awareness of how to fix things, including gay-boy relationships. On a special note, a lesbian character is the very first *Star Trek* character to actually fix the ship with duct tape: there's a reason why *Star Trek* is so well loved, especially in marginalized communities. – Chip H.

33

What Movie, or TV Show, Were You Obsessed with, as a Child or Teen?

—————▽—————

Southend-on-Sea (UK)

Lawrence of Arabia because there's an S&M aspect to it. It's a beautiful movie, beautifully filmed. He gets raped in it by Turkish guards. I remember that. I may have gone to the cinema to watch it with my parents, actually. – Martin

—————▽—————

Indianapolis, IN (USA)

It could hardly be considered stereotypically gay, but my favorite movie when I was a kid was Steven Spielberg's first full length film *Duel;* the road rage thriller starring Dennis Weaver as a traveling salesman being terrorized by a psychotic truck driver on a lonely desert highway. I saw it as an eight-year-old when it originally aired on the *ABC Movie of the Week* in 1971. I was completely mesmerized; it was the most exciting thing I'd ever seen. I like cars, and action, and there was plenty of that, but another thing that captivated me was the scenery. As a kid growing up in a big city, I'd never seen a desert before, and was fascinated by the terrain, and the feeling of all that open space. And then there was Spielberg's wildly imaginative use of the camera, and refusal to reveal the trucker's motivation, or even show his face. It was the perfect mysteriously suspenseful action movie, and I became completely obsessed with it. I'd watch every rerun, even if it was at 2AM on a school night with the sound turned down. *Duel* not only turned me on as a movie, it turned me on *to* movies as an art form. It inspired me to write dozens of original screenplays, illustrate numerous storyboards, and actually make several short films of my own. – Xavier Bathsheba-Negron

—————▽—————

Southern California (USA)

There has to be several because I've always obsessed over things. I loved *Harry Potter*, I loved *Lord of the Rings*, stuff like that. The thing I was obsessed with growing up was definitely anime in general. I was more into reading comic books and video games. My one obsession was *Kingdom Hearts*. That was my life, I could not put the controller down. I just played, and played, and played, and played. That was all I did. The same with *Warcraft,* I would play that for 12 hours. Don't eat, don't sleep, just play. – Bambi

What Movie, or TV Show, Were You Obsessed with, as a Child or Teen?

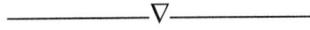

—————▽—————

New York, NY (USA)

Laugh-In. "Goodnight Dick." "Who's Dick?" That's what got me to watch it every week. That whole period of the '70s was very liberating, not only for me but for the gay community as a whole. – Juan-manuel Alonso

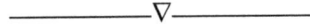

—————▽—————

Mississippi (USA)

Cagney and Lacey. I was glued to that show and I did not know why. Of course, I know now. I was an avid *Charlie's Angels* fan growing up. Even 'til this day my mother will point out, "You know, you watched that show a lot." … "Yea mom." – Jade

—————▽—————

Southern California (USA)

Funny enough, me and my mom were obsessed with *RuPaul's Drag Race.* We would watch that religiously, back when we had the cable television. My mom have DVR setup in case we missed it. We told my dad and my sister "If you guys don't want to watch it, go eat dinner in the kitchen. We're going to be in the living room watching RuPaul. Very devout followers of RuPaul. – Hayley

—————▽—————

Riverside, CA (USA)

I loved watching *Sailor Moon* growing up. Obviously pretty, strong women, fighting crime in really cute outfits. Mostly because at that point in time, I could escape into a world where, "Oh my god, they can transform into powerful women, fighting crime, in cute outfits and look amazing doing it." One of the characters actually had short hair and they referred to her as able to be a boy at one time and a girl at another time. I could relate to that because there wasn't a lot to relate to as a closeted trans woman growing up. It was kind of like me. – Chloe DeCamp

—————▽—————

What Movie, or TV Show, Were You Obsessed with, as a Child or Teen?

Boston, MA (USA)

The *Sonny and Cher Comedy Hour* and it was because I was in love with both of them. And I was coming out, and I wanted to take care of Chas. I wanted to be Chas' babysitter. I wrote them letters, told them they could stay at my house, use my bunk beds. Crazy stuff. Anyway, I got my grandmother to take me to a Sonny and Cher concert. When I was a teenager at Boston Garden and I dressed in the hippie furs, the whole thing. I really do think it was about me learning about myself and what that meant. He was cute, but she was hot … what does that mean? Related to this story, I can tell you when I was a kid that there was something about Chastity. I knew when they brought her on in those little pink frilly dresses that she was going to hate their guts someday. She looked so awkward and uncomfortable, unhappy to me. I think I had some kind of … relating to her going on too. I think the *Sonny and Cher Comedy Hour* and Chastity Bono was about my coming out. Isn't that weird? – Leslie Tisdale

———————∇———————

White Deer, Texas Panhandle (USA)

I was not allowed in my mind to dwell on a man's body or masculine features. I would notice they had on a pair of pants, but I would not notice a bulge or an ass, if they had clothes on. I didn't have a crush on anyone on TV, but we lived in an isolated part of Texas and we didn't get TV until I was 14. Even then there were only three channels. They signed off at 10 o'clock at night. They repeated a lot of shows to have something to broadcast and on Tuesday night – and we would watch everything as a family – on Tuesday night was Tuesday night wrestling. I would watch it with the family, my mom, included. I remember leaving the TV room and going upstairs to masturbate. So seeing those fit men in their tight trunks wrestling was very erotic to me. – Don Rockwell Coffee

———————∇———————

Palm Springs, CA (USA)

Absolutely. *Magnum PI*, Tom Selleck. The most gorgeous man. When he was doing that, he was gorgeous. Now, I don't like the dyed hair. And Sean Connery. Oh, stop it! He's aged very well. James Bond where's he's tearing his shirt … oh stop! – Jack Farquhar Halbert

36

What Movie, or TV Show, Were You Obsessed with, as a Child or Teen?

—————∇—————

Northern New York State (USA)

The first thing that comes to mind is *Wild, Wild, West*. I was clueless as to why I liked it so much. The fellow's shirt was always off. He was a hot guy, I never connected it until later. I was really into that. – Paul

—————∇—————

(USA)

Westerns (*Gunsmoke, Wild Wild West, Bonanza*, all the classics). Obsession was the clothing, and a bit of the romantic ideal of the old West. But if it's jeans and cowboy hats, I'm in! – James S

—————∇—————

Mineral Ridge, OH (USA)

I was not obsessed with a specific movie as a child, but I was with *The Tonight Show with Johnny Carson* and soaked up every interview and story he had with so many big stars, authors & other raconteurs. – Mike Gifford

—————∇—————

Santa Cruz (Chile)

One movie that was meaningful to me was *Hedwig and the Angry Inch*. Anything that had a man in drag, men wearing women's clothes, was totally banned. I had no access to that. But for weird reasons I saw this movie and became obsessed with it. So, I was looking for more materials and the music. I was living in the countryside at that point, in Chile. It just so happened that the owner of the land where my parents worked, had a satellite. He captured this Argentinian channel and there were old artsy movies. Another movie was *Xanadu*. I was a child at that time, dictatorship time. All the movies and everything we were seeing was passed by the Consejo de Calificación Cinematografica. They literally have these old bitches seeing every single movie and they decide, "This is not appropriate." They publish lists and that kind of stuff. *Last Tango in Paris* movie was banned. So they had afternoon movies, but they don't have many movies to show, so it was four or five movies shown over and over and over. One of those movies was *Xanadu*. I watched *Xanadu* maybe ten times because it was always on. In *Xanadu* they had skating, music, and I loved all of that. I was fascinated that they were roller-skating because I was living in the country, so we didn't have roller skates, or streets. I wanted to have roller skates and I wanted streets to roller skate on. It was so distanced from our farmland in Chile. Later I learned that the guy who did the programming was actually gay, so he picked up some of those movies that were glamorous. That's why we had musicals on rotation. – Ives

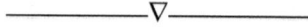

————▽————

London (UK)

There were a few. I was a *Dr. Who* fan from the very first day because I love science fiction. Then there was an Australian soap opera that was on when I was in my teens. Which was *Neighbors*. The good part about that was that men kept taking their shirts off, so that was one of the reasons I watched that. Then *Dallas*, just the whole cowboy thing was a big plus for me and some of them took their shirts off too. Generally speaking, any series where men take their shirts off. – Tess Tickles

————▽————

(USA)

The Wild Wild West. I had a macho streak. Also, I was fascinated by what today we would call the steampunk aesthetic. It seemed to take place in a 19th-century idea of the future. I'd never seen anything like that. I also loved *Johnny Quest* for similar reasons. – David Pratt

————▽————

Central Illinois (USA)

Cat People or *Rocky Horror Picture Show*. – Terry Gaskins

————▽————

Rugby (UK)
Bath (UK)

I was never really a movie buff. I liked disaster movies in the 1970s, perhaps because it made my own crap life seem so much better. *The Rocky Horror Picture Show*, which I first saw in 1982 was a revelation. Great songs, shamelessly pro-sex and a precursor of punk attitude. Wow! Since meeting my current partner, I've become a big fan – how predictable – of Bette Davis movies. He does quite a good impression of her in *All About Eve* but he actually sounds more like the camp vicar in *Dad's Army* (Britain's all-time favourite TV comedy), than Bette Davis. – Diesel Balaam

———▽———

Chicago, IL (USA)

Any old MGM musical, but mostly *On the Town*. I had a crush on Gene Kelly for years. – Rick Karlin

———▽———

Los Angeles, CA (USA)

It was a Mae West movie called *My Little Chicakadee*. I was in love with Mae West. The first time I saw her was when I was in elementary school. This was back in '76 that I was introduced to that movie. It was, "Wow! Who is this woman?" I've seen the movie since and I thought, "What the hell did I see in this movie?" – Felix

———▽———

Chicago, IL (USA)

The Wizard of Oz was a magical story and back when I was a kid, they played it once a year, so it was more of an event. The film's conversion from black and white to color was magical and the characters were all so interesting. It was the original feel good story with Dorothy finding out that what she was seeking was right under her nose all along! There's No Place Like Home indeed! – Robert Castillo

———▽———

Elyria, OH (USA)

My childhood obsession (which has followed me thru life) has been with the totality of cinema. I can't point to a single film – although *The Wizard of Oz* was the first movie I remember seeing and the one I've seen most often. – Alex Gildzen

What Movie, or TV Show, Were You Obsessed with, as a Child or Teen?

—————▽—————

Seattle, WA (USA)

It was mostly movie musicals and it was more the music I was obsessed with. I loved *Pajama Game* and those kind of romance movies. – OT

—————▽—————

Chicago, IL (USA)

1964. *Mary Poppins*. I think it is the first film I remember going to in a movie theater with my family, and my Grandmother was there, and it was so full of joy and excitement, and color. As a child my family did not have a color TV until I think I was in my mid to late teens, so the colors were glorious. Just like the first time going to Bozo's circus. His hair was so red, and his costume was also so bright. I think the obsession was color and how vivid it all was. – Dean Ogren

—————▽—————

Chicago, IL (USA)

A Buster Crabbe western where he is tied up in a chair shirtless. – Anonymous

—————▽—————

Northlake, IL (USA)

My best friend Roy (still to this day after 57 years!) and I were obsessed with *Gone with the Wind*, so much so that we actually made our own home movie version over one summer when we were 12 years old! It was called *The Story of Whispering Oaks* and was filmed with a hand held Kodak Brownie camera. We enlisted the help of my friend's brother, also gay, and a few neighborhood kids. We made sets, costumes and Roy wrote the script. I starred as Sheila O'Hara in a stiff blonde mannequin wig and a ruffled voluminous hoop skirt made from old white bed sheets. It was also my first foray into drag and I thought the movie and my star turn were EVERYTHING! Sadly, the movie has been lost, but other early attempts at movie making survive and we occasionally have a great laugh watching them again after all these years. – Paul Mikos

What Movie, or TV Show, Were You Obsessed with, as a Child or Teen?

————————▽————————

Milwaukee, WI (USA)

The Poseidon Adventure. Glamour, disaster, and more. I even recreated the entire movie, playing all the characters on a cassette tape. – Anonymous

————————▽————————

Niles, IL (USA)

Family Affair - I wanted to live in a NYC high rise, and *That Girl*, I wanted to live in NYC and have my own Donald. – David Plambeck

————————▽————————

New York, NY (USA)

I was never obsessed by a movie, but one that had a huge impact on me was *Cabaret*. The Michael York character being Gay had an impact on me. Plus, I was hugely attracted to Michael York at the time. Because of that movie, I stopped dating girls and eventually came out. – Ian H

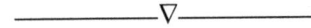

————————▽————————

WHAT'S THE WORST DATE YOU EVER WENT ON?

San Fernando de Henares (Spain)

My worst date was a man who I met in San Fernando de Henares Comunidad de Madrid, Spain, 2004, and when we finished he asked me, "What kind of awful things did we do?" And I answered him, "What you wanted to do … fuck me." – Dr. Eduardo Levaggi Mendoza

————∇————

Independence/Kansas City, MO (USA)

The worst date I ever went on? As you get older, you realize that the guy who got arrested by the police at the end of the date really wasn't the worst date. Things went well until then. Arguably, I was judgmental; he would have been paroled by now.

No, the worst date was in Independence/Kansas City, Missouri. I had just returned from a trip to Tokyo, Japan, and a man said he wanted to hear about my trip. He was thirty minutes late arriving to his house (I was driving.) We had to sit in the bar at Chili's because he needed to watch "the game," while apparently ignoring my Tokyo tales. We went to a local bar, where I caught him kissing another guy. At this point, I decided to see how bad this date would go. After the club, he had me run him through a drive through (he didn't offer to buy me any food.) When he asked me to park in a cruise park, I told him that I would leave him there. I don't need to cruise. I drove him home and asked to use his restroom. While in the bathroom, contemplating my options and realizing that the Chili's was hitting, he busted down the door, pushed me aside, and promptly began using the toilet. I ran

42

out of his house. He instant messaged me a few days later wanting a second date. He took offense when I said, "No." He then began lecturing me on the enslavement of African Americans in the founding of the United States. Yeah…that one is still the worst. – Thomas Bottoms

—————▽—————

San Francisco, CA (USA)

I had gone up to San Francisco to spend a weekend with somebody that I was seeing, and he flat out told me, "I don't love you." He was thinking that we should probably go to one of the bars so that I could find somebody else to go home with. Of course, I was probably getting too emotionally involved with him, but he really wasn't interested, so that was awful. I left early the next day on my motorcycle, Santa Ana wind the whole way from San Francisco all the way back to Los Angeles on a Sunday. I was absolutely exhausted. I must have looked like hell when I stopped in at the Gauntlet, which is now the Eagle – I think it's the Eagle, up in Silver Lake. I stopped there just for a rest stop, pit stop, get something to drink. I was wearing a leather jacket, a bandana on my head – no helmet law back then – chaps … just exhausted from fighting the wind all the way back down from San Francisco. I got hit on three times that afternoon, and I was too exhausted to do anything about it. I had to tell the guys, "I just rode my motorcycle back from San Francisco, I'm exhausted. I'm sorry." That never happened to me before, three different guys … it was extraordinary. – Tim Barela

—————▽—————

Denver, CO (USA)

I tried to repeat a date with a guy I met at Charlie's. He was strictly a one-night-stand sort of guy. He spent the entire second date trying to frighten me. He didn't succeed in that, but I got the message and didn't call on him again. – Louis Flint Ceci

—————▽—————

Chicago, IL (USA)

Guy who ate with his mouth open … salad flying everywhere … paid the bill and left through the kitchen. – Don Strzepek

—————▽—————

43

What's the Worst Date You Ever Went On?

Fort Lauderdale, FL (USA)

Though more of a hook up it was at the Marlin Beach Hotel in Fort Lauderdale in the early '80s when I went to the room of a guy I had just met, we were lying in bed and he pulled out some poppers, my head was flat on the pillow, after he opened the bottle he proceeded to drop it on my face, the poppers went in my eyes, up my nose and into my mouth. After flushing my face at the bathroom sink the mood was gone and I high tailed it out of there. – Robert Hansen

———————▽———————

Greenwich, CT (USA)

I never really dated much but there was one guy who, the moment I picked him up from his job, started doing cocaine in my car. The whole night he was bragging about how amazing he was. I had to call a friend to make a distraction so I could get the hell away from him. I left him at the bar. – Thomas Autumn

———————▽———————

Palm Beach, FL (USA)

I don't remember how I met this guy. We were introduced at a party, I believe. This was long after I was divorced. He was an anesthesiologist. Older Jewish man, divorced from his wife, three sons, which was typical as I had three children. The first time we went out we went to dinner and it went well. It was pleasant, it was OK. Then he invited me to come to Palm Beach to his home there for a week. I said, "OK." It was a disaster. I never spoke to him again after that. The story is that we went to Palm Beach and I found out his ex-wife was staying at the house when we got there. I loved her, I thought she was awesome. She was a wonderful woman. We had a great time. We were similar personality-wise. I would have had a better time that weekend hanging out with her, laughing, drinking, dancing and doing whatever. He was horrified that I got along so well with her. It really put a cramp in his style. He was so bent out of shape that I called a taxi and took myself to the airport and flew back by myself and told him to go fuck himself. It was really ugly. – Joseph S.

———————▽———————

What's the Worst Date You Ever Went On?

Detroit, MI (USA)

I picked up this really good-looking guy in a Levi/leather bar. The way I'm supposed to be is a top. He didn't live very far from the bar, so we went to his house. We were undressed in bed, not really playing, and it's just like, "I'm not performing tonight. I was not able to perform." – Dan Brazill

—————∇—————

Chicago, IL (USA)

About 10 years ago, dinner with a man who spent the entire time either on his phone or looking at his phone. – Kbro

—————∇—————

Chicago, IL (USA)

A person I casually met, took me to a weird hotel in the Loop. The room was very surreal with a bed centered in the room under a large skylight. I thought to myself, this may be fun. About fifteen minutes into the encounter, I heard him say "Oops" and found out the gum he was chewing was transferred to my pubic area. The mood was definately lost. Every time I saw the person after that, he was always chewing gum. Oh well, I could have been the best thing that ever happened to him. – Gary Chichester

—————∇—————

(USA)

When I was 17, with a girl. I was scared to death. I have never really been on a gay date. – Driveshaft

—————∇—————

Philadelphia, PA (USA)

I've had so many, how to compare them? The guy that stalked me? The guy that was wearing a diaper when I went to his place or the guy who expected me to blow him in a theater while watching some boring mainstream movie. I have awful taste in men, they are either creepy alpha types who turn a little nuts, or the soft and fluffy liberal dudes who are so boring, any interest turns to dust. There is one guy who stands out in the soft and fluffy "run for your life" category, Joe (not giving his last name) was a psychology instructor at Princeton. He was built like a brick shit-house, dripping with beefy manly ruggedness, SO HOT! He invited me to dinner at a fancy restaurant in like 1994, in Center City Philadelphia. Before the first course arrived, he was in tears. Joe spent the meal telling me how he'd hidden in his laundry room behind the washer, afraid of everything frankly. He had panic attacks and almost didn't want to take me out. Turns out the only reason he went on the date at all was he liked the way I gave blow jobs. I never gave him one again. – Daniel Fisher aka Raid

———————▽———————

Palm Springs, CA (USA)

I had just dyed my hair black. At 25 years old my hair was silver already, so I dyed my hair black and went to this guy's house for dinner. I guess I didn't wash the dye off my face, I had all this dye on my face. He kept looking at me. I was like, "Why are you looking at me like that?" So I go to the bathroom, and I came out and said, "Oh my God, I'm so embarrassed." We just laughed about it. From that point on I stopped dyeing my hair. – Rory

———————▽———————

New York, NY (USA)

Red took me to BBQ in the West Village, we ordered red wine and waited for dinner. His chewing was loud and he spoke with his mouth full. He asked the waiter for a cup of ice and subsequently dropped a few cubes in his wine glass. I excused myself to go to the bathroom and walked out of the restaurant. Never heard from him again. – Dale

———————▽———————

Long Beach, CA (USA)

I've got a funny one. I'm not that tall, I'm about 5' 8" but this man had to have been about 5' 5" and certainly had what is known as the Napoleon Complex. He was supposedly straight – I let individuals sort themselves out, whatever they want to call themselves is fine with me. I'm interested only if they're interested in me or if we're going to do something. Then I get interested, other than that it doesn't really matter. Either we're going to be friends or we're not going to be friends. Anyway, I had seen this man in one or two gay bars, and I had seen this man in a straight setting. He seemed to

be with this woman ... sort of, sort of not, using that swagger he had. It was that whole situation ... that swagger, that machismo, sort of thing. Anyway, as time goes on we talk and the next thing you know he wants to come over. Then he wants to have sex. We are engaging in that. Of course, dealing with his fantasy of being with a black man is hilarious. He wanted me to call him his bitch, this and that. Then he was going to be this strapping boy and I was going to take advantage of him. I was laughing and he got mad, "I'm serious, I'm serious." I tried. He had this whole little scenario, this speech, and I was trying not to bust up. How he was going to be taken as this sorry little bitch.
– Kalvin

———————▽———————

San Diego, CA (USA)

When you ask that, it brings up so many feelings of expectation and what I would always hope for when I met Mr. Right. I can remember a time, only a year ago ... I'm 66, right. I was 65 a year ago when I had a date that was disastrous and it was disastrous because we hanky-pankied a little bit, had a little bit of sex – he was from out of town. He went home. Then I called him up a little while later. We're chatting, "How are you?" Then by way of talking, he said, "Oh I was over at the Desert AIDS Project and they were treating me for chlamydia." I go, "Wait ... what?! Wait a minute." He never thought to call me and tell me. Just in passing he's going to mention he has chlamydia. I did the prudent thing. I go get checked and I was OK. I felt so angry. He actually phoned me up a couple of months ago and said, "Oh I've moved to San Diego, can we get together?" I said, "I don't want to be your friend." Doesn't he get it? – Bill

———————▽———————

(USA)

I'm not sure I had a worse date, but a couple of times ... I liked this guy, he was nice, went home, and he had the most horrible body odor that you've ever smelled. I really tried to overlook it but after three dates I just said, "I'm not in love with you." I've never smellled anyone so horrible. – Ron

———————▽———————

Petoskey, MI (USA)

I met a guy on Bear411 when I was living in Petoskey, MI. He was working

47

midnights at a Home Depot. He worked the night before the date and would come around 2pm that afternoon to my place. I was working at a college and my apartment was off the lobby of the residence hall. He arrived at my outside entrance. We sat on the coach and had some nice small talk. He then said what do you have planned for us today? I said, "Well I thought we could take a drive up towards Mackinaw City and then have dinner somewhere." He said, "That all sounds great and everything, but I am wondering if I could take a nap for a bit on your couch." It was a weird request, but I said ok. He then stretched out and fell asleep. Two hours later I tried to wake him up and had no luck. I thought, "Are you fucking kidding me?" I then walked out the door to the lobby of the residence hall and my friend Susie, who was staying in the residence hall for the summer from California asked how my date was going. I said, "Come in and have a look."

She walked in my apt. with me and we stood over him like he was a dead body and she said, 'Well, he's good looking." (All the while laughing.) She left and another hour passed and I shook him to wake him up and said, "Josh, I am hungry and going to order a pizza." He said ok and faded back into his slumber.

I was working on things at my desk and eating pizza and finally had enough. I walked over after over three hours and said, "Josh, you need to go. I have been waiting over three hours and this isn't working." He replied, "No?" He got up, put his shoes on and turned around to shake my hand and said, "Sorry, man." He then left.

The next day Susie placed a children's book in my apartment titled, *The Adventures of Rip Van Winkle*. It was hysterical. I never heard from Josh again. – Greg R. Baird

——————∇——————

London (UK)

I was in drama school and this guy was hanging around and he would pick me up when we came out in the evening. He was so boring, it was terrible. We would go off and have a meal near Baker Street, somewhere in a restaurant there, and that was a date. He took me to meet somebody else who became a very dear friend of mine called Bernard ———— . We went up into this apartment and he introduced me to Bernard. I thought, "Well at least Bernard is nice guy." My date was really bloody dreary. Bernard said to me, "You know what's going to happen, don't you?" I said, "What?" He said, "He wants to stay the night in my guest room with you." And I said, "That's not going to happen." And it didn't. – Bob Brown

——————∇——————

What's the Worst Date You Ever Went On?

Washington DC (USA)
San Diego, CA (USA)

My Navy lover got orders back to sea and I was retiring from the Navy and there was this fellow who was a smooth talker. He was nicely equipped. We started seeing each other but it turned out he was a pathological liar, manipulator. Since I was relatively new to gay life, I went along with it. He wound up following me to California and created all sorts of problems. Finally, after I pulled him out of the 11th floor window in the apartment complex I lived in, that was it. He was a drama queen, but he was sitting there on the floor with his legs out in the open air. I pitched him back into the room. Took the bottles of drugs that he was taking and pitched them across the room and out into Balboa Park. The homeless people thought it was manna from heaven. "Drugs!" I took his Chivas Regal scotch and upended it into the sink." – Hal

————————▽————————

Key West, FL (USA)

I never really dated. Most of the time when you make a date with a gay man they don't show up. When I lived in Key West, I arranged to meet a couple of people and they never showed up, so you learn not to make dates. – Laurie Cowall

————————▽————————

Florida (USA)

At the time I was dating someone, so it was a date with this guy. It went south pretty quickly. We had been dating for a while. I hadn't dated a lot of people in my life at this point. We used to go out at the weekend and have a good time. It wasn't a serious relationship, it was just a guy I was seeing. We were on the way home and he decided he wanted to eat, so I said, "Wherever you want to go is fine, it doesn't make any difference to me. I couldn't care less." He wanted to stop at Taco Bell, so I said, "Sure, go ahead, whatever." We get to the drive-through and we're discussing what we're going to order. I said, "I'll have a chicken quesadilla," … something stupid like that. The first thing that comes out of his mouth is, "You're not having that." I said, "What do you mean, I'm not having that? Why not?" … "No, you're not having that, I want you to have this instead." … "What's the reason?" … "No, I don't like you having that kind of food. You're going to start eating this from now on."

49

What's the Worst Date You Ever Went On?

I said, "OK, so just order for yourself, I'm not going to have anything. I decided I don't want anything." I wasn't going to argue with him. I was in his car. I was away from the house and I have to get home. That was the first thought in my head, I've got to get back. Not to let it escalate, I said, "That's cool, order whatever you want. I'll pay for it, don't worry." But once we got back to my place, he wanted to come in. "No, no, no, you had the food that you wanted. I'm going inside, close the door behind me, and you're going to go home. I'm done with this." His personality would flip periodically, so this was just another one of those times. It was the worst flip. I wasn't going to be talked to in this way. No! Life's too short for that. – David Vega aka Lucifers Axe

———————∇———————

Palm Beach, FL (USA)

I was approached by a guy who was full of himself. So full of himself, it wasn't funny. He wanted to go out with me, and I wouldn't give him the time of day. I had my clique of friends, and one of my friends knew this guy. So, Betsy says, "Go out with him, what have you got to lose? Go out, have lunch." Alright, I gave in. I went out. Oh my god! We went to a restaurant on the strip there with outdoor seating. Schvitzing to death in the summertime, so already I was cranky. I was polite. The guy wasn't bad looking but he was just a pompous jackass. He started with such an arrogant attitude with the waiter. I'm a hairdresser. I was in the service industry. It rubbed me the wrong frigging way. I tried saying something and he got worse. This was one of those times – I always drive myself, but this was the first time I let somebody drive. I was done. Second round, when the waiter came over he got even more rude ... I said to the waiter, "Don't even bother bringing my stuff," I said, "Because this dude is an asshole. I'm sorry but I'm out of here. Bye. Don't bother me anymore." That was the worst date I ever had. – Keith Kollinicos aka Missa Distic

———————∇———————

Sydney (Australia)

The worst date I ever had was when I was asked to meet up at the beach. I didn't realise the beach we went to was a nudist beach (Reef beach in Sydney harbour). I had never been to a nudist beach before, so I was instantly uncomfortable. The guy I met up with was a performer in the theatre and was telling me about his latest role and then suddenly stood up and started singing opera to me at the top of his voice like you see in the movies. This drew the attention of everyone on the beach, I was so embarrassed and desperately wanted to leave, but I didn't want to walk over to the rocks to get my clothes because everyone was watching. So I politely sat there for 3 hours until every inch of me was sunburned to a crisp. I was in so much pain that I had problems getting dressed to go home. I ended up with heat stroke and spent a few days in hospital. We never ended up getting together. – Ian Davies

———————▽———————

Chicago, IL (USA)

We had sex at his place. When we finished, I just wanted to go home. I was much younger then, and I thought it would be rude to just leave, and he'd realize I didn't want to see him again. So I stayed awake all night and left in the morning. The things you need to learn. – Mark Zubro

———————▽———————

North Carolina (USA)

Every date that was aborted when I explained that I had AIDS. Each one hurt more than the previous, until I stopped dating for many years. – Gavin Geoffrey Dillard

———————▽———————

(USA)

There's so many. One of them was someone I met online. She was going to come to my house and we were going to barbecue. I had two friends there. She came in – my house is very eclectic, it's like a strange, odd, pop culture, museum. Not a normal … baby heads and weird … so she came in and she just went from room to room looking around. Just not knowing what in the hell it was. Not identifying with any of it. She said, "Oh it looks like a museum." Having to sit and have dinner with her, I couldn't wait for her to leave. It was horrifying. She totally judged me, like I was crazy, which I am – so it was kind of a compliment., but it was a back-handed compliment. I'm sure there's been more bad dates. I've had a slew of them, they're all rushing to get to the front, like little people in my head. – Siouxzan Perry

———————▽———————

What's the Worst Date You Ever Went On?

Levin (New Zealand)

There's only been Greg, and Jason, and Art, ah! … Henry. Probably Henry. I'd just discovered I wanted to do hairdressing, I don't know why, it just hit me. I was dating Henry, I was 22 and he was an older man, a travel agent in a little town called Levin. I moved in with him. I was 22 and he must have been 40. He was a nice man, but sexually there was nothing there. I realized after a couple of months that he was a bit "my way or the highway." I haven't dated many people, I've just had tricks. – Gib Maudey

——————▽——————

Near Calais (France)

More of an encounter. It was an S&M one with a French guy. I went across the channel from England, not really knowing where he was. He collected me from the port and took me to his farmhouse. I thought, "What on Earth am I doing? I don't know where I am, so nobody else knows where I am either." So, I tied him up and he started having a seizure and collapsed. I thought to myself, "I'm somewhere in France with a dead body, I think." Wasn't absolutely sure at the time. "Nobody knows where I am, I could just leave." Then he came around. He was ok and he said, "Oh I should have mentioned that. I quite often have a little seizure at times. Did I not mention that I have seizures occasionally?" I thought he was dead, which was a bit worrying at the time. – Martin

——————▽——————

Ventura, CA (USA)
Yucca Valley, CA (USA)
Palm Springs, CA (USA)

It's a combination of worst and OK date. This is before Charlie and I, we've been together since 1987. In '86 I had just moved to Ventura, California, and I met someone on a telephone chat line who lived in Yucca Valley. We were commuting back and forth, one week he'd come to Ventura, one week I would go to Yucca, for eight months or so. Turned out he had a very serious drinking problem. And as it became apparent, I decided I did not want to see him anymore. So, I decided the next time I go to Yucca Valley I'm going to break up with him. Well, on the way to Yucca I decided to call that gay chat line and I got to talking to somebody who said, "Hey, well, if you go out to Yucca Valley, why don't you come and pick me up and we can have a date and spend the night in Palm Springs. I thought, "OK." So, I stopped somewhere in LA and picked up this really cute red-haired guy and I left him in Denny's in Palm Springs and I drove up to Yucca. It was a very bad scene because my ex was drunk, I told him I didn't want to see him anymore. He was blocking the door and it became very close to becoming physically violent. I managed to get out and I came back down to Palm Springs, to the Denny's where the cute red-haired guy was. He said, "Oh I'm glad you came back, I thought I was going to be stranded here. I wasn't sure how I'd get back to LA." This was 1986 and there was no Uber or whatever. So, we went to a hotel and, of course, we were having sex, and this was the first time I'd ever been with a redhead. He got naked and I started laughing because he had this fiery red bush. I couldn't stop laughing. We had a great time that night. We went home the next day, dropped him off in LA. I went to Ventura and on my front door is this awful note from the guy I broke up with. He had apparently got in his car right after I left and went to Ventura. It said, "I'm pounding on your door, you're not here, where are you, you motherfucker." Blah blah blah. Long story short, that was a combination worst date and fun date all rolled into one. I never saw the redhead again." – Cody

———————∇———————

Chicago, IL (USA)

It wasn't a date so much as a desperate pick-up in Chicago's Boystown. I found a guy at a bar, "went home" with him, and spent a substantial part of the night listening to him dry heaving in the alley behind my apartment. At a lull, I flagged down a cab and made sure that he was taken *somewhere else*. – Chip H

———————∇———————

Palm Springs, CA (USA)

That one is hard because there's so many to choose from. There was one date I went on with this guy. He was well-off financially and I'm on the other side of that spectrum. But it doesn't matter. We met in a restaurant and he continued to talk about himself for an hour. Would not let me say a word. The waiter kept coming over and asking, "Are you ready?" ... "No, we're not ready." I just had to sit there and listen because I'm far too passive to be able to say, "Hey! I'm hungry, I want to eat." I sat there and listened to him talk and talk. Shortly after we ate, he said, "Let's go walk around." I said, "Oh I have somewhere to be." So, I ducked out of that one. – Hayley

What's the Worst Date You Ever Went On?

—————∇—————

Southern California (USA)

This was a couple of years ago. I met this person on an online dating app. We were really, really, good, going back and forth. It was cool. I was maybe talking to them for two or three days. I generally have a rule that I talk to them for a month, before I hop in their car and go somewhere. I was like, "Oh whatever, it's fine." So they hit my curb and I hop in their car and they start telling me about how they are a furry. And that they also used to have problems with consent. So that was a little terrifying. They said, "When my partners were asleep, I used to just do my thing." I'm thinking, "Oh shit!" My brilliant reaction was, "I'm going to do a lot of drugs right now, I'm not here for this. And I'm going to smoke all their weed. This is me charging them for my time." So I'm in the car and they just keep talking at me. I'm sitting there absorbing and listening. I'm a counsellor, right. I wasn't certified at the time, but that's my personality. He tells me he's looking for a packhouse and "I identify as a cat." I'm like, "Whoaa!" He says, "I'm actually a cat." I said, "OK. Cool, this is totally normal. I'm OK, everything is great." We get to the venue and we're going to see a Prince tribute – he'd just died – and apparently they didn't accept cards. So there's a panic attack at the register trying to get a coffee with me. I said, "Relax. I've got money." I paid. We're talking back and forth and they're unloading all their childhood trauma onto me and I'm thinking, "This is a totally normal first date." He said, "This place sucks, let's get the fuck out of here." I said, "Alright, I should probably go home soon." … "No, let's go shopping." So I said, "OK you're the one driving, I've got no choice at this point." So we went to Target. They told me they used to be in fashion, a fashion designer. My biological mom used to live right across from FIDM [Fashion Institute of Design & Merchandising] and I used to watch their runway shows in the garden. This person was not in the fashion industry. I would watch stuff at FIDM all the time. We get to the register at Target and I'm by myself. They have another meltdown at 11:59 at night in Target at the register. They are just screaming melting down because their card isn't working. They have a full cart, a mountain of crap. You could tell this person was probably a hoarder. I felt bad for the workers because they had to put all this junk away. We got to the car, they calm down, and I say, "Listen, it's kind of late, I should probably go home." I said, "I've got to let you know that furries are a trigger for me. I kind of have a problem with that. And I'd especially like it if you didn't talk to me about that, especially in regards to bestiality. That's a hard stop for me. I don't have many but that's a major one on my end." They said, "I totally understand." We're right down the street from my house. And they go, "Totally not into bestiality, I promise, but sometimes cats are sexy, right?" I was like, "Oh, ok."

So I smoked more weed. They decide as they're pulling up to my house to also smoke and then they say, "I'm too high to leave." I said, "OK." I invite them back to my place to sleep on my couch, to come down. I was staying in my parents' garage. So I had my bed way over there and a sectional couch on the other end. I said, "You can go sit on the couch, I'm going to sit on my bed." I was not going to sleep while they were there because they already told me they had a history of assaulting people in their sleep, so I wasn't going to do that, to put myself in a bad situation. They're there for three hours. I said, "Surely, you've come down from your high." My cat, who is my service animal, hops down and they see him and they say, "He's so cute." So I start freaking out. "DON'T touch him! Leave him alone!" It was bad and they were like, "Oh I think I'm too tired to drive home." I'm like, "Oh my parents say I can't have anyone over." They're like, "But you're 23." And I say, "Oh it's this huge thing, my parents cannot know. You have to go." They text me the next morning, "Oh my god, you showed me the best time. You are so good at listening, can I please take you out to a movie?" I never responded.
– Bambi

———————▽———————

Riverside, CA (USA)

I was talking to this girl online and I told her I was trans. She said that she's never dated a trans person before, but she would definitely give it a try. So we met and she wouldn't look me in the eye or anything. But we still went over to a place to sit down and eat. We didn't really have a lot of conversation even though we tried. She kept looking at other places, then half way through us eating she looked at me and said, "I can't date a trans person." Then she got up and walked away. I sat there, and I was very embarrassed, and I thought, "This is just terrible." Everyone was looking at me. She kind of outed me in front of all those people, so it was a little bit embarrassing. – Chloe DeCamp

———————▽———————

Portland, ME (USA)

It was with a man. I remember it like it was yesterday. I was coming out of a marriage, I was dating on the Internet, and I met a man who was a flight attendant. We went out for drinks and I wasn't even attracted to him. I went home with him and I thought, "Is this what my future is going to look like, a bunch of shitty dates?" His penis size was terrible, his kissing was terrible. I can't tell you that I was drunk, but I might have been. I don't really think that's an excuse but that was probably the worst date. Although I had a couple of other pretty bad ones with men. I've only been out a short time and my wife is only the second woman I've been in a relationship with. I've been attracted to other women, I've kissed other women, but I've only had two female relationships. – Cathy Melton

―――――∇―――――

Boston, MA (USA)

There's alcoholism in my story, so I might not remember. I was hanging out in a bar in Boston called Jacques. An old drag queen bar. I was just coming out. I asked Sean, and other people that I knew who were gay, "Where do the women go?" He told me about a bar called 1276. I went there – I got up the courage and went there by myself – and that began my coming out process. My worst date was, I had befriended a gay male couple and one of them was a drag queen – beautiful, beautiful Asian guy, beautiful woman when he did drag. To my knowledge he was not MTF or trans or anything like that, just a drag. They point me in the direction of this bar called Jacques. By day it looks like an old Italian place, with an Italian bartender, in this crazy bar. I started going there and befriended some of the queens. I was the patch-up person, because when they were getting terrible dates, I would be the one to patch them up. Cleaned 'em up and sent them on their way again. This particular queen and I were buddies. I think I spent some time at their house with his boyfriend. We did a double date with a guy from the bar. We had to prepare ahead of time, "What are you going to do, what am I going to do. How is this going to work if this is a three-way kind of thing?" It completely fell apart. It never really happened the way we thought it was going to happen. That was the worst date I went on. – Leslie Tisdale

―――――∇―――――

Albuquerque, NM (USA)

Oh yeesh ... most of the really bad events are from a time in my life where informality reigned to the point that nothing was ever designated "a date" ... assuming I can use those, I got picked up by a Differently Behaving Woman in Albuquerque, circa 1980. (Note: I'd only very recently realized I was gender-inverted didn't know precisely what to look for, but knew to watch for women who seemed Different). She invited me to her house and kept up a running monologue interspersed with questions and was good company, so far so good, until we got onto her block and a neighbor woman said something to her; all of a sudden my "date" propped her hand on her hip, cut loose with screaming and exaggerated mocking akin to how a four-year-old would taunt a disliked schoolmate and felt embarrassed to be with her; she beckoned me towards the house and then started demanding that I buy groceries and informed me that if we were going to get married I had to do this and do that ... I began backing away, trying to ease back out the front door, making apologies for misunderstanding; she followed me out and proceeded to scream at me and throw things at me. – Allan Hunter

————————▽————————

San Francisco, CA (USA)

This guy in San Francisco, we dated a couple of times. I tried to make him dinner one night and I tried to make fresh pasta and the thing just turned into a big clump. All he did was rag on me the whole time about it. He thought it was so hilarious and I got really hurt from that. That was the end of that. – Paul

————————▽————————

Beavercreek, OH (USA)

If I had to choose one it would be with this Irish gentleman when I was 24 years old. It all began when we met on a dating website called Plenty of Fish in the spring of 2007. This was our third date and the Irishman was going to make us dinner and asked me if I would bring some wine. When I asked him what kind of wine he thought would pair best with the meal he responded, "The kind in the box."

When I arrived at his condo the Irishman was finishing up cooking but was a little horny. He shoved me up against the island in his kitchen and pulled down my pants to suck me off, which seemed quite great in the moment. That was until he took a ferocious bite of the sensitive skin next to my shaft. I shoved his head away from my tattered johnson and cried out in pain. Biting is not for me. After the kerfuffle was awkwardly settled because I apologized for being bit, we sat down for dinner.

The Irishman thought it would be fun for us to watch his high school musical review of Stephen Schwartz's *Pippin* on VHS while we ate. It was fun for him.

Back to the boxed wine. It was obviously disgusting, so I didn't have more than a sip. By contrast, my Irish homosexual host was guzzling that boxed wine down like it was a bottle of Château Cheval Blanc 1947.

Now it was time for games. The Irishman suggested Uno. Whatever ... He asked me to retrieve it from a closet. I noticed a rather heavy small box on top of the board games and asked my host what it was. He replied that it was his father. Yes, he kept his father's ashes on top of the board games in his closet.

This is when I should've left but I was young, he was a hot soccer guy and I was still swept up in the accent thing. What I'm saying is that I was a shallow faggot because there was clearly some serious faggotry afoot.

We tried to have sex but the box of wine was empty and there's not much fun to be had with a limp foreskin, no matter how ambitious. So we went to bed. A few hours later I awoke and realized I was lying in a quite large puddle of urine. Yes, the Irishman had not only wet the bed but had managed to soak most of my person in urine as well. When I politely woke him, he leapt out of his bed laughing & crying out, "I'm wet, I'm wet!" He then demanded I get out of the bed so he could yank the piss-covered sheets off and roll around on the floor in them. I am an atheist but I prayed to god in that moment. My prayers were not answered because I didn't die.

We then slept the rest of the night on a hide-a-bed in the living room. In the morning the Irishman asked me if he'd ever see me again. Rhett Butler style, I kissed him and said with no conviction whatsoever, "Yes, I'll call you when I get home." I never spoke to him again. – Mike Gifford

——————▽——————

London (UK)

There's been so many. My favorite worst date was just after I split up with my first partner. I used what then was the only online app that was available. It was on Yahoo and you could meet people through the groups there. I met this guy and he seemed very nice when we chatted online, so we set up dinner. Dinner went very well, he was kind and pleasant. But at the end of the meal he removed all the silverware and pepper shaker from the table and put them in his pocket. Then he leaned over and whispered to me, "I'm sorry, I should have mentioned that I'm a kleptomaniac." – Tess Tickles

——————▽——————

Santiago (Chile)

I was living with my sister in Santiago. I hooked up with this guy on the Internet. He was having a party. It was supposed to be just us two but suddenly five other people turn up. They show no interest in me the whole night. They are drinking in this posh apartment. They were talking about art and literature. I didn't understand because I grew up in the country and they were talking about all the marvels of the world. Speaking in different languages and that kind of thing. The guy was really hot so I put up with all the shit for three or four hours that night. I wait until the end of the night and I think, "Now it's going to happen." I wanted to have fun. Then the guy didn't get an erection, so I had to put up with all that shit for nothing. – Ives

———————▽———————

New York City, NY (USA)

1994. A perfectly likable guy, but so nervous I had to tactfully cut the date short after an hour or so. It was so hard just to be in his presence. – David Pratt

———————▽———————

Weston-Super-Mare (UK)

There was a guy in Weston-Super-Mare, in Somerset, England. We walked along the beach at night and, like Dr. Foster, I fell in a puddle right up to my middle. Later, at his place, I found out he had a thing for eating food during sex and passing it into the mouth of his partner. Ugh - No! The only time this was surpassed for sheer awfulness was when a hot date starting snorting methedone and asked me to shit in his mouth. Ugh! No! No! Nooooo! All chemsex drugs are vile. At least he didn't chop me into little pieces and eat me, so I'm grateful for that. – Diesel Balaam

———————▽———————

Los Angeles, CA (USA)

I met the guy at a drag bar in Los Angeles called Plaza, it's still there. They did drag shows and it was easy to get in. I heard about it from friends at the Alibi East, "Oh the doorman is cool and it's easy to get in," so we started hanging out in Los Angeles. So, I met this guy there. At the time I had a thing for white men. I was young and Latino and it was rare for me – my boyfriends were always Latin. So, I had a thing for white men, and I started thinking, "Let's see what happens." I met this guy at the bar. I'd seen him before, and we started going out ... not going out but just meeting for dinner and stuff. So, he said, "I'll meet you this weekend. I'll pick you up." He had a VW bug and he picked me up. We went for dinner and he said, "How about a movie?" I said, "Sure," so we were in his bug and started messing around, just kissing, and all of a sudden he started getting aggressive, and I said, "Wait a minute, I don't know you. I'm closer to my home, I can walk home, you don't have to take me home. Leave me the fuck alone. I don't want to mess with you. I'm getting out." He said, "No, no, no, I'll take you home." Then later in life I started realizing that this guy was a little bit strange and maybe he liked young guys, very young. So that scared me. – Felix

———————∇———————

Elyria, OH (USA)

A girl asked me to go on a church hayride when I think we were still in junior high school. – Alex Gildzen

———————∇———————

Seattle, WA (USA)

It was a long, long, long, long time ago and it was an encounter with a friend of a friend. Went to his apartment and as we started to shed our clothing, he took off his clothes and is body was riddled with eczema and psoriasis. I'd never seen that before and I was thinking, "He's a human being, this is a part of what he looks like" … but I couldn't get past that. So I said, "You know, it's getting late and I have to go." – OT

———————∇———————

Chicago, IL (USA)

I have never been on a bad date. Granted I didn't date much but luckily, all the men I dated were usually friends, so we were generally pretty comfortable with one another at that point. I was probably on a few dates I didn't realize were dates because of the friendships. – Robert Castillo

———————∇———————

New York, NY (USA)
Boston, MA (USA)

I find myself sitting on the fence, not quite knowing whether to interpret the word "date" as actually going out on a real date for dinner, etc., or going home with a guy I picked up in a bar, because I have a doozy for that one. I guess, I'll interpret it as going out for dinner or a movie.

I was hanging out in Julius's, a Gay bar in Greenwich Village, just standing around cruising. This guy came up next to me and started talking to me. He had a really whiney-nasal-fingernails-on-the-blackboard sort of voice. On top of it, he wasn't my type at all. He kept talking to me and I would nod, or grunt, a one-word reply. His name was Sheldon. So, here I am, leaning against the wall, hoping that Sheldon would go away, when he says to me with in that nasal-whiney voice, "You know, you're nice. You're not like other guys who just try to ignore you and hope you'll get the hint." I then start feeling all guilty for poor old Sheldon and make an earnest effort to engage in conversation. Next thing I know, he's asking me out for a date, and could we go to dinner the next night, punctuating it with how nice and kind I am. Me, feeling guilty actually say yes, and we arrange to meet in a Chinese restaurant in the Village.

I show up for dinner and Sheldon with a voice that could strip paint off a car is getting on my nerves. He also has his little catch-phrase, which is, "I'm amenable," but you have to imagine those words coming out of a screech horn. Every other sentence that comes out of his whiney mouth is, "I'm amenable. I'm a very amenable person."

I'm thinking, how the hell do I get myself out of this? Then Sheldon asks me what kind of sex I like. In a flash, I decide to be as outrageous as I can think of, so I say to him, "Well, I really like fist fucking guys."

There's a pause. Dead silence. Sheldon, blinks once. Sheldon blinks twice. I think I might have finally gotten rid of Sheldon. Then Sheldon says, "You know, with the right guy I'd be very amenable to that."

I suppose my second worst "date," was with a guy I met in the now gone Gay bar Sporters in Beacon Hill when I was going to school in Boston. It was a pick-up and not really a date, but it was a doozy. As I said, this guy picked me up in Sporter's. I though he was cute, so when he suggested we go back to his place across the Charles River. I readily agreed.

We got to his place and started talking and without a doubt, he was one of the most BORING people I had ever met. He worked in city planning for the City of Cambridge and insisted on walking me through city planning manual after city planning manual. It was pretty late, and a miracle I didn't fall asleep. FINALLY, he suggested we go in the bedroom. We made out for a bit and he then went down on me. He was all teeth! I don't mean just a little scraping here and there, it was like my penis was stuck in a meat grinder. Heavy, heavy teeth. I finally climaxed. I attribute that to me being only 21 and it was much easier for me to reach a conclusion in those days.

I had to sleep over at his place, and early the next morning, I made my way back across the river to my dorm. I stripped down to go and shower and then saw IT. My penis was black and blue. Not just a little black and blue, my entire cock from tip to base was one angry dark purple bruise.

As luck would have it, later that day, I started to have severe abdominal pains, nothing to do with my cock, and I had to go to student health services. The nurse put me in an exam room and told me to strip down and remove my underwear. Her eyes went wide and she just stood there, staring, transfixed on my cock.

I sheepishly smiled, shrugged, and said, "What can I say? Rough sex." – Ian

—————▽—————

TELL US ABOUT THE FIRST TIME YOU CROSS-DRESSED?

Temecula, CA (USA)

When I was a little kid, three or four years old, the neighbor next door gave me a pair of her old high heeled shoes – I remember sparkles and they were plastic – and they fascinated me, but that was about the extent of it. I was just a little kid. I can't remember any desire to do anything but get into leather and look as masculine as I could. – Tim Barela

——————▽——————

Chicago, IL (USA)

I wore a blue ball gown which set off my red beard to a meeting of the Church of the Sub-Genius. It was a comic take on a revival and I took a healing by the laying-on-of-hands but refused to fall to the floor in the dress. – Vincent Rideout

——————▽——————

Cleveland, OH (USA)

Hindsight is 20/20, and in the age of LGBTQ, I am O for obvious. My family lived in an apartment complex in Cleveland OH. My mother always slept in and I was an irresponsible child. I had just graduated head start and was eager to start kindergarten. I would put a dish towel on my head and strut in the apartment complex in my pajamas, claiming I was a girl. I would shake my boyish hips side to side, thinking I was so pretty. Most adults thought I was strange. Oddly, it cost me a friendship with a neighbor boy; his mother wouldn't let him play with me since I was "weird." My later cross-dressing attempts would at least have more effort and, fingers crossed, be much prettier. – Thomas Bottoms

———————▽———————

Norfolk (UK)

Murder Mystery party at my parents' holiday house in Norfolk. Well, four of the eight of us had to wear dresses. Not sure what the neighbours made of it. – Matt D

———————▽———————

Greenwich, CT (USA)

The one and only time I put on full drag – hair makeup and wearing my mother's cotillion dress – was to the *Rocky Horror Picture Show*. I was Janet from the wedding scene. – Thomas Autumn

———————▽———————

Chicago, IL (USA)

As a child I dressed as a woman one year. After that, it was for a play. I was Shelley Winters in a Poseidon Musical. – Kbro

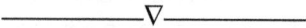

———————▽———————

Chicago, IL (USA)

I was around 18, and some friends were throwing a dance party. Some of the theater girls were dressing up. They knew I was gay – and found it somehow fascinating. As they were getting ready, they asked me to join them and started applying makeup to my face – blue eye-shadow, and red rouge and lipstick. We all agreed I should "dress" for the party. As I was a bigger "girl" they somehow helped me squeeze into a girdle and emerald green dress that fell to the middle of my thighs. There were no heels that would fit, so I wore flats. They filled my cups with pantyhose and we went to the party. The party was memorable, because in that darkened basement room, men kept coming up to me and reaching under my dress and squeezing my ass. The whole evening ended in incredible sexual frustration, for me.

Later, in my 20's I would "dress" having learned to apply my own makeup, and finding a couple of corsets that fit properly, and go out to club Berlin in Chicago. With all the other goth and crazy kids, I would dance in my heels and occasionally my lipstick covered lips would spend an evening on some man's body. Good Times. – Steve K

—————————∇—————————

Wilton Manors, FL (USA)

It was four years ago. I had no intention of ever doing it. I did want to feel what it felt like. I did a Halloween thing in Wilton Manors in Florida. I wore high heels, I had stockings on, I did the whole thing. I wore a feather mask and I had a beard on my face. Remember them doing this when they first started coming out and the guys were wearing high heels and stuff, but they still had beards. I wore a big fancy hat with my hair pulled back, so you couldn't tell if I had any hair or not. I enjoyed every minute of it. I did my own make-up because I was a stylist for years. Big bright red lips, big long eyelashes, it was awesome. I never did it again. I have no desire to ever do it again, but those fucking shoes will kill you or cure you. They cured me because I never want to wear them again. EVER. And I hate the feeling of stockings on my legs … itchy. Hated it, it was terrible. – Joseph S

—————————∇—————————

San Francisco (USA)

I did Patsy Cline in San Francisco. I lived in Santa Rosa at the time. It was Halloween, we had a designated driver, and me and my roommates went down to San Francisco. I had a cream chiffon dress on and a wig. I remember coming back and I was so wasted that I had to pee so bad. The designated driver stops at this truck stop. I went behind this truck and slipped in some grease. It was a mess. I've only done drag twice. – Rory

—————————∇—————————

Chicago, IL (USA)

I was underage and had friends who were going to attend Costumes on Parade at the Aragon. They convinced me if I dressed, I wouldn't need to have IDs. Being young, I was cute, but carried myself like a truck driver. It was a true learning experience, but boy did my feet suffer. – Gary Chichester

Tell Us About the First Time You Cross-Dressed?

──────────▽──────────

(USA)

When I was about five years old, I used to put my grandma's dresses and high heels and jewelry on. – Driveshaft

──────────▽──────────

Yellow Springs, OH (USA)

I was 16, made a dress out of my grandmother's brown and white flower printed tablecloth (the thing was ugly) with this lacy fringe all over it. Me and a couple of friends were driving to Antioch College for an open-mic performance at an Anarchist community conference. We wrote a ten-minute play about coming out as teenagers in the Midwest and did the make-up in the car. We were terrible. Probably should have rehearsed, but we wanted to be spontaneous. Also, I wasn't sure my parents would let me use the car that night. Good thing they didn't check the odometer, as far as they knew we went to a friend's house and not across state lines. – Daniel Fisher aka Raid

──────────▽──────────

New York, NY (USA)

I have always worn articles from every gender in my every day wear. My very first show in NYC was the first time I was head to toe in "female attire." The rest is history. – Dale

──────────▽──────────

Seattle, WA (USA)

I went to a Radical Faery gathering. It was Memorial Day, we camped – so to speak – at a commune, an "intentional community" they call it now, in the back country behind Seattle. We did a Dance to the Moon one night and a procession. We were all got-up in all kinds of whatever. I had put together my ... I figured we're Radical Faeries, so I'm going to dress as a fairy. So I had these little pointy shoes, striped like elves would wear, and a big cod piece and flouncy top and a wild hat. It's interesting because that's the only time I've ever done drag. I did it there in a context that was very meaningful to me. It wasn't just about me being outrageous. It was about stepping outside a boundary to really connect with the joy of being alive. It's hard to put it … this intentional community was founded on the idea of honoring Aphrodite. They even had an area in their commune, a love nest, but it was considered sacred space. You would honor the Goddess there, so this was a special place that we were doing this. It was very meaningful to me. – Bill

———————▽———————

Chicago, IL (USA)

I do/did it for every Halloween … lots of work … first time took the heels off at 3 am … on Halsted!!! – Don Strzepek

———————▽———————

Long Island, NY (USA)

I tried on my mother's high heels once but that was it. – Ron

———————▽———————

Traverse City, MI (USA)

I dressed up in drag for Halloween to go to a gay bar in Traverse City, MI. I had just started dating a guy and we decided to dress up like we were prom dates. I had a ballroom gown on, and he was in a tux. Since I have experience in make-up, I did my own and looked pretty damn good. That wasn't the last time I did it. – Greg R. Baird

———————▽———————

Amersham (UK)

I was about eight. I had two dresses that my mother had given to me, one was my afternoon dress, the other one was a tasseled 1920s that she picked up somewhere where she was working. She gave me that. I kept them in a paper bag in the house. I used to go and play with my girlfriends across the street. One girl, I really liked very much, Pam ———— . We would go to her house and sit on her lawn. I would put my dress on, and we would have tea parties and discuss things. That would be it. – Bob Brown

Tell Us About the First Time You Cross-Dressed?

——————∇——————

Key West, FL (USA)

Never really, accept one Halloween in Key West. A negligee, jacket and high heels. It wasn't very successful. – Laurie Cowall

——————∇——————

New York, NY (USA)

My partner asked me that and I had to think because I couldn't remember. We were going through old photographs, aged five, and we found a photograph of me with long hair, dressed like a little witch. That was the earliest I could find a photo. Around the house, if I could get away with it ... you know, when you're young they don't leave you alone much. If I was playing in my room, I had to be really careful. I couldn't put anything on because I couldn't get it off fast enough. When I was five, I remember I went out in public, I went out in the neighborhood. Halloween was always a good time of year because you could be yourself for anybody who was different, according to the rest of the world. I got all done up as a witch. It didn't go over well but I was always strong-willed and had thick skin even as a child. I wasn't the type where you were going to take the belt and beat it out of me, it wasn't going to happen. I was going to do what I wanted to do, and I did. Most of the people in the neighborhood didn't know who I was. I went out with a couple of kids from school and there was the usual, "Ha Ha." But one of the girls was dressed as Batman. So, I'm dressed as a witch and she's Batman. Later in life she's a lesbian. I'm complicated. – Keith Kollinicos aka Missa Distic

——————∇——————

New York, NY (USA)

I don't know if I would call it cross-dressing. I would call it being young and experimenting. My mother was known for wearing wigs all the time. It was the '70s and '80s, she always had a different color on. So she had a ton of wigs and I used to play with the stuff but I didn't ... I don't know if I would call it cross-dressing but I would put on her wigs, and shoes and make-up. I would put her long dresses on, just to experience it. But it wasn't like I was doing it because I felt like I needed to do it. Or it was inherent inside of me. It was just fun. That was in the South Bronx, early '80s. – David Vega aka Lucifers Axe

Tell Us About the First Time You Cross-Dressed?

————▽————

West Hollywood, CA (USA)

My first Halloween in Hollywood. With my buddy Craig – He was *Señorita Costa Rica*, and I *Señorita Jalapeño*. I have a brilliant shot of us two by Greg Gorman. – Gavin Geoffrey Dillard

————▽————

Sydney (Australia)

Cross-dressing wasn't any fun for me because I wanted to be a "drag queen" when I did it and people used to think I was really a girl. I was so often mistaken for a girl that I once shaved my head and the first time I went out I was feeling pretty self-conscious about it. A guy that was talking to my friend asked him "what's her problem?" I wasn't even wearing anything feminine. – Ian Davies

————▽————

(USA)

I was touring in a Broadway show and we did a Broadway Cares/Equity Fights AIDS fundraiser and I staged a number, it was the *Cell Block Tango ...* "he had it coming" ... from *Chicago*. I used all Asians and we were all in drag. It was the first time I did drag. The first time you do it, you think, "I look like my mother." I think that's people's model, the first time they do it they do their mother. My mother was hot. – Simeon Den

————▽————

(UK)

Actually, my mother hated girls, and she told us. She dressed us like boys, and cropped our hair as small kids, probably as we also lived in the countryside and were outdoor kids. I often used to get mistaken for being a boy when introduced to my parents' friends which would make me cringe. So, when you see photos of us, I look quite boyish. Nevertheless, when I played, I would dress up as a cowboy, rather than a cowgirl...or maybe I didn't know I could have been a cowgirl. – Helen Macfarlane

Tell Us About the First Time You Cross-Dressed?

—————▽—————

Palm Springs, CA (USA)

I've never cross-dressed unless you consider leather cross-dressing. I threatened a friend of mine, if I ever got into drag – he was Australian, dead now, he loved Wagner, which I detest. So, I said to him, "If I ever do drag then my drag name is going to be Brunhilde." – Marc

—————▽—————

Napier (New Zealand)

I did drag three times only. I sold my share of a business to my partner back in 1995. I had a Gib (Heart) UCU party. I was on a chaise longue at the top of the stairs as guests arrived. I was dressed in drag. A friend who was in the industry did my make-up. I looked like an Italian brothel owner meets … I had a leopard print jacket on and this big red skirt and she painted my … I said to her, "You're not plucking, tweezing my brows." I had on this long sleek blood red wig. It was in New Zealand in a town called Napier in Hawkes Bay, which is the Art Deco city of New Zealand. It has a population of probably 100,000. – Gib Maudey

—————▽—————

Baltimore, MD (USA)

Probably the first and only time. I must have been 12 years old and I was alone in the house. Home from school early, I guess. My brother wasn't there. My parents were working. I just put on my mom's underwear and a sun dress. I didn't think I looked very good, so I took it off and never went back there again. It wasn't something I was interested in. I don't anticipate that I ever would be, at least not for any kind of gratification. Maybe for something comical I would. – Cody

—————▽—————

Baton Rouge, LA (USA)

When I was in elementary and junior high. This would have been in the 1960s and early 1970s, but it had been going on for quite a while. There were these things that schools put on called Boys' Beauty Pageants, where the guys would get dressed up in drag and be judged as though it was a beauty contest.

Football players, everybody, and it was taken quite seriously. The football players would get their girlfriends to make them up. They would try to look as pretty and poised as possible in order to win the crown. I did that one time when I was in junior high, so I must have been 13. I made a very ugly woman. I still have my junior high yearbook and there's a picture of it. – Michael Wayne

—————▽—————

Chicago, IL (USA)

The first time was a few days before Gay Pride, Chicago in 1999, and again at the Pride Parade itself. Drag isn't my thing: not enough pockets. – Chip H

—————▽—————

Chicago, IL (USA)

It was with the Chi-Town Squares group years ago. They knew I was into leather and one of them asked me if I'd ever been in drag and I said, "I find that quite threatening." I didn't like that concept so they decided I should. So, I picked a little black mini kilt type of skirt, had a white top but with a leather harness and boots. One of them said, "You look butcher in that outfit, you look less in drag in drag than you do out of drag." But Quentin Crisp said, "We're just naked and everything else is drag." So, when you say drag, you could say leather or anything. – Martin

—————▽—————

South Beach, FL (USA)

It was Halloween. Two other friends and I decided to do drag, the three of us for the first time. I made my own clothes and they made theirs. My alter-ego was Natasha who was a Russian princess who immigrated to Paris, ran out of money, and had to become a dominatrix. I made a dominatrix outfit. We three of us were dominatrix and it was so much fun. Not only getting dressed but being out in the street and bumping into people I knew from San Francisco. I remember Anne Rice was signing a book called *The Queen of the Damned* outside Books & Books on Lincoln Road. She was the neighbor of a lover of mine in San Francisco, so we knew each other. And here I am dressed like a dominatrix and I put my foot on top the table where she was signing and she said, "You're tall, who are you?" She heard my voice and she said, "Juan?" I said, "Yes." She said, "You're doing great PR for this, stay around." So we stayed around the table outside the bookstore dancing on the poles of the awning. Then someone came with a boom box and it was a scene for her to sign her books. Which was really cool. That was one of the best times I had with weeks and weeks of preparation. – Juan-manuel Alonso

———————∇———————

Southern California (USA)

I'm trying to think. I'm sure I did it when I was a kid because I loved to dress up outside of Halloween. I loved just dressing up as characters I liked. But the first time I can think of was in high school. I think I was a freshman, and it was opposite gender day to be a fundraiser. My dumb ass was in this striped shirt, I was wearing two sports bras, jeans and boots. I took eyeliner and I'd drawn a crappy little fake mustache with the little twirls. I called myself Pierre, and that was my first time cross-dressing. I was so clever at 14. – Bambi

———————∇———————

Southern California (USA)

When I asked my mom if I was supposed to be a girl, they did not react well to that. I suppressed that. Being a rebellious teen, I moved out at the age of 17 and I moved into a house that was a big old party house of LGBT people. Everyone would say, "Oh you'd be really pretty as a girl." I finally had a friend do my make-up, hair – they said you can't see yourself until you're done. Basically, growing up looking in the mirror I never liked what I saw. Seeing pictures of me it was like looking at a stranger. When my friend finished with my hair and make-up, I looked in the mirror and I started crying. I thought, "That's who I've been looking for." That was the very first time I cross-dressed. – Hayley

———————∇———————

Riverside, CA (USA)

I wouldn't say I was cross-dressing. It was more that I was dressing to how I felt. I would say I was more cross-dressing wearing what everyone told me to wear. I had been dressing as my true self, on and off since I was 5, over time it got more intense. My freshman year in high school I went out and bought a lot of clothes, started dressing more as my authentic self, but secluded. Once I graduated it was almost all the time except for work because I was afraid of getting fired. It was really tough in that situation because I didn't even know what transgendered was until I was about 19. That's the first time I heard the word, actually understanding what it was. I actually wrote my mother an email when I was 11 saying "I should have been a woman." Because we had no information, she didn't say anything, so I thought I was disappointing her and I never brought it up to her, so I kept all my dressing and stuff to myself. Secluding myself in my room and going out with friends. – Chloe DeCamp

—————∇—————

Vicksburg, MS (USA)

It had to have been 2nd grade. I remember I liked to play the butch part, the male part. I loved that role. Even though I love being female, I loved that role as a kid. I remember going out onto the playground and there were these squares – I don't remember what they were for, some game or something – but we made that our house. Now what I knew of a man, probably from my own biological father, is that I had on a shirt that had buttons at the front. I unbuttoned my shirt because that's what men did. They walked around with their shirt open. So that was to me my first experience dressing as a man, without dressing in "men's" clothing. I had a phase I went through where I dressed real masculine, but it was because I was being hit on by a lot of guys. I think that it was my way of saying, "You don't want to hang out with me." I went through a period at that time, in my 30s, when I hung out with my gay boys at the bar when my hair was short and I wore a baseball cap all the time. I would get hit on by all these little twinks all the time. My friends would say, "Hey dude, she's a girl." – Jade

—————∇—————

Palm Springs, CA (USA)

I can almost give you an exact date. It was my birthday. I'm a leap year baby so I only have a birthday every four years, I've only had nineteen. So those times are pretty significant. And oftentimes they stand out. So, I had these friends in New Mexico. They were bringing some gifts for my birthday and I was to open them in sequence. I would open one and there would be a garment and I would put in on. That was part of the whole thing. It was in a confined safe environment but then when I had all that drag on, they said "OK, we'll go to Toucans." So, I went to Toucans and I already was not myself. I was in costume. So, I just released myself and picked up a trick in twenty minutes. I had to go in drag to get laid. – Don Rockwell Coffee

Tell Us About the First Time You Cross-Dressed?

———————∇———————

Gloucester, MA (USA)

Oh my god! I was probably 20 years old. I worked for a company called Raytheon. I can remember wearing a suit and feeling so empowered in a suit. I remember thinking, "Wow, let me put on a hat with that suit." I felt powerful. I sometimes think I have a voice and a walk that makes me feel even more powerful, but I was surprised at how a suit made me feel. Although, I could feel that same sense of power in a skirt suit, as I did in a pant suit. – Cathy Melton

———————∇———————

Weymouth, MA (USA)

I must have been tiny. I must have been a little girl. I never was comfortable in dresses and I was always uncomfortable in school until – I don't know what grade it was, but it was in elementary school when they started to let girls wear pants. I rarely went back to anything like dresses or skirts or anything like that. I always felt out of place dressed in female garb. I would tell you that I'm a jeans and T-shirt kind of a girl. Also, a dressy kind of a girl, in that when I go on cruises, I like to wear suits. And I look right in them. I would tell you that I've always cross-dressed. I would call myself gender-nonconforming. – Leslie Tisdale

———————∇———————

London (UK)

I remember toddling around when I was four or five in my mother's high-heel shoes. Then over the next five or six years we had a big old play box, a dress-up box in the spare bedroom. I made use of veils and hats and anything else in there. There weren't any real women's clothes, like dresses. The first time I did that was kind of upsetting in a way, because I was 16 or 17 and I was in the school choir and we'd been asked to go and sing at an Old People's Home near the school. The matron, or whatever she was, the woman who ran the place, said they'd had a drag act – she called it a female impersonator – and all the old people had loved it. So, if we could do that it would great. For some reason or other the choir voted for me to get dressed up as a woman. I wore this beautiful red sequin dress and I donned that and put on a wig. I didn't have any facial hair at the time. So, we did this whole thing and I did a solo, *Big Spender* of course. At the end they all clapped politely but the woman running the place, said to me, "They don't know you're a man." So, I took the wig off and they all clapped louder. – Tess Tickles.

—————▽—————

Albuquerque, NM (USA)

When I wear clothing that is conventionally associated with female people, it's not cross-dressing, it's me signifying gender. But assuming that's what you mean anyway, I coveted a pair of pants of my sisters when I was about 10; they were made of a fabric that none of my boy-pants had, and I discovered that I could fit into them. Or do you mean in public? First skirt in 1980, wore it on campus and out and about on the Albuquerque sidewalks the spring that I came out. – Allan Hunter

—————▽—————

San Francisco, CA (USA)

A friend of mine had me do it. He really wanted to go as Edina from *Absolutely Fabulous*. He dressed me up as Patsy for Halloween, the tall blond … One of the questions was, "When did you last eat food?" … "It was in 1963." We went to a party and then we went to Edge bar, or one of those places down there and hung out. Then I took the shoes off and walked home barefoot. Those damn heels I couldn't stand them. That's the only time I did drag. – Paul

—————▽—————

Windsor, CT (USA)

Mid-1960s. As a kid I put on little shows where I wrapped myself up in sheets and blankets that were like gowns, but I have never done actual drag. – David Pratt

—————▽—————

Elyria, OH (USA)

I wore a cousin's first communion dress to a Halloween event in elementary school. – Alex Gildzen

Tell Us About the First Time You Cross-Dressed?

————▽————

Milwaukee, WI (USA)

I used to love to wear high heels, mom's clip on earrings, and fashion towels into turbans. That felt like me, but I also knew that this form of play was a huge taboo and that this innocent form of fun was, in ways I didn't understand, very wrong. I never thought to question why until years later. – Anonymous

————▽————

Chicago, IL (USA)

In 6th grade, we had to come up with a product and act out a commercial for the product in front of the whole class. I came up with the idea for Breasto-Bras, comfortable bras for women. Our work group consisted of four males, two who would open the commercial with a song and dance, and me and my friend M———, who would come out in drag to talk about the bras. When the day of the commercial came, we both dressed in the coatroom then had a few of our female friends come in to do our makeup. The minute we stepped out of the coat room and into the classroom, the whole class erupted in hysterical laughter. I barely got my lines out but managed to extoll the virtues of my Breasto-Bra. I lost it when my friend M——— without skipping a beat, blurted out: "Are you kidding me?! This bra is hugging my breasts so tight, they can't get any air!" That was quite a fun experience and am glad that I was able to have such a cool teacher and cool classmates. – Robert Castillo

————▽————

New York, NY (USA)

A Halloween party in 1975. Got dressed up at a friend's house (his parents were out) and I put on some of his mother's clothing and a wig. The party was supposed to be a costume party. We got to the party and NOBODY was in costume or drag. – Ian H

————▽————

HAVE YOU MET ANY GAY OR GAY-FRIENDLY CELEBRITIES?

Denver, CO (USA)

In February 2000, I drove nine hours from Kansas City to Denver to meet Pam Grier. She was so personable and friendly. She autographed my *Coffy* movie poster and Japanese movie book for *Jackie Brown* (something she had never seen!) – Thomas Bottoms

——————▽——————

Chicago, IL (USA)

Yes, quite a few ... from Billy Porter to Chef Art Smith. – Don Strzepek

——————▽——————

Los Angeles, CA (USA)
New York, NY (USA)

Ben Casey, [Vince Edwards] he was a big hot guy. I remember I was in LA and we ran into him at the racetrack. I have a cousin I'm very close to who is a TV producer for many, many, years and she knew everybody. So she would point everybody out. Then, I was at the Regency Hotel in New York. I used to scout out the interior design things and go to Bloomingdales and see the rooms and we were sitting in the dining room having breakfast and O.J. Simpson was sitting there smiling. Then when he was leaving, he introduced himself and we shook hands. But he was still a celebrity then. – Laurie Cowall

Have You Met any Gay or Gay Friendly Celebrities?

———————▽———————

Chicago, IL (USA)

I got to meet Joan Cusack years ago and thought she was incredibly friendly and outgoing. Always heard she was incredibly open minded and gay friendly. – Jim

———————▽———————

Fort Lauderdale, FL (USA)

My first long term boyfriend (two years 1980 -1982) was a radio station disc jockey so we'd always get back stage passes to all of the big concerts, John Cougar, Joan Jett, Point Blank, Lover Boy, even drank hot Saki with Rod Stewart, who's manager was a gay man that asked for my number, when he heard I had broken up with Buddy and moved back to the Chicago area he called and set up a tryst at the Raphael hotel on Michigan Ave. with me when he was in town for a concert in 1983, a few years later heard he passed from AIDS sadly. – Robert Hansen

———————▽———————

Chicago, IL (USA)

The answer is definitely yes, back when I worked for Borders Books on Michigan Avenue in Chicago, this was when the first season of *Queer As Folk* was released on video. The three actors who played Michael, Melanie, and Ted came to the store for interviews with *Windy City Times* and to sign copies of the video for customers. I was in charge of watching the large buffet set up in the green room and I got to hear Melanie's interview with the reporter from the *Times*. When they had finished signing, the trio was down in the green room and the two male actors came up and introduced themselves to me. Michael even told me that I looked like the man who was president of *Showtime*.

Another time, I also got to meet, albeit from a distance, RuPaul when he came to sign one of his new books. He wasn't in drag, and he was very tall. I do remember a customer screaming very loudly, the words: *"Lord Jesus, now I can die and go to heaven."* The shocked look on my store manager's face; *priceless.* – Jerry S

———————▽———————

Chicago, IL (USA)

I wouldn't say I met her, but I ran smack into Megan Mullally, who had just finished playing Karen Walker on *Will and Grace*, outside the men's room at Soldier Field in Chicago, Illinois. I was there to participate in the opening ceremonies for the 2006 Gay Games; she was there to deliver a gay-supportive speech. I nearly bowled her over (I'm 6'3" and she's … not). I flushed, stammered an apology, and hurried back to my assigned position in the pageant. – Louis Flint Ceci

———————∇———————

Provincetown, MA (USA)

I've met many actually, because I worked in the business for so long. I met Patti LuPone six years ago in P-Town. Sat next to her husband in a one-on-one program she was doing with Seth Meyers. She was being interviewed and I was sitting next to her husband. We hit it off very well and he introduced me to her at the end. We chatted a little bit and I told her I was a fan and I really enjoyed her presentation. That same summer I met Armistead Maupin and his husband in P-Town. I had coffee with them, his husband's a doll. He, himself, is a regular down-to-Earth kind of guy. He's a storyteller and that's what he likes to do. He was even telling stories at coffee. I've always been a fan of his. Those were two of the most recent, but I've met some in the past too. – Joseph S

———————∇———————

(USA)

Nothing too memorable. I met Dick Leitsch once – and promptly bought him a drink. I got into a screaming match with Larry Kramer once or twice … but who hasn't? – Steve K

———————∇———————

Los Angeles, CA (USA)

Johnny Mathis. My first partner and I were in Los Angeles, being hosted by a guy who was a friend. We were driving down Santa Monica and next to us comes a fabulous Mercedes, not these real low convertibles, this was a high one, the big top folding back. James said, "Oh look there's Johnny Mathis."

His security guy was almost as big as the car. Just this huge man. Our host says, "I know where they're going." We took a short cut and got to the bar first, just moments before. In they come. Our host had met Johnny Mathis before, so I was introduced to him. – Dan Brazill

―――――∇―――――

Chicago, IL (USA)

Richard Chamberlain. Meredith Baxter. Various porn stars when I bartended at Roscoe's. – Kbro

―――――∇―――――

(USA)

I saw George Takei at a convention when I was like seven, but we went to get James Doohan's autograph, so I never met Sulu. Burl Ives when I was six, I thought he was a peddo, and stank like scotch. Met a ton of politicians but they're politicians and in no way would I consider any celebrities. Other than that, I don't know, if I have, I didn't know who they are. – Daniel Fisher aka Raid

―――――∇―――――

San Francisco, CA (USA)

I met Sir Ian McKellan in San Francisco – Driveshaft

―――――∇―――――

San Francisco, CA (USA)

I met Lily Tomlin. I bought a ticket to see her at the Palace of Fine Arts. I sat in the third row. She did her show, and, in the intermission, I started talking to the guy next to me. I told him that I really loved her, watched *Laugh-In* all the time as a kid. He said, "I'm her brother, do you want to go back and meet her after the show?" I said, "Oh my God, yes." So, I went back, and she had a bunch of people there and it thinned out until her, and her partner, and her brother, and myself sat there and had a glass of champagne and I got my picture taken with her. It was fun. – Rory

Have You Met any Gay or Gay Friendly Celebrities?

———————▽———————

(USA)

I have been very fortunate in regards of meeting many celebrities. Including Miss Winfrey who I know has quietly helped gay people. It's hard to say that one is better than the other. Chuck Panozzo of the rock band Styx is a dear friend and I care for him deeply. Openly gay and living proof of how to overcome many obstacles that can be thrown your way. The list goes on and on. A book of its own. I can't leave out Kristen W. Who doesn't love her? She's done so much for our community. She is a survivor! – Tripp

———————▽———————

New York, NY (USA)

I met Phylicia Rashad at the Metropolitan Opera when I was in the chorus, she came backstage and was amazingly gracious, she took time to acknowledge those who were not principals. I just stood there frozen. – Dale

———————▽———————

(USA)

Yes, many with my work. Leslie Jordan is a friend of mine, Chad Allen, Gary & Larry Lane, Dr. Ruth Westheimer, Judy Shepard, Jeannie White-Ginder, Sharon Gless, Norm Kopi, Meredith Baxter, Esera Tuaolo and Billy Bean. – Greg R. Baird

———————▽———————

Hollywood, CA (USA)

When I worked for a film company in Hollywood. My undergraduate work was in filmmaking. Actually, it was in academic film history, but I ended up working for an animation studio in LA. It was mostly animation work, so it's not like we were meeting celebrities. We also did music videos and I remember once we did a video for Alice Cooper. I was just a gopher, at the bottom of the totem pole, but I loved being in the film world. I was meant to go and make sure we were stocked up on Coca Cola … Alice Cooper was addicted to Coke … Coca Cola. So I had to have cases of it sitting there. It was a studio shoot. I never actually met him because the filming was to be later. I was there to prep. It was thrilling. Because I love animation, what was more thrilling to me, I was also the delivery boy – this is before computer animation – I had to deliver film stock and film takes and to be able to drive into Disney or Universal Studios to deliver films. That's as close as I can get to meeting celebrities. – Bill

—————▽—————

East Hampton, NY (USA)
Sayville, NY (USA)

A couple when I lived out in the Hamptons. What was his name? He played opposite Bo Derek in that movie *10*. Oh, I dated one of the Village People. We met in a bar in Sayville Long Island. When we first met he wasn't a part of the group yet, but he was auditioning for it. He was the second cowboy. We dated for quite a while and when he got the part, he wanted me to move to San Francisco and I said, "No." I just remembered, it was Dudley Moore, I met him at parties in the Hamptons. – Ron

—————▽—————

London (UK)

London at Wig Creations, the first one to really take a shine to me was Noel Coward. He used to come in for his hairpiece to be cleaned, or if he was doing a movie or whatever, we always did wigs for him. He took a shine to me. He was having an affair at that time with Graham Payn who was living in Switzerland. Noel was in London making a film, this was 1963. He came to Wig Creations and I went in with Stanley, my boss, and Noel was very attentive and rather sweet and charming. Stanley said to me a couple of days later, "Why don't you take the wig down to Noel, he always stays at the Savoy Hotel." I said, "Yes." Stanley said, "He might ask you for dinner." I said, "Fine." So I went home and put a suit and tie on – we all put suits and ties on in those days. I went down to the Savoy with the wig box, up to Noel's suite. He was sitting in bed and said, "Would you like a drink?" I said, "That would be wonderful." He said, "Help yourself." So I poured a gin and tonic and he said, "Why don't you come and sit in bed with me?" I said, "OK fine." And so, I did. I undressed and we had a conversation in bed having our drinks. And I fell in love with him, absolutely enchanted. We didn't even think about sex. That went on for three years. On and off, whenever he was in London, he always called me, and our code was, "Why don't you bring the wig down." – Bob Brown

—————▽—————

Have You Met any Gay or Gay Friendly Celebrities?

Washington DC (USA)

I spent a lot of time in DC with a gorgeous gentleman who became a star in the X-Rated film industry. He left DC, went to West Hollywood, or LA, and was in a number of films. He died of AIDS in 1985. Basically, he used his own name, Mike Morris. His best film was a Joe Gage film, *El Paso Wrecking Corp.* He was also in *L.A. Tool and Die*, and his ex-lover from DC was also in that film. – Hal

—————▽—————

Phoenix, TX (USA)

Rusty Warren, "Knockers-Up." She was a comedienne. She lived in Phoenix. I had an aunt who knew her, so I became friendly with her. – Laurie Cowall

—————▽—————

West Hollywood, CA (USA)

This is an unfair question for me. Tom Hulce was a buddy in high school. Paul Rubens was my roommate in college. I've dated/escorted Christopher Isherwood, Gore Vidal, Elizabeth Montgomery, Bianca Jagger, Dolly Parton, Lily Tomlin, David Geffen, Philip Anglim, Barbra Streisand, Bud Cort, Tony Perkins (the real one, not the dickwad), Jimmy Buffett, Ethel Merman, Larry Kert, Hiram Keller, Peter Allen, Divine … and hob-nobbed and partied with Elton, Jack Nicholson, John Lennon, Blondie, Cher, Bette Davis, Timothy Leary … – Gavin Geoffrey Dillard.

—————▽—————

Chicago, IL (USA)

There is actually a huge LGBTQIA following for the actresses who have decorated such late night cable efforts as *Creepozoids*, *Sorority Babes in the Slimeball-Bowl-o-Rama*, *Sorority Girls and the Creature from Hell*, *Dinosaur Island* and many other juicily inventive titles. I guess the minority always finds the minority and while cinema scholars may not appreciate such offerings, many a celluloid worshipping outsider does. Linnea Quigley, who has starred in some of the better known of these genre offerings such as *Return of the Living Dead* and *Night of the Demons*, has become a pal. I've interviewed her multiple times on stage at different events in Chicago and she has a huge gay following.

Have You Met any Gay or Gay Friendly Celebrities?

I actually have a funny story about her. A group of us had coordinated an appearance at Alley Cat Comics in Chicago with her one December and, afterwards, we all went to a cozy neighborhood bar to hang out for a bit. The backroom of the place was laden with loads of comfortable couches and thrift store chairs. There was a fireplace glowing in the corner. We settled in and were chatting when these two drunken straight guys stumbled over to us and ingratiated themselves into our party. They were so intoxicated; I don't even know how they were able to make out our forms in the room. After a period of small talk and the realization that they weren't departing anytime soon, Linnea started asking them questions. Were they from Chicago? How long had they been out partying that night? One guy explained he was from the suburbs and that he was heading home that morning. Linnea breathed a sigh of relief and said, "Good!" "Why?" the guy slurred out. "Because they're going to start spraying the city tonight. You don't want to be around for that," she replied. She then began to go into great detail about how bad the spraying would be and how relieved she was for him that he was escaping its effects. My friend Ralph and I gave each other puzzled looks and began trying to earnestly figure out what the city could be possibly spraying. We knew that they poured green dye into the river in March for Saint Patrick's Day and I had seen them hosing down the streets in Wrigleyville in preparation for Cubs season in the early spring ... but what could they be possibly cleansing in the winter? The guys eventually stumbled off and we settled onto other topics. Still, that burning question remained .... I remember looking around the city the next day, hoping to spy some errant mists flowing and figure out what was going on. Nothing, though. Well, it turned out that Linnea was actually fucking with these guys for stumbling into our little celebration. She had merely taken a clue from *Return of the Living Dead*, in which chemically induced rains are a huge plot point, and was just screwing around with a couple of obnoxious drunk straight guys. It was goofy and weird, and most probably appropriate, and endeared her to me forevermore! I also think it's hysterical that I got, momentarily, conned as well due to her coolly convincing attitude with those (harmless yet intrusive) idiots. – Brian Kirst

——————∇——————

San Francisco, CA (USA)
Los Angeles, CA (USA)

I toured with Lena Horne for a year. We did a production of *Pal Joey*. It was a remake of the show and it was supposed to go to Broadway and it never did. The try-out back then was San Diego, LA, and San Francisco. It was an interesting situation because it was supposed to be an inter-racial cast. It was 1978 when you didn't have a singing chorus and a dancing chorus, but you had an ensemble, and, in this case, because she was black, it was going to be inter-racial. It turned out to be half black and half white. I was the only one in between that wasn't. So I guess she took me under her wing. I traveled with her. I remember I'd given her a flower on the first day of rehearsal and it turns out her son had just died, the flower was from Hawaii. She made a connection between her son dying and the flower. The flower was on his coffin. After working with Yul Bryner for a couple of years, who was an asshole, she was like mother, grandmother, best friend, sister, mentor. It was a very different kind of relationship.

In San Francisco at a White themed Party in 1975 I met Quentin Crisp. He was in town to do one of his staged readings. And what stands out from that memory more than anything else, the white themed party was a dessert party of all white desserts. AND it was hosted by a nellie queen from South Africa. I was the only non-white person there but I'm pretty sure that any political subtext was missed by all ... except the hostess. In 1978 when I did the Lena Horne production of *Pal Joey* in LA, I was invited to a sit-down dinner at Johnny M's Hollywood Hills home. Johnny was a very good friend of the choreographer, and one of my mentors, Claude Thompson. Also in attendance was Martin Sheen, known for his Progressive politics and activism (as is Johnny) and he came with his three children – his daughter and his two now famous sons Emilio Estevez and Charlie Sheen, who were 9 and 11 at the time. Johnny and I flirted at the table the entire evening and after dinner we all retired to the living room to have dessert. Midway through dessert I went to the powder room and before I was done, Johnny opened the door and stealthily slipped in ... the powder room. We were both giggling and started going down on each other to a point where we were completely undressed and 69ing on the bathroom floor. ANYWAY, when we were done, we put our clothes on, turned off the overhead light so as not to draw attention to our coming out of the loo together AND LO AND BEHOLD, Martin Sheen, his three children and my mentor were sitting patiently and all eyes turned towards us with expectation. It turns out that desert was long over, the Sheens were waiting and wanting to go home, but all of our cars were parked in the driveway and MY car was blocking everyone in. – Simeon Den

———————∇———————

New York City, NY (USA)

One evening when in my early thirties, I was at the Eastside Club, a bath house. After a fairly uneventful evening, I was walking down the stairs to the lower level for a last looksee when a cute chubby older guy with thick, black-rimmed glasses beckoned me into his room. I always liked cute chubby older guys, so I went in. He shut the door, dropped his white towel, sat on his cot, looked up at me, and removed his glasses.

As he roamed his hands over my torso, I looked down and realized, Oh my God, one of my idols! "Edmund?" I blurted out.

He dropped hands to side, gave a polite smile and cute head tilt. "Have we met?"

"No, but ... but ... you're Edmund White!" As if he didn't know.

We chatted a little, played a little. He'd come from a party where he'd had way too much to drink, and I was so star struck that ... well ... not the friskiest of encounters for either of us. As we were saying goodbye, he asked, "Did you know it was me before you came in?"

"No," I replied honestly, "I didn't."

He grinned and gave me a tender kiss on the cheek. – Daniel M. Jaffe

—————▽—————

West Hollywood, CA (USA)

My Russ Meyer connection. It started back when I saw *Beyond the Valley of the Dolls* and I started dating one of the women in the film, Erica Gavin. At the time, 1970, there wasn't any video. As time went on videos happened and I would buy a blank tape, then I'd go to the video store and rent the video. Then I'd take the thing apart and take the video, then return the blank tape to the store. I had the master. I'd show it and turn all my friends on to it. Then more and more of the films came out. Then I started thinking this should be on DVD ... time passed. Nobody was doing anything with Russ Meyer's films and they're brilliant, absolutely brilliant. I got this notion in my head that I'd start gathering members of the cast. I wanted to find Erica again because I hadn't seen her for years. So I started gathering all the different cast members and the people that sang. Everybody, we started touring on the road. We finally got it on DVD, did a double box set, and at the time I met more Russ Meyer people. I was working with Cynthia Myers, playmate 1968, I was doing her website. I was kind of taking care of her in a managerial way and she said, "Why don't you be my manager." I said, "Well, I don't really know how ... " ... "You're already doing it." – So we started doing autograph shows back in the early '90s. Everybody started saying, "Will you work with me too?" So I did a show with a whole bunch of the Russ Meyer people, from all the different films, and Tura Satana was one of them. I didn't really know much about her because I was so into *Beyond the Valley of the Dolls*. She called me two days after the show and said, "Hi this Tura Satana and I've made up my mind that you are going to be my manager." So I said, "OK." And then she said, "You'll be getting some packages, I'll talk to you later." And boxes started arriving with pictures and costumes, so it ran its course.

We ended up being the best of friends and she was everything to me. She died on my birthday and we were in the middle of making her documentary. So now we're in post-production of her documentary *Tura*. We're going into a feature film after that. She left everything to me, the kids didn't want any of it. I salvaged when they were throwing things away. I am actually Tura now because I've registered the trademark. – Siouxzan Perry

———————▽———————

New York, NY (USA)

I used to live in Philadelphia, I've lived all over the place, and I used to go to New York once a month or so. The only person I met was Bette Midler at the Continental Baths. This was way back when, before she became famous. – Marc

———————▽———————

(New Zealand)
San Francisco, CA (USA)

Robin Williams, Cameron Diaz, Terry McMillan, there's a few in New Zealand I worked with, celebrities, public figures, television personalities, some models. Rachel Hunter … there's so many. When I lived in San Francisco, I had an agent, and he booked me for some editorial or fashion magazines. Terry McMillan … we were working on celebrity weddings filmed in her home in Marin County. She's a black lady who wrote *How Stella Got Her Groove Back*. I felt a bit intimidated by her, because she was quite powerful. I could tell she was gay friendly. I was doing hair and make-up. – Gib Maudey

———————▽———————

Milwaukee, WI, (USA)
Chicago, IL (USA)

I had a major crush on Judith Light when she was at the Milwaukee Repertory Theater, and when she moved to another regional theater across the country, we exchanged letters a few times. Then she came back to the Milwaukee Rep for a show, and we were going to go have dinner after a performance, but while I was waiting in the theater for her, a long lost friend or relative of hers showed up and she ended up going out with them. Years later, I got an opportunity to say hello to her at a Point Foundation event and reminded her of her long-ago correspondence and failed excursion; she had no recollection of it whatsoever! – Yvonne Zipter

—————▽—————

New York, NY (USA)

I'm sure I have. I think the most obvious one was when I met Harvey Fierstein. It was at a stage door after a performance of *Hairspray*. We knew – my husband and I – that we were going to see the show that night. I sent him a note of congratulation because the reviews had come out and they were really good. I wrote, "This is going to be the first Broadway show my husband sees and we're so glad it's you." He sent me back a lovely personalized autographed picture. So when he came out of the stage door I said, "Thank you so much for the autographed picture. I didn't expect it when I sent you that little note." He said, "Well you know, I'm like Ethel Merman, I answer every piece of fan mail I get." – Michael Wayne

—————▽—————

Palm Springs, CA (USA)

James _____ . I'm a sober member of Alcoholics Anonymous and I met him through there. That's about all I can say about that. I didn't even know who he was. He was at our meeting and everyone was pointing him out and I'm like, "Who the fuck is James _____ ?" I knew him when I recognized him, I'd seen him in a couple of movies. But everyone else was all gaga over him. I walked up to him and said, "I'm sorry dude, don't know who you are, but I guess you're pretty famous. I've seen you in movies. Glad you're here. See you later."– Jade

—————▽—————

Riverside, CA (USA)

I've met a lot of different people, I couldn't say whether they were gay or gay-friendly, other than they were always friendly toward me, whether I was "dressed" or not. I have played a lot of music. I was in a band that toured a little bit on the west coast. We met a lot of different bands that were very friendly, some of them were very alternative, so very open-minded people that had gay friends or trans friends. These people are very accepting, and I think being in an alternative band, it lets you open up to the possibility of leading an alternative lifestyle without judgement. – Chloe DeCamp

———————▽———————

Chicago, IL (USA)

I met the poet, Nikki Giovanni, who knew (at least casually) the author, Samuel R. Delany. The topic of his sexuality came up during a brief conversation I had with her while drinking coffee. – Chip H.

———————▽———————

London, (UK)

Jean Paul Gaultier cruised me, but I wouldn't say I met him. That was in a leather bar. I was cruised in a tobacconist by Rupert Everett before he was famous. He was doing a play in the West End, before any of his film acting. I was so shy at the time, I'd really only just come out. I just ran. So it didn't come to anything. But I didn't speak to either of them. – Martin

———————▽———————

New York, NY (USA)
Chicago, IL (USA)
London, (UK)

Well, I work in the fashion industry, so yes. I met Halston at Studio 54. I remember saying to him, "I never get picked up." He goes, "You're standing in the wrong place, come with me." We stood outside the men's bathroom on the mezzanine. He lit a cigarette, put it in my mouth and says, "Through here, everyone … whether they're going to pee, poop, or have sex, or do drugs, they're gonna come through this door, so this is the best place to meet someone." And he was right. Celebrities, a lot of them I had sex with without knowing who they were because I'm clueless. I was in New York and I walk into a bar and they were playing the Annie Lennox song *Some of them want to abuse you. Some of them want to be abused.* As I came into the bar dressed in leather, I looked around to see whose eyes were looking at me. I saw him, went straight up to him and said, "We're going home right now." We went back to the hotel in New York and we had a wonderful night and he gave me his phone number. The next day in Chicago a friend of mine says, "Let's go and see a movie. When we got to the movie, this man I had sex with the night before was in the film. I said, "Oh my God!" My friend said, "What's the matter?" I said, "I had sex with him last night." It happened again with someone else in Old Brompton in London. – Juan-manuel Alonso

———————▽———————

Palm Springs, CA (USA)

I really like the TV channel HGTV. In Las Casuelas Terraza on Palm Canyon. I'm sitting in there with my mother and I was like, "Oh my god! There's Josh [Altman]." He was from *Million Dollar Listings*. I was so excited to meet him. I went up to him quietly and casually and said, "Are you Josh?" He said, "Yes." This was about five years ago. I said, "Can I take a picture with you?" I took a picture, I still have it. I felt like I was 12. He is a realtor, and such a queen. I've seen him on the TV show, and I think, "Relax dude, it's not that serious." I was so excited, I just loved it. – Cathy Melton

———————▽———————

Provincetown, MA (USA)
Palm Springs, CA (USA)

Linda Gerard was the co-owner of the Pied Piper in Provincetown with her partner, Pam Genevrino. She was a torch singer and she was Barbara Streisand's stand-in for *Funny Girl* on Broadway at the time. She did tea dances and sang and performed high-camp. I also reconnected with her here in Palm Springs. I moved to Palm Springs in 2011 and she was here and doing the same kind of things at the Ace Hotel. – Lesley Tisdale

———————▽———————

Chicago, IL (USA)
Milwaukee, WI (USA)

I've met Andy Bell in both Chicago and Milwaukee, RuPaul at a screening in Lakeview, Margaret Cho at Sidetrack, Hal Sparks at Sidetrack, Amy Sedaris outside Border's on Michigan Avenue, Jim J. Bullock while shopping at Gay Mart on Halsted, Monica Reymund at Chicago's Reeling LGBT International Film Festival and the Chicago PRIDE Parade and I met George Takei and his husband Brad at Frontrunners Proud to Run, held the day before PRIDE. The next day I ran into George and Brad and ended up giving them the rainbow flags I had brought because they didn't have any. It made me proud to see them carry and wave them in the Chicago Pride Parade the year Takei was Grand Marshall. I'm sure there were more but the folks mentioned stand out for one reason or another. – Robert Castillo

———————▽———————

Albuquerque, NM (USA)

A few. The most obvious name would be John Waters. I met him a few years ago, we had dinner with him because my husband was at the performing arts center in Albuquerque. And guest speakers would be taken out for dinner after each performance. I was part of the group and I was asked to go and pick him up at his hotel. On the drive over to the restaurant we struck up a conversation where I explained to him the joys of naked gay square-dancing. He said, "That might end up in one of my books." I said, "Please do." – Tess Tickles

———————▽———————

New York City, NY (USA)

About 1994. Lots of LGBTQ authors. A huge favorite, as many of my friends know, was the late Leslie Feinberg. I got to meet her at a reading when her second novel, *Drag King Dreams*, came out. And I did get to shake Taylor Mac's hand after his show. He was on vocal rest so he couldn't say anything, but he smiled very warmly. – David Pratt

———————▽———————

Chicago, IL (USA)

Lots. I worked for *Gay Chicago* so I took many photographs. Possibly Boy George, John Waters, Annie Liebovitz, Chuck Pannozza and Elvira to name a few. And Billy Jean King and Elizabeth Taylor. Sylvia Rivera at Stonewall Inn for 25-year anniversary of Stonewall. – Terry Gaskins

———————▽———————

Chicago, IL (USA)

The only one I'll mention is, I went to see the one man show, *Alan Cumming Sings Sappy Songs* at the Oriental Theatre. After the show my friends and I joked that it would be funny if we bumped into Alan Cumming in Boystown. Well we ended up at the Lucky Horse Shoe go-go bar to visit a bartender friend and when I plopped down on a stool I was sitting right next to Alan Cumming. He was a very nice man who definitely seemed to like the bearded dancers, but who doesn't, and fun was had my all! – Mike Gifford

Have You Met any Gay or Gay Friendly Celebrities?

—————▽—————

Milwaukee, WI (USA)

Clive Barker impressed me with his kindness and the time he took for everyone who came to his book signing. – Anonymous

—————▽—————

Bath (UK)

No, not really. Not a great fan of celebrities in general. The actor Michael Cashman (now Sir Michael Cashman) was nice. We first met in Bath Spa when he came along to a Gay West social event while he was appearing in the play *Bent* at the Theatre Royal, then a few years later we met again at a Gay Humanist dinner in London. He has since become a patron of the gay charity, of which I am Treasurer, the Pink Triangle Trust. – Diesel Balaam

—————▽—————

Palm Springs, CA (USA)

John "Smokey" Condon, I never knew he was a singer until I saw some pictures of him and then researched him. It was nice because he became my friend. – Carlos

—————▽—————

New York, NY (USA)
En route to London

I'm not into the whole mystique of celebrity and could not care less about it. But two people spring to mind, though I'm not so sure they would be classified as "celebrities."

The first takes place somewhere around 1975 or 1976 on Christopher Street. I was out prowling the streets with my friend Jim, and we came across this little group of people. It may have been in Sheridan Square or perhaps across the street on Seventh Avenue. The group leader was a drag queen named either Marsha or Bambi, I forget which, but she was one of the drag queens at Stonewall and had been involved in STAR (Street Transvestite Action Revolutionaries). She was a very well known drag queen on the streets of the Village.

By this time, the Stonewall bar was long gone, and a bagel restaurant called Bagel And occupied the space.

This drag queen had made her own "Historic Site" plaque. Jim and I joined the group and Marsha (or was it Bambi?) lead this rag tag little band up Christopher Street to Bagel And. She then read a proclamation she had written proclaiming it a historic Gay site. Someone handed her a hammer and she proceeded to nail this handmade wooden sign to the side of Bagel And, then put a candle on the ground and lit it.

There were only about 15 or so people, so I guess I must be one of the only people around who remember this "historic" event.

The other "celebrity" I met was in the very early '80s. I was flying to London and was lucky enough to be in business class. I took out a book to read, which happened to be *Nicolas Nickleby* by Charles Dickens. The guy sitting next to me struck up a conversation. He asked me, "Have you seen the play?" (It was on Broadway at that time and tickets for that time were pretty expensive) I said, "No. I figured I'd read the book and save $80."

He thought that was funny and we got to chatting. He told me his name was Chris. We got around to talking about what we did for a living and he told me he wrote plays. I asked him what plays he had written. It turns out that he was Christopher Durang. I LOVED Christopher Durang's plays. He was my favorite playwright! I then became a babbling fool and started gushing. I never gush. I told him I never gushed as I was gushing. And proceeded to go telling him I never gush and kept gushing. I think he thought it was very cute. The story would be better had he or I made a pass and we ended up in the bathroom as part of the mile-high club, going at it, while he quoted from his plays to me, but that didn't happen. He was, however, a very nice and interesting guy and made for a very nice flight. – Ian H

—————∇—————

HOW DID YOUR PARENTS REACT WHEN YOU "CAME-OUT" TO THEM?

Chicago, IL (USA)

They told me, so they were fine with it. – Don Strzepek

—————▽—————

Aurora, CO (USA)
Parker, CO (USA)

I have a rough relationship with my parents to this day.

I came out to my father at 17 in Aurora Colorado. He took the news well, although I noticed he stopped hugging me.

My family was living in Parker, Colorado at the time.

My mother found out I was gay by going through my room looking for "overdue library books." This was a blatant lie and my father chose not to protect me. My mother outed me to the entire family. She began to openly call me "faggot." She one time barked in front of company, "Why don't you go get AIDS and die!"

Sadly, the situation got worse. On what will probably always be the worst day of my life, she had to drive me to my high school orientation in Lakewood, Colorado. I was transferring high schools my senior year; I hated Parker that much. She took it upon herself to call me "faggot" and insult me continuously. I asked her to stop. I asked if we could drive in silence. I asked her to pull over and let me out of the car. She was insatiable in her attacks, getting crueler with every breath. I eventually had to tell her that if she did not stop, I would have to hit her. She called my bluff. I told her this was the final time. She called me "faggot" and I slapped her.

She did not run out of the vehicle for safety. She did not order me out of the car. Instead, she turned the car around, passing a crowded grocery store parking lot, passing the police station; etc to drive all the way home, to grab a knife and to call my father.

I did eventually get enrolled for my senior year of high school. I graduated. I got a college scholarship.

To this day, I still don't talk to my mother. – Thomas Bottoms

———————∇———————

Temecula, CA (USA)

Well, I didn't really come out, we didn't have a moment, it just sort of happened by osmosis. They just figured it out. It went pretty much unspoken. I do remember that I was having my motorcycle worked on, it was in the shop. My mother was giving me a ride to pick it up and she started getting really … she started talking about weird stuff. She was talking about these friends of mine that I brought over. Occasionally I introduced them to her. She was talking about these gay men that I hung out with – she knew they were gay. "Haven't you ever thought of a girl, a Mexican girl, even a black girl?" She thought it was her fault, that she did something." I told her, "No, no, no. It's not your fault, you didn't do anything." As far as my father was concerned, we never really talked about it. When my second book came out – I was pretty successful at that time – I was nominated for a Lambda Literary Award in the Humor competition. I had just done a book-signing up in San Francisco. I came back and had pictures of me signing books for people. I remember my sister-in-law was over at the house, really excited looking at my book, and my niece who is nearly 30 years old now and has kids of her own. She was a little girl at that time. My sister-in-law handed her my book and said, "Uncle Tim made this." My father was sitting there, on a Sunday afternoon, looking on. My sister-in-law said to him, "Aren't you proud? Tell Tim that you're proud of him." My father just sat there and never said a thing. – Tim Barela

———————∇———————

Chicago, IL (USA)

It seemed to be easy. I slid the names of guys I dated into conversation. I always hated the 1980's sit down coming out stories and felt we as gay people deserved to have it be as big/little of a deal as we wanted. I'm blessed and was very lucky to have such supportive parents. – Jim

How Did Your Parents React When You "Came-Out" to Them?

———————▽———————

Montevideo (Uruguay)

My parents gave me a wide freedom about my personal life, so they don't like my sexual orientation, but they knew they must accept it accordingly to their beliefs. – Dr. Eduardo Levaggi Mendoza

———————▽———————

Madison WI (USA)

"I thought half as much" is what my mother said. Dad never addressed it. – Vincent Rideout

———————▽———————

Chicago, IL (USA)

My father passed when I was seven, my mother took it well, but curious to find out why she contacted the doctor who performed hernia surgery on me as a newborn, thinking maybe that had something to do with it. – Robert Hansen

———————▽———————

Milwaukee, WI (USA)

My mother said, "Oh, good. Now we can be friends." My father (who had remarried when I was four) nodded solemnly, and then launched into an unrelated political anecdote. After about an hour, he asked me not to tell his wife (a conservative Lutheran) or his other kids. I told him his wife was entirely his business, and that it was too late about the kids. "I told them first and asked them how I should tell you." We didn't speak about it again for 10 years. (His wife eventually found out anyway.) – Louis Flint Ceci

———————▽———————

Greenwich, CT (USA)

I told my mother I thought I had HIV because I had anal sex for the first time (I wish I had Internet back then). She cried and cried, made a really big

96

deal about it, she said she would tell my father. The next morning I ran into him in the kitchen and he gave me a really sweet look and nudged me with his shoulder, never said a word and we never discussed it. He welcomed my first boyfriend and treated him as family. – Thomas Autumn

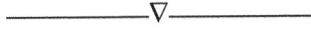

———————∇———————

Yosemite, CA (USA)

My mother was OK. I came out to her through a sister. I came out to one sister, but I told her I wanted to tell my mom, but I didn't want to tell her face to face. So I had this one sister feel her out and then she told her, and then I went up there and visited and we talked about it. I think we drove up to Yosemite that day, and mom said, "Well that's a pretty hard choice you made." I didn't want a big debate over whether it's a choice, so I just let that go rather than turning it into an argument. So, she ended up being accepting of it. We went to a gay restaurant together. I never told my father, but he was in the Navy for 21 ½ years. He wasn't stupid. Out of the whole family I had no negative, "You're going to hell." – Dave

———————∇———————

San Diego, CA (USA)

When I first came-out, my mom wasn't surprised, but she was angry that I hadn't told her directly, that somebody else told her first. Basically, I got challenged by my sister who found out I was gay. "You tell them, or I will." She didn't directly tell my mom, but she led her on pretty well. When I came out to my mom, she said, "Fine, but you have to tell your father. I'm not going to be the one to tell him." My father got home, and I told him. He sat there in stunned silence, lit up a cigarette and said, "Leave." For the next eight years I didn't talk to him. I stayed in touch with my mom and my siblings. No contact with my father whatsoever. My father was in the military, a Navy Petty Officer. He was on a cruise and one of his employees – whatever you want to call them – came to him distraught and wanting out of the Navy because he was gay. My father spent the night talking to him and saw what he was going through. The man's partner had committed suicide in San Diego, he wanted to go home, didn't care what the Navy would do. My father counselled him to not tell the Navy he was gay. Told him he'd arrange emergency leave and send him home. Once he got everything sorted out, he could come back. So, I was summoned to my parents' house and my father told me he didn't know if he would understand it, but that I was still his kid and we'd work on it. And I'm glad we did because less than a year later he died. That would have remained unresolved otherwise because I wasn't going back. I didn't want anything to do with him, because if the fact of who I am is that big an affront to you, then I don't need you in my life. – Art Healey

—————▽—————

Hoboken, NJ (USA)

I told them before I told anybody, together. Even before I told my wife. They were going to get the repercussions of everything that would come down after that, and I thought they should be prepared. I was the only son of an Italian woman and the only son of this very strict Marine Corp drill sergeant. I wanted them to hear it from me and not anybody else. I remember my mother crying and saying to me, "I just don't want you to be alone." I said to her, "Alone is not important. I like my own company. Alone is your issue." She said to me, "You're right, it is my issue. Just be happy." I said, "I'll make myself happy. I'll be the happiest I want to be. Whatever that means." And my father … I don't think he quite understood it. He kept saying to me, "But you have kids, you're married. You have a wife." I said, "Yeah." I'm thinking, "You're a marine, you never saw anybody get fucked up the ass during World War II." I'm sure he did, because he was a handsome, beautiful marine and I'm sure he must have seen something. I don't think he was shocked by it. I think he was OK with it. No-one screamed and yelled and carried on and told me they didn't love me anymore. There was none of that nonsense. It was not totally accepted, but it was a matter-of-fact, "So what?" It was weird, it wasn't very comfortable. My father was a blue-collar guy and my mother. They were not the most intelligent and educated people, but they were loving and kind. – Joseph S

—————▽—————

Detroit, MI (USA)

My father was already dead and when I told my mother, it was, "Oh my God, what did I do wrong. What could I have done to change this?" She got used to seeing me with other men, she was very genial. I don't think she ever got over it. I really don't. – Dan Brazill

—————▽—————

Chicago, IL (USA)

They sent me for counseling at Catholic Charities. Sounds funny now but at the time there were very few options. Then I was "cured." At least for a few months ... – Kbro

———————▽———————

Chicago, IL (USA)

Coming out when you are bisexual is complicated. I never came out to my homophobic/asshole dad and, as I was always dating some girl, I never needed to. Came out to my mom in high school and she thought that being bisexual was "just a phase." Ever since then, about once every five years, I have made mention of my bisexuality and she has acted surprised, as if I have never mentioned it before.

Mostly the rest of the world just thinks I am like them. I married a woman, had three kids, and straights just think I'm like them. Queers see the way I dress (I'm a leatherman), and the way I carry myself, and think I am like them too.

The problem was always my wife. When she liked me, then I had no past. When she was angry at me then, "The problem with our marriage is that you're a faggot!"

My oldest daughter is also ashamed that I am bisexual, but my son and younger daughter are bisexual, just like me, but smart enough to hide it; especially from their mother. – R.M. Schultz

———————▽———————

Chicago, IL (USA)

My father was already deceased, and my mother was going through the "Where did I go wrong?" syndrome. I always said if I was asked, I would not hide the fact. But, as I found out, it was an ongoing process. That process actually brought us closer together over the years. – Gary Chichester

———————▽———————

Santa Rosa, CA (USA)

Mom died when I was in my twenties, but I think she knew. I lived out West and I went back to see her before she passed away. My dad re-married the step-monster and we went out to dinner sometime. They came out to see me in Santa Rosa. In the middle of dinner, she goes, "Your dad wants to know if you're gay or not." She wanted to know, not my dad. I said, "Yes." My dad looked at me and said, "I don't love you any less." – Rory

How Did Your Parents React When You "Came-Out" to Them?

—————▽—————

Nashville, TN (USA)

I was 18 years old and living in Nashville and my mother one day asked me if I liked men. I said I liked both. Then she proceeded to get me made up in drag. LOL. It was never discussed with my father. – Driveshaft

—————▽—————

(USA)

I didn't really give them much choice other than to accept it, or I could do without them in my life. My mom had the hardest time but mostly because she had questions. I was watching Geraldo Rivera (yuck) at like 3:00 am, my mom came in the room to bum a smoke. We were both nocturnal, so both were always up late into the night. It was his first Gay Prom episode, so he was trying to shock middle America because these kids wanted to go to prom … Scandalous!

I just turned to her and told her I was gay. After some time, I gave her the spiel, not her fault, not a fad, blah, blah and the blah. After a few weeks and some dumb questions, she was okay about it. The kicker was when she asked about me having two girlfriends. I said there are no absolutes in the universe and that shut her up. My dad was way more pragmatic, he thought I was coming out as a communist. When he found that I wasn't he was fine. He accused me of being a communist a lot, so that's normal??? – Daniel Fisher aka Raid

—————▽—————

(USA)

When I came out (not long after my first gay bar experience), my mother lost it. Did not except it well at all! That being said, my mother had a lesbian sister and niece. So it somehow ran in the family, I guess. Driving down the interstate one day, she blurted out, and I quote "I never thought that I would raise my one and only son to grow up to suck another man's dick." I wanted to jump out of the car right then. But as time went on, I couldn't have asked for a better parent. She loved me and my husband. I was very blessed to have her in my life. She was definitely an outspoken person. – Tripp

—————▽—————

How Did Your Parents React When You "Came-Out" to Them?

Trinidad (West Indies)

Fortunately, I never had to come out to my parents, it was just who I was/am.
– Dale

———————∇———————

San Diego, CA (USA)

I remember exactly what happened. I was away at college. I came back for Easter vacation. I wanted to have a chat with my father. We went out to eat and I told him I was gay. It's very interesting, he stroked his chin and said, "What role do you play?" Then there was a long pause and before I could answer, he said, "Oh I guess it doesn't really work that way, does it?" We actually had a decent talk. I said, "Maybe we should now talk with mom." He said, "No, let me tell her, she's going to be very upset." In fact, later he told me she was very, very, upset, angry and upset, cried and cried. I didn't experience that. He was with her through that. Later my mom came around. It really was no problem. It's interesting because many guys have the reverse of my father and mother. – Bill

———————∇———————

Los Angeles, CA (USA)

I don't think that was ever necessarily. They knew I was different from the beginning. I knew it to. So we never had that conversation. I just started bringing boyfriends home and they acted as if it was the normal thing. It was never one of those situations where it was a big deal. It was part of who I was. I guess because I have been blessed enough to be authentic most of my life. – Kalvin

———————∇———————

Chicago, IL (USA)

After a night of drinking with my dad, he cried, told me not to tell by mom or siblings. Before he died, he said he loves me, but can never accept me being gay. When telling my mom, she was emotionless. – Martin Mulcahy

———————∇———————

How Did Your Parents React When You "Came-Out" to Them?

New York, NY (USA)

My dad was already dead by the time I started living my gay life. My mother was fine, she said, "Well I never would have known unless you said something, but you're still my baby." My mother was an incredible person, it was like living with Auntie Mame. She liked creative types. She loved decorators and all that stuff. It was a lot easier for me because I had a gay older brother. My mother tried to set me up with the daughters of her women friends and I finally sat her down and said, "OK I love you but I'm not coming over here anymore." She said, "Why?" I said, "Because you keep trying to fix me up with all these girls. And mom, I have to tell you, I'm gay." – Ron

———————▽———————

Imlay City, MI (USA)

My Mother was not good. She had lots of negative influence from the church and my stepfather was very homophobic. I could come and visit my home, but I needed to stay in a hotel at night as my Mom did not allow gay people in her house after dinner time. My stepfather also had a huge influence in her decisions. When my Mom died, my brother and I were not put in her obituary. I had to call the funeral home six hours after she died to have our names included in her obituary. My stepfather was the one who omitted us. He died five years later alone and angry and we never saw him during the time he lived in our childhood home. It was a wonderful closure when he passed and we sold our home this past year.

My Father is still alive and lives with my brother in Florida. He was the most bigoted and closed-minded man growing up. He is not now and accepts my brother and I. – Greg R. Baird

———————▽———————

Amersham (UK)

I never came out to them. They assumed. My parents never talked to me about gay. My dad called me a poof and a ponce when I was four years of age. So I grew up with that title. My eldest brother used to call me a poof and a ponce. Then when I said I wanted to be in the theatre, they knew. The only time my dad ever, ever, said anything about gay to me was when AIDS came out and Bob Robinson and I were down there for the weekend and my dad was in one of his pissy-assed moods. He said to me, "This AIDS thing that everybody's getting, is all for the queers. They ought to be put on some island somewhere." I said to him, "You know, we're human beings. You can't do that." That was the end of the conversation. The next time he ever said anything about gay to me was when I was moving back to New York to work and we were down for the weekend more or less saying goodbye. Bob Robinson and I lived together for 17 years. My dad said, "Can I ask you a personal question?" I thought, "Oh Christ, here we go." He said, "Well, are you and Bob Robinson breaking up?" And I said, "Yes, that's what's happening." And he said, "Well I think it's a bloody shame." – Bob Brown

———————▽———————

San Diego, CA (USA)

My step-dad was deceased. Actually, my mom outed me to herself. I used to say that my mom was a woman of the earth, and in many respects that's true. She was 8 ½ months pregnant with me when she and my father were married in Yuma. She truly loved him all her life, even though she was good to my step-dad and I think she loved him, but she was always in love with my father who's name was David. Later in life she had rheumatoid arthritis severely and they gave her a lot of Prednisone, that destroys the immune system because it's a steroid. One day she had to go into a hospital, she had a little infection on one of her ankles. So they had to go to hyperbaric oxygen chamber in order for the healing to go. Well, it was in walking distance from a small business I was managing, so at lunch I went up to see her. We had a lot of conversations, and there was a flaming queen nurse in charge that my mother didn't like. She said, "What's the term I want? Oh he's too nelly." I choked. Then she's just sitting up there in her bed and she gets this shit-eating grin on her face and I said, "What?" She said, "Oh I have to tell you, I have on the graveyard shift here at the hospital, two male nurses who are so cute and I've told them all about you, and I wish you could get together with them." Well, pick me up off the floor." – Hal

———————▽———————

Chicago, IL (USA)

I said to my mother one day that I had problems and couldn't talk about them with her, She said, "Why don't you talk to the rabbi." So I did. I said, "I'm gay," and he said, "If you were my son I'd want you to tell me." So I went home and I told my mother, but I never told my father. I told my mother and she did the laundry on Thursday and the cleaning lady came on Friday and ironed. I went upstairs and she was crying, and I said, "What are you crying about?" And she said, "I'm going to have to be doing your laundry for the rest of my life." She went and got therapy, talked to someone about how to deal with it. I suppose that at some point she told my father, but it was totally accepted. I had no trouble coming out. Then I decided I wanted to go into therapy, so I started seeing a psychiatrist. He said, "At some point you're going to have to decide either this is what you want, or this is what you don't want." He said, "It's pretty hard dealing with something that gives you so much pleasure." I chose gay and after telling my mother, I told my close friends, after that it was simple. When your friends are Jewish and you live in a Jewish world, most of us are liberal and open. Then it wasn't a problem. The only discrimination I felt, I cast upon myself, but I never felt it from anybody else. – Laurie Cowall

———————▽———————

New York, NY (USA)
Pompano Beach, FL (USA)

When I came-out to my mom was about the time-frame I came-out to my brother, Danny. It all happened at the same time. I think my mom knew, but she never really talked about it. She was religious and very quiet about things. So when I came-out to my brother, Danny, one of the first things he said was, "Have you talked to mommy yet? Did you tell anybody else in the family?" I said, "Well no, you're the first one in the family I've talked to about this." After that I spoke to my sister, and she said the same thing, "Did you talk to Mommy yet?" … "No, I didn't talk to mommy yet. When I'm good and ready, then I think she's good and ready." My father actually found out first. I was at my oldest brother's house, and I had come-out to them. And he said, "You can talk to poppy because he's coming to visit." I said, If I choose to talk to poppy about it, that's my choice. I don't think he's going to have a problem with it." Which he didn't. Actually, my sister-in-law outed me to my father. He was like, "So what?" It was not a big deal. But when I came-out to my mom, it was a little bit different. I was living in Florida at this point. She was living in Connecticut and at the time I was dating someone I thought was "the one." I thought this was the guy I was going to be with. I wasn't thinking about future, I was thinking about the present moment. I called her up and said, "Mommy, I got to talk to you about something," because at the time I was considering getting married to this person. I thought, "Maybe if this goes that route in my path of life, I'm going to have to eventually tell mommy, because if I get married to someone she's got to know." I wouldn't want to keep that from her. So I called her and said, "I'm thinking about getting married." … "Oh David, I can't believe it. It's about time. I was wondering about you. I was afraid this day would never come."

When I was growing up, I was very masculine, butch, I didn't have what would be considered feminine tendencies. Even though I had them in me, I suppressed them, because I was a Hispanic kid growing up in the South Bronx. The last thing you want to do is show femininity because you see what happens to everybody else. So I hid it all for years. But when I eventually came-out to my mom she kind of accepted me but not really. It was, "You're my son and I'll always love you ... blah, blah, blah." That's not accepting somebody to say those words. I've been with Keith for 17 years and she's never been here. She doesn't want to ask about it, she doesn't talk about it on the phone. She doesn't want to go there. She knows and I'm not going to hide it from her. I tell her all the time, "Keith says hello." That's as far as it goes ... "Goodbye mommy, I love you." ... "Me too." I get a 'Me too,' I don't get an I love you too." But that's ok, she's set in her ways, in her 80s now. I waited until I was of age, I was over 21. – David Vega aka Lucifers Axe

———————▽———————

North Carolina (USA)

My dad shrugged and said it wasn't news to him. My mom was a total cunt about it. When I brought a black girl home one afternoon, Dad later confessed he'd rather see me with a white boy than a black girl. He apologized and said it was simply how he was brought up. I told him that was unacceptable and soon left home (at 15). I never knew what my Mom's issues were, but they invariably revolved around what the evil bitches at church would think. – Gavin Geoffrey Dillard

———————▽———————

New York, NY (USA)

Not well. Not well at all. I was always playing with boys all through school. I got caught in the 2nd grade by Mrs. Goldberg and mommy got a phone call. I was caught in the bathroom with Michael Kirk doing bad things. Well, what they thought was bad, I thought was fun. I had a bag of marbles and I was putting them up his butt. I thought it was fun. I didn't come-out then, I got punished. That generation would punish their children. Later on, when I had seen more of life, a little bit older, I went to Fire Island and there was no keeping me quiet after that. So, I came out. But I waited until my grandmother's funeral. My mother had everybody back at the house because that's what they did ... 2:00-5:00 and 7:00-10:00 at the funeral home, then everybody back to the house. Well, I waited until the end on the third day and then my mother was coming out of the kitchen with the food, all the

aunts are there. I said, "I have an announcement, I'm gay!" CRASH! The tray of food. They all lost their shit. I laughed my ass off because I thought it was fucking hysterical. I thought it was hysterically funny. That was my big, "I'm out, fuck you." They were all together and I figured this was the best time to speak to relatives who were not normally together. Weddings and wakes or you don't see some of them. This way I did it for all of them. And I was out. I was always flamboyant, so there was no putting the genie back in the bottle.
– Keith Kollinicos aka Missa Distic

———————▽———————

(UK)
Salzburg (Austria)
Cyprus

I had two run-ups with mum who was always very open and down to earth. I remember I was 23 and my mum and I were sitting on the bed and I was just about to say, "Oh by the way … " when she said, "You know, your brother, he's never had a girlfriend." And my sister said, "Well maybe he's gay mum." I'm sitting thinking, "Oh God, this is my big moment." Then mum said, "Well, if he's gay, that's the way it is, but not under my roof." So I thought, "Oh I'll just leave it for now then." In my late-20s I moved in with my girlfriend in Salzburg and my mum came to visit. In fact, they got on very well and there was never a moment when I thought she didn't accept it. So that was ok. My parents had been divorced for 15 years, but my father had lost his wife very suddenly in about 1995 and I went to the funeral and I hadn't told him because he lives in Cyprus and we just hadn't seen each other so I could tell him. I did tell him around that time, but he was grieving and not in a very good way. He wasn't upset or shocked. But then when I took Eva over a few months later for a visit, he took us to his rambling group. And we're standing in this circle and you have to introduce yourself. He goes, "Let me introduce my daughter and my daughter-in-law." It was just like that. He's been lovely ever since. – Helen Macfarlane

———————▽———————

Honolulu, Hawaii (USA)

I told my mom first. My sister was getting married. It was 1971 and I came home and said to my mother, "I'm just like you, I like men." I was trying to make a joke out of it. She said, "Yes, I know. Did you tell your dad?" I said, "No." My parents were divorced, before I was born, I think. There was a period when I lived with my dad and a period when I lived with my mom.

Mostly I lived with my mom. My dad was an immigrant who couldn't read, not because he was stupid but he'd never learned how to read or write. He came from the Philippines. He came to work the fields. My dad used to be a part of the Filipino Mafia when he was married to my mother. Not that he killed people, but there was a whole organized gambling thing and he was part of that. When he married her, she made him quit, just because of respect for the kids. He ended up being a dishwasher at the Royal Hawaiian Hotel forever. So I said to my mom, "Should I tell dad?" She said, "You'll be surprised how open he is." But I never told him. What happened was, later on he was in a care facility, when he was older, before he died. I remember coming home from New York for a while and I went to visit him, and he was really friendly. I spent the day with him. The nurse told me he only speaks Filipino to her and he likes to watch the Filipino station on TV. We spent the day together talking and then I said, "Ok dad, I gotta go." I gave him a big hug and I left. Just before I was leaving, I heard hm say really loudly to the nurse, "Who was that bald-headed guy?" And I laughed, I thought that was great. I never came-out to him because at that point there was no reason to. I put myself through college, I paid for everything. They never supported me after high school. Whatever I did was on my own. I think they respected me for that. I never felt that I needed his approval. – Simeon Den

——————∇——————

Maitland NSW (Australia)

When I "came out" my parents weren't in the picture, at that time I was 17 and living with my older sister.

Once I understood that I am gay, my feelings made sense and I was happy. I still didn't know about homophobes or that it was even a problem, so I proudly announced it to my sister and her husband.

That was the last day I felt like part of the family, it got real ugly, really quickly.

I knew they wouldn't be happy about it, but I thought they would eventually accept it.

I was so wrong, at this point the church got involved and began preaching to my family about my sins.

My sister contacted all family and friends to warn them about me, because they were all starting their families and I could no longer be trusted around children. By the time everyone heard, I had no relationships with anyone. My father called me a poofter and my mother never spoke to me again, (both my parents have passed away now). I couldn't stay there anymore and had nowhere else to go, so I moved to the city.

Things almost got to a civil point until the AIDS outbreak and the public hysteria, at this point I was considered to be diseased and infectious and it all escalated into constant abuse until I stopped coming back.

That all happened over 30 years ago and not much has changed, we talk on the phone every couple of years and have meaningless conversations about nothing, while we make out that none of it ever happened. – Ian Davies

————————∇————————

Mokena, IL (USA)

"Do you think it's a surprise?" … "We love you." – Mark Zubro

————————∇————————

Princeton, NJ (USA)

During the spring of my senior year at Princeton, Mom and Dad visited and I asked them to sit down in my dorm room because I had something to tell them. I sat on my narrow bed, Mom sat beside me, Dad pulled over my wooden desk chair and sat.

"I've joined an organization," I said. I knew that because of my concentration in Russian Studies and my having spent the previous summer studying in the Soviet Union, they would immediately assume I was declaring membership in the Communist Party, the most horrific affiliation they could possibly imagine. Or so they might have thought before I quickly added, "I've joined The Gay Alliance of Princeton."

"The what?" spat Dad with a suspicious squint.

"The Gay Alliance of Princeton."

"Why? Do you think you belong there?"

"Yes."

Dad was dumbstruck.

Mom reached her hand out and took mine. "Is this why you had difficulties years ago?" She was, of course, referring to my freshman year suicide attempt, the reasons for which I'd never shared.

"Yes," I replied. Years before, I'd concluded that being gay was incompatible with being Jewish, that God hated me as an abomination, and that the only way to be a good Jew was to kill myself and thereby show my devotion to God's teachings.

Sitting on my bed now, Mom clutched my hand tightly.

For years, we went through several difficult conversations while Mom and Dad struggled to understand. Nevertheless, they always welcomed any "friend" I brought to their home, and they later grew to love the man who would become my husband, Leo.

How Did Your Parents React When You "Came-Out" to Them?

Thirty years or so after I first came out to them, as Mom suffered from Alzheimer's, she went through a period when she'd refer to me in third-person as her mind flashed to some moment in the past. Sometimes, she'd start weeping and ask me desperately, "How is he? How is he?"

Knowing that she was referring to me, I'd reply, "He's okay, Mom. Really, he's okay. He's happy now."

"Really?" she'd ask, her voice straining with hopefulness as she clutched my hand the same way she had that day I came out at Princeton. "Really?"

"Yes, indeed. He's happy as can be. He has a good life."

"Oh, oh thank goodness," she'd say, wiping her tears, pressing her cheek against my hand. "I'm so glad."

Around that same time, as Dad was recuperating from cancer surgery during what would be a month before his death, he sent Leo a birthday card, urging him to enjoy life ... and love.

Dear Mom and Dad. – Daniel M. Jaffe

—————∇—————

Manhattan Beach, CA (USA)

My dad was a policeman in town, very well known. He was freaked out because he thought everyone was going to say, "Perry's daughter is a lesbian ... ughh!" Mom was kind of ok because she used to tell me that men are horrible, except for your father. They took me to the family doctor, and he said, "There's nothing wrong with her, let her alone." And they did. They got into it and they started letting me have parties with all these dykes at my house. They were fine with it. After a while they didn't care because my dad was an actor, very prominent here in Palm Springs, he was into the music and acting, so he was pretty into that, and my mom worked in a nightclub called the Horn in Santa Monica. She was at Jim Nabors and Rock Hudson's wedding that they had after hours at the club. So she was fine. She knew I loved Kim Novak and she would come home and say, "Kim was in tonight." ... "What was she wearing, did you touch her?" I remember having a crush on John Travolta, and she said, "Oh honey, he's gay." So they couldn't care less unless I did something horrible. – Siouxzan Perry

—————∇—————

(New Zealand)

My mother said, "Oh dear, I want you to get married and carry on the name." That whole English thing. It was probably around 1988. I remember sitting up at night with my father and getting to know him as a person and a friend. I said, "You know dad, I'm gay." He said, "For God's sake don't tell your mother, whatever you do." Then one day I had a bit of an argument with mum, and I said, "I'm gay, I love men." But then when I met Art he came to New Zealand for 10 days. I took him on a tour, and I took him to where she was, and she looked at him with a seal of approval. But it was not a talked-about subject, even though she probably knew, but she gave him the look. I think she was looking at him and thinking, "God he's handsome." My mother did admire fine men. When I told her, it was just pushed under the carpet. "Oh but dear, I'd love you to have a wife and children." I said, "I'm still your son, it doesn't change the fact that I'm your son." It was probably because I was a very expressive person. But with my family, it was all pushed under the carpet, no arguing. I would say to myself at the age of 14, "When I grow up, I'm going to express." That's why people have issues today because they suppress too much. – Gib Maudey

————————▽————————

South Bend, IN (USA)

My father never acknowledged it. He still loved me. My mother always knew I was different. In fact, one of my aunts said to me, when I came out to her. She said, "It's no surprise to me, I always knew you were different." – Marc

————————▽————————

Florida (USA)

Well, my dad was military, so I certainly wasn't going to come out to him. I came out to my mother and the way it happened was ... I was already 16 years old and sneaking off to the bars. Me and a bunch of friends we used to sneak off to the Parliament House, the Loading Dock, and all those places. And if you were underage you had to do favors for the door guy, or you weren't getting in. My mother asked me straight out. She said, "Where are you going? What kind of clubs do you go to?" That kind of thing. I said, "What are you asking me?" She said, "Do you go to meet boys or do you go to meet girls?" I'm in the middle of eating cereal, about ready to dash out the door. So I said, "If you ask a question like that, you're ready for the answer either way. Are you ready for the answer either way?" She said, "Yes." I told her and she flipped out. She completely flipped out. And I resented her for it because she went through all of the normal ... "What did I do? Where did I go wrong?" Just all of that stuff. I felt betrayed by that. I had always been myself, I didn't change. But everybody else changed. I didn't talk to family for a while. I short-changed my dad because everyone told me not to tell him. They said, "Don't tell him. He won't understand. He's old school." So I didn't tell him for years. I kept my life hidden from him. Then one day, this was after I found out I was HIV Positive, I decided to tell him. Just everything, just all of it, unloaded the whole thing about being gay, HIV, all of it. And he immediately responded with kindness and understanding and support. I couldn't believe it. It was the complete opposite of what everybody told me. And because of those fears, I didn't have much of a relationship with my dad at all for a long time. That was a shame. – Bart

————————∇————————

Baltimore, MD (USA)

I smile when I talk about that because my family was incredible. I had already been with Charlie living in California for maybe four or five years. We got together when I was 27. I was in my young 30s and I would go back to Baltimore to see my parents once a year to visit. They knew that I had a roommate, they knew I was in the process of purchasing a home. It was late in the evening and my dad had gone to bed, and my mom asked me, "Are you going to have the same roommate?" I said, "Yes." Then she said, "Are you gay?" I said, "Yes." She cried a little bit, so I said, "Do you want me to wake dad up and we can have a family talk?" She said, "No, I'll tell him in the morning." So my mom went to bed and I went to bed and the next morning I was in the kitchen pretty early. I don't think I slept at all that night, because I wasn't sure what to expect from my dad. I'm sorry I'm going to get emotional here. My dad came in the kitchen and he said, "Your mother tells me you're gay." I looked at him and I wasn't sure what to expect. If he was going to backhand me, or what. I said, "Yes." And he gave me a hug and said, "You know, that's OK. That's just fine. Thanks for sharing." The kicker was, and this is where it gets a little silly, my mom comes downstairs and says, "I just saw a commercial for Oprah Winfrey, they're having gay people and their parents on. So we're all going to watch it today." I thought, "Oh God." So, of course, Oprah has on the most effeminate guy in the world and the most butch, severe, short-haired chick on with their parents. And I thought, "No, this is not the way I wanted this to go." My parents have been great ever since. My whole family knows. They insisted that I tell my brother, which was just as difficult, if not more difficult, than telling my parents. My brother and sister-in-law were fine from Day 1. Grandparents, aunts, uncles, cousins, you name it, it was a welcome. I think the reason I was so closeted and into myself when I was younger was because – like I said, my parents were pretty liberal, nothing was ever hidden in the house. I remember the book by Dr. David Reuben, *Everything You Always Wanted to Know About Sex: But Were*

Afraid to Ask and that was a really whacked-out book. I just remember reading the part about homosexuals, godawful stuff, and I thought "Oh this is horrible, this is what my future is?" I tried to pray it away, I remember going to bed at night and just praying that I would wake up attracted to women. Of course, that didn't work. – Cody

——————▽——————

Milwaukee, WI (USA)

I never got to come out to my parents. I was estranged from both my biological father and stepfather (now both deceased), and my mother died when I was just 24 and only beginning the coming out process. I like to think she probably knew and was OK with it, but I'll never know for sure, of course. – Yvonne Zipter

——————▽——————

Southend-on-Sea, (UK)

I was very worried about telling them. All my friends at the time said I was mad because they were the coolest people on the block. They were artists, they knew gay people, vegetarians in the 1960s. It wasn't that unusual but it's still one's parents. I told my mum first in the kitchen over a cup of tea. She sort of realized anyway. Then she said, "Whatever you do when you tell dad, pretend you haven't told me first. Tell us both at the same time." Over a Sunday lunch I told them. Mum was a little bit upset at that point but that was more "not having grandchildren," that sort of thing. They were fine with it. Now I've taken them to sex shows, drag joints and all sorts of things. So everybody else was right, there was no difficulty, but it's still your own parents. – Martin

——————▽——————

Chicago, IL (USA)

I never did. There's more to the story. I wanted to come out and then my mother got very, very, ill. It was going to be a very slow decline. I felt that telling her would just put a burden on her. Then after she passed away my dad came to visit Tim and I, my husband. He stayed with us, he stayed in one bedroom and Tim and I stayed in our normal bedroom. Nothing was ever mentioned. Then we drove him back to the airport, dropped him off. He called me when he got home and said that he'd had a wonderful time, and then he asked to talk to Tim. He said, "I'm so glad that Michael has you in his life." Then during my 50th birthday party, my husband's sister drank a bit back then. We called her Loud Patty because after she had a certain number of drinks she got loud. I was opening presents and I told Tim that I wanted a snow-blower. Now my birthday is in August and they weren't in stock. So he gave me a lovely card with a picture of a snow-blower on it. This was when we were living in Chicago and shoveling snow was quite a task. So I showed it to everybody – I had my Southern Baptist family there. I said, "Tim gave me a snowblower." And Patty said quite loudly, "A snow blower!! What the hell kind of present is that for a gay man." So my sister-in-law officially outed me to my family. – Michael Wayne

—————∇—————

Chicago, IL (USA)

I'm not out to my biological father. My mother pulled a "bait and switch" and told me, after a prolonged period of time, that it was okay that I'm gay. She has since lived on a swinging pendulum between shrill, religious insanity expressed as homophobia, to grudging "tolerance" when periods of religious insanity subside; they never subside for very long. – Chip H.

—————∇—————

Chicago, IL (USA)

I made a decision early on, as I was coming out to friends and other family members that I would wait until my parents broached the subject, before I discussed it with them.

To my surprise, it was my father who asked me first. He took it unexpectedly well. My mother, on the other hand, had a much harder time with it. She eventually came around and has attended Pride parades and even rode with me and my husband Rick on the Chicago Gay and Lesbian Hall of Fame float a couple of times. – Gregg Shapiro

—————∇—————

New York, NY (USA)

They were OK, no questions were ever asked. I was married, but I was living with a man. My parents came to visit, they asked no questions or anything. When my dad died, my mom was in the hospital and she said, "I have to tell you this … " My wife had called my parents to let them know I was gay. My father answered and said, "We don't care what our son is, he's our son and we love him for who he is." That was the best answer. Less than a week later mom passed away. They never asked any questions because it was ok with them. So I was lucky. – Juan-manuel Alonso

———————∇———————

Hattiesburg, MS (USA)
Vicksburg, MS (USA)

I was with my first girlfriend. We lived in Hattiesburg, Mississippi. It was my mom's 50th birthday and we were having a big party for her. We drove up to Vicksburg, got a hotel room – there was no way in hell that I was staying with my parents. No way. I knew I needed to tell them because we were going to be moving to Florida. I wanted them to know before I left. I waited during the party, it was held at the Knights of Columbus because my parents were such good Catholics. I decided to take my dad into the bar. I was drinking at the time. I took him into the bar and I sat him down and I told him, because I knew if I told my stepfather, it would take the punch out of telling my mom. I told him. He didn't care. He's very open minded and it didn't bother him. But I said, "I gotta tell mom." He said, "When are you going to tell her?" I said, "Probably after the party." He said, "Good idea." We went home to my parents' house, I took off my shoes, sat on the couch, and we chatted … my little brother was 14 at the time, he was down there, yak, yak, yakking. Finally, it was getting late and I sent my brother upstairs because I didn't want him to know at the time. I put my shoes back on because I knew I might have to run. I proceeded to tell her. She didn't say a word. That's worse than anything. The silence. There was just silence. Everybody else tells stories, "Oh my whole family, when I told them, they said, 'Oh we already knew.'" My mom, you could just see the devastation on her face. I looked right at her, "I know this might upset you, but you got me married once." That was my line. I left and I didn't speak to her for four years. Then 9/11 came, right after 9/11 my mom reached out to me. She said, "You're coming home, I need you to come home. I need to see you." That's how it's been. So, my parents are ok with me being gay from afar. But don't bring it to Mississippi. – Jade

———————∇———————

Southern California (USA)

There's my coming out as bi, then there's my coming out at trans. Then there's my biological family and then the people I call my family. It's a little complex, so I'm going to cherry pick. When I first came out as bi to my father, I was terrified and I said, "Dad, I think I like girls." He said, "What a coincidence, so do I." So he helped me write a love letter to my best friend who I was in love with at the time, when I was 12 years old. He was also the first one I did my soft coming out as trans to. There was my soft, my official, and then my re-coming out as non-binery. So I've had four different coming-outs. The first was, "Dad, I think sometimes I need to be a boy." He said, "Alright, let's go get you some new clothes, so you can experiment. This is how I think you'd look most androgynous. Let's get you some glasses, get you some beanies and we'll pull your hair back." When I came out as trans, my dad was initially, "What do we need to do? What do you want to be called?" My biological dad has always been 100 percent supportive. Coming out as non-binery was nothing, it was like, "OK change your identity, that's fine." With the person I call my mom, she's always been 100 percent supportive. She calls me her son. She tells me to let my freak flag fly. Whatever crazy fashion choices I feel like pulling off, "Just go ahead and pull those stunts." So I really appreciate my mom and my dad. My biological mother felt heartbroken that she was losing her daughter and even after she had seen me with a chest compressor and a full beard, still called me "she" and by my dead name. Then told my friends, "I don't know why she's using the men's bathroom when she looks like a bearded lady. As if my friends wouldn't tell me that my mom was talking smack about me. So that really hurt. The rest of my family are just coming to terms. One of them, my brother, went back and blocked me. When I initially came out, he said, "I have a little brother now, yeah!" Then it's been almost a decade and he's decided that I'm his sister, schizophrenic, and crazy because I'm trans. – Bambi

———————▽———————

Southern California (USA)

Technically I came out three times. I came out as bi first, then gay, then trans. With the whole bi gay part of it, my parents were totally fine with it. Never an issue. But when I came out as trans after I'd moved out, I went two years without talking to my father or my sister. It wasn't until I was going to be getting married that I gave them an ultimatum. I told them, "I'm happy now. I've been depressed throughout my whole life, I'm marrying my best friend. You can choose to be there and be a part of my life, or if you're not there, there will be no repairing things. My mother, on the other hand, has always been my biggest supporter. I wouldn't be where I'm at today, if it hadn't been for her. – Hayley

———————▽———————

Riverside, CA (USA)

It was interesting because they thought I was just going to come out as gay. They were confused because I've only ever been attracted to women. It was a weird thing for them. When I came out as trans I was expecting my mom to be like, "Just do it," and my stepdad would say, "Well ok, but I've got some questions." It was actually the opposite. My stepdad was like, "Cool, what's next? What do we do?" and my mom said, "I have some questions." She was very supportive the whole time. I had to learn that it was not only a transition for me but a transition for my parents as well. Throughout the whole experience, everyone was very encouraging and I'm very fortunate. – Chloe DeCamp

───────▽───────

Palm Springs, CA (USA)

My father is deceased, and I do wonder if my father would have still loved me. Knowing that he was a racist, I wonder if he would have opened his arms to me. 2014 was the first time I was with a woman and I can remember introducing this woman to my mother. Even though I told my mother that was my girlfriend, I don't think she really understood but when I married Leslie, that's when she began to have the craziest conversations with me. She would say, "Cathy, now Cathy, tell me how you can go from being with men all your life until one day you say, 'I love women?'" I said to her, "This is what I would tell you, for me it's not about the part, it's about the heart. So it's not gender-specific. Although being with a woman, I get things I never received from a man." And she says, "Like what, Cathy? Tell me." I said, "She knows my body because it's her body. She knows how to caress me because it's her body. She knows where it feels good and I don't have to direct her, I don't have to put her hand here, I don't have to say anything. Our bodies are the same." Then she said, "Cathy, your wife is the least feminine woman that I could ever imagine. How could you love somebody like that?" So I said, "She's got a vagina and she's got tits, both of which I'm attracted to." Again, she's like, "Cathy, Cathy, you've always been with men." I said, "It's funny mom, you never asked me if I've ever been with a woman, or am I attracted to women. And I would tell you now, I'm almost 60 and I love a good rack on a woman. I love boobs. I love the way a woman smells, I love the curves of her body, I love everything about this woman. And this is the most important thing, I am almost 60 and this is the first time I have found happiness and it's unconditional. She loves me unconditionally, as I love her." I see my mother frequently, at least once a week if not more, and we've been having this conversation for at least four years. Every time it's the same conversation. And every time my answers don't deviate at all, but the funny thing is, around the time I came out, my daughter, who is 17 years younger, came out too. When I met my wife, she met her wife, and it was almost as if she was in a race to marry a woman before I did. She always flirted more openly with women than I did. Don't get me wrong, I flirted with them – I remember being in a strip club flirting with a woman. I look back at it now and I think, "Gee that was a little sleazy back then." My mother doesn't understand it at all and I just think it's because I was always with men. I think it would be easier for her to swallow if I was openly bisexual and she saw me with a woman, but she's only ever seen me with men prior to my first girlfriend. – Cathy Melton

—————▽—————

Norwell, MA (USA)

My parents were both deceased when I came out. My grandparents were my caretakers after my dad passed last. He passed between my junior and senior year of high school. Crazy dysfunctional family stuff, but my natal grandmother and grandfather took care of me after he died. I came out to them. I made a process out of it. I said, "I need to talk to you," and we went onto their back porch, a screen porch. This was their family home. I just said, "I need to tell you something. I'm gay." They said – quiet, quiet, quiet, nothing, saying nothing. Shortly afterwards my grandmother said, "You never have to tell us that again." I said, "You're right, I don't. I just needed to tell you who I was." – Leslie Tisdale

—————▽—————

Melbourne, Victoria (Australia)

It's 2005. Mum and I are fighting. She asks me if I'm dating my then girlfriend. Even in the fight I don't want to lie, I said, "Yes." She of course took it badly. Dad was fine but it takes a lot for him to lose his composure. Finding out I was bisexual didn't even cause a ripple. – Anita Morris

—————▽—————

Palm Springs, CA (USA)

Well, I never did. That was a part of my journey. My dad would have been devastated. He was fine with it if we didn't talk about it, didn't discuss it. He would have not known what to say and I don't think my mom would have known what to say either. I did not come out until both of them had died. I was married, in my 50s, 58, my wife was 54. She was a pediatrician and she gained a lot of weight and died. By that time my big brother had died, my mom had died, my dad had died, and it kind of set me free. The people that would have judged me were dead. I really grew after that, I had acceptance, that's when I came to Palm Springs. I said, "I've got one more lifetime to live." I was 58 and now I'm 79, so I'm 21 years into that lifetime. It's been totally different to my previous life, but my previous life prepared me for what I am now. – Don Rockwell Coffee

————▽————

Bellwood, IL (USA)

My mother instinctively knew that I was gay but never wanted to admit it. When I told her, she naturally felt guilty and thought she did something wrong as a mother. I assured her that wasn't the case at all. I told her I realized I was different and I came to accept it. If she couldn't, I was prepared to move out of the house. She said no, that wasn't necessary. She supported me and was always concerned about me, particularly when the AIDS crisis surfaced. Mom was inquisitive about gay life and one of her first questions to me was, "Who puts what where?" I reacted with shock upon hearing this, but she obviously had no knowledge of the mechanics within gay sex, and simply responded, "Well, I want to know."

As for my father, my mother told him and his reaction was short and simple: "There are worse things to be in this world." Dad was never a great communicator but his message was clear: it didn't matter.

Both of my parents accepted my two partners and they were considered to be part of the family. It was wonderful to experience this. – Yehuda Jacobi

————▽————

Albuquerque, NM (USA)

I did come out to them in 1980, but not in the normal fashion. I'd figured out that I was a heterosexual sissy, a femme girl kind of person who was male and whose attraction was to female people, and it was definitely hugely DIFFERENT. Lots of liberal tolerant college friends had been after me to come out and accept myself all year long – assuming I was a gay guy who wasn't out yet – and my Dad said something in passing that made me think they were letting me know that they knew and that it was OK with them. So

118

How Did Your Parents React When You "Came-Out" to Them?

I broke the ice and spoke of the nice supportive college kids who were ready to accept me as a gay friend and classmate, and said that maybe they (my parents) thought that, too – because unlike the rest of the world they had never hassled me about being feminine. But that it wasn't that; it was something else. They denied having ever thought anything of the sort, but they seemed embarrassed and relieved and awkward. And they heard the part they were comfortable hearing ("not gay") and ignored the part that made them squirmy ("I'm a feminine boy/I'm different in a fashion similar to how gay people are different but it's something else"). Not many people were coming out as "trans" back then yet and I don't think that possibility even occurred to them, and even if it had, I didn't identify as trans either – back then the only trans people were the ones who get surgery and change their sex to fit their gender and I wasn't doing that, I was identifying as a male sissy, a girl with a male body who didn't consider the "girl" part or the "male" part to be inappropriate or wrong. – Allan Hunter

———————▽———————

Detroit, MI (USA)

My mother said, "I already knew that." She always knew. They've got two gay sons, now they've got a third one. I told him, "You're not going gay uh uh." He's been married to this woman for 15 years. I consider her my sister. Now he wants to go fuck around. He showed up at my house wearing a dress … he looks like a witch. – Jack Farquhar Halbert

———————▽———————

London, (UK)

I didn't. My father died in a car accident when I was 21. He was drunk and drove his car into a lamppost on the North Circular. I wasn't out to anybody at that point. Although, I was out by the time my mother died in '87. I never came out to her directly. But she was dying of lung cancer and I remember sitting with her one evening in her apartment and it was probably only a month or so before she died, we were watching a quiz show on TV and she turned to me and said, "I don't suppose there's any point in me hanging on for you to get married." And I said, "No, I don't think there is." That was the only conversation we ever really had. I mean, it was understood. – Tess Tickles

———————▽———————

How Did Your Parents React When You "Came-Out" to Them?

San Francisco, CA (USA)

I sent them a seven-page letter. I wrote them shortly after I arrived in San Francisco. They guessed it anyway. My brother, my younger brother, is gay. He came out to them before I did. He's nine years younger than me. My mother is quite religious, so she wrote back and said, "We're wondering what we did wrong to have two gay sons." But she's reconciled it, I guess. My father was nondescript, just sitting in the background. She was the one that did all the talking. He accepted us, I think. – Paul

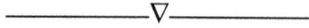

————∇————

Columbus, OH (USA)
Willard, OH (USA)

My parents would never turn their back on me but they were not sure how to react when I came out to them, so we did nothing. We didn't talk about it for a long time and there was a lot of distance between us. Then later my younger brother and younger sister came out and my parents and siblings are just a big gay happy family! – Mike Gifford

————∇————

Santiago, (Chile)

That was interesting. I was at the point where I was thinking, "If I die today, you won't know half the people at my funeral." That would be odd, so I decided to fix it. I came out and told my parents. My mum turned it around, so it was about her, so I said, "This is my thing." She was stealing my thunder. My mom's first reaction was, "Oh this is going to be hard for me and your dad." She gave me a speech about, "I'm cool but I have to think about it myself. What are you doing to me?" I asked my dad what he thought, and he said, "You're my son, so I'm cool with that." – Ives

————∇————

New York, NY (USA)

1994. I was on the phone with my mother. I actually had to point out what I had just told her. Like, "Do you get it?" She was perfectly suitable, as we say in WASP-y New England, but she moved the conversation on to other topics as quickly as she could. – David Pratt

How Did Your Parents React When You "Came-Out" to Them?

───────▽───────

Central Illinois (USA)

My mom said she did not care as long as I believed in Jesus. – Terry Gaskins

───────▽───────

Chicago, IL (USA)

Neither was particularly surprised. My mother didn't want me to tell anyone else. When I protested, she said, "It took you 25 years to come out, don't expect me to do it overnight." Within a few years she was talking about it on television. – Rick Karlin

───────▽───────

Weymouth, (UK)

Badly. I was 19 and between a rock and a hard place. With hindsight, I can see that I wasn't ready to come out and could have handled it better. But I was with an older partner and not being out, with all the lies and subterfuge that entails, was disrupting our life together and unfair on him. It came to a head one Christmas, which I felt I had to spend with my parents, without him, of course. When I phoned my partner on Christmas Day, he responded with a foul-mouthed rant at how selfish I was being and told me to fuck off. My parents eventually came 'round to the idea and are now fully supportive of me and my new partner. I was annoyed with them for a long time, as they presented themselves as open-minded, liberal, educated people, but their reaction at the time was selfish, petulant and bigoted. They were unfair on my partner of the time, whom they sought to blame for me being gay and I was rather frozen out of their lives for several years. Their reaction still rankles. My father has recently apologised several times (including in print), but my mother never has. Annoyingly, she recently asked me to intervene and offer support to a gay male friend of my sister, whose own parents are giving him a hard time over his coming out. Grrrrrrr! – Diesel Balaam

───────▽───────

Chicago, IL (USA)

I came out to my parents the way they say you shouldn't; in anger. My Mom and Dad used to leave for work early in the morning (around 5am) and one morning after I had just broken up with my "secret" boyfriend, my straight friend was dropping me off in his car and I broke down and told him about the breakup and I started crying. My friend put his arm around me to console me and that is when I noticed my Dad staring at us through the front windshield. I was doubly horrified when I also saw my Mother, and I hurriedly exited the car. My Mom continued walking down the gangway, but my Dad had stopped and I was face to face with him when he angrily asked, "What are you? A sissy?" I wasn't having it, so I huffily replied, "Yeah!" He told me to get in the house and I responded with a defiant and loud "No!" He left in a huff and my "secret" was no longer a secret. We didn't discuss it for a while but later my Dad, who loved to work on cars, would tell me, "It's not like you're a car with a bad carburetor and I can just go to the junkyard and get a new carburetor, so I guess I'll just have to live with it." My Mom, it turns out, seemed nonplussed by the news and later I would find out why. I'll just end the story there. – Robert Castillo

—————▽—————

Niles, IL (USA)

I used to work out with two gay priests at the Body Shop gym. My mother found a *GayLife* periodical in my bedroom. She drove to one of the priests and discussed my lifestyle. (They later told me). They supported me but my mom brought up John Wayne Gacy – and that era – and said she didn't want to see me dead. My father was very supportive. – David Plambeck

—————▽—————

(Venezuela)

It's interesting because I never came out to my parents. I left the country in 2008 and some of my cousins, or most of my cousins, knew that something was going on with me. They kept pushing my mom and she blew up. My mom met Robert, my husband, before. He spent some time with them, and they visited us in Guadalajara. Anyway, my cousins were bothering my mom. When I talked to her eight months ago, she said, "Someone was bothering me, they kept asking, 'What do you call Robert?'" He's my husband and we're married. And my mom said, "It's none of my business, Robert is married to my son, so he's my son-in-law." When she told me that, I cried on the phone. That was so touching. Of course, she knew, but I never came out to her. – Carlos

—————▽—————

How Did Your Parents React When You "Came-Out" to Them?

Elyria, OH (USA)

The conversation was in our eyes and heart. – Alex Gildzen

─────────▽─────────

Milwaukee, WI (USA)

They said it changed nothing, but we never spoke of it again other than when they said, "And we aren't going to tell any of the neighbors." – Anonymous

─────────▽─────────

Chicago, IL (USA)

I never did. – Anonymous

─────────▽─────────

Seattle, WA (USA)

My father had died in 1986. My mother was in her 90s and I was divorced and living with my life partner and my mother knew him and there was a point at which I said, "I really need to tell my mother because I want her to know." And my mother was a very liberal, very progressive woman growing up in the 1900s, so I knew that she would not be condemning. I had a whole speech prepared and I drove all the way up to her assisted living apartment. I told her I had something I wanted to share with her. And I got there, and I started sharing this. I was sweating and nervous. When I finished, I said, "So, I'm gay." She said, "Well, I was pretty sure that you were." I said, "Mom why didn't you say something?" And she said, "Well, I really felt that was something for you to be ready to tell me when it was your time." I could have strangled her because there was so much anxiety. She was very accepting but because she lived in a retirement community that was sponsored by a Christian organization, she said, "Now, I cannot let anybody else here know this." So I said, "I understand that." Then she said, "But I have no problem with this." I'm sure that my mom, although we never discussed it, somewhere among all her acquaintances with women, probably knew some lesbians, and probably gay men. My brother, when I told him I was going to have this talk with her, said, "You can't. You absolutely can't tell her. It will be bad for her, she's in her 90s. Don't do this." It turned out fine. – OT

How Did Your Parents React When You "Came-Out" to Them?

—————————▽—————————

New York, NY (USA)

In a few words, not well. I came out to my father, but never came out to my mother. I came out to my father in anger. It was Yom Kippur 1973 and I was in synagogue with my father. An orthodox synagogue. My family was orthodox. My father, who rarely showed any interest in me, started prying into my personal life. He wanted to know if I needed rubbers, because he would buy me some. I said to him, "I'm afraid I wouldn't have much use for them." He then, after a while, said, "Are you a homosexualist?" And I told him I was. There we were fasting and praying, and I came out. I came out almost as a way to punish him. I've regretted the way I did it. – Ian H

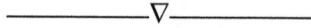

—————————▽—————————

WHAT WAS THE FIRST GAY BAR YOU WENT INTO?

Iowa City, IA (USA)

It was 1979 and I was 18 and in my 2nd semester at the University of Iowa when a lesbian friend invited me to meet a friend of hers at a place called That Bar on the edge of Iowa City and the area's only gay bar. I was banging a French TA at the time, nine years older than me and I didn't want to go to a 'gay' bar. My girlfriend told me to go ahead, that I'd have a great time; she'd been to several gay bars in Paris and said they were fun. Reluctantly I went, and so nervous that I sat in this dark, little bar at a cocktail table and consumed seven beers in the first two hours. I was blonde and thin and at least two men had tried to get me onto the dance floor. Finally, my friend said I should go ahead and dance with someone; she said I liked to dance, and it didn't mean I was gay just because I was dancing with a guy. So the next offer I got, I was just buzzed enough to say yes and I began to loosen up and have a good time. Later, as I stood at the bar waiting for another beer, someone tapped on my shoulder and I turned around to politely decline another dance, and I fell in love. But that's for another story. – Timothy Juhl

———————∇———————

London (UK)

The Black Cap, Camden, London summer 1981 just after leaving school. – Matt D

———————∇———————

What Was the First Gay Bar You Went Into?

Chicago, IL (USA)

Broadway Limited on Broadway ... sheet metal dance floor. – Don Strzepek

———————▽———————

Denver, CO (USA)

The Foxhole in 1992. I was underage and they were the bar that didn't ID. No one went to that bar; the Paradise Garage next door was much more happening. I went one night and met a guy from out of town. I must have done something right because he moved to Denver a few months later AND got me a fake ID. Certainly made my teenage years better. – Thomas Bottoms

———————▽———————

Belmont Shores, Long Beach, CA (USA)

I can't remember the name of the place. It was on the beach in Belmont Shores, Long Beach. It was not my type of bar. It was the type of bar where everyone dressed nice, but it was pretty. I guess it was back in the late '70s. It was down the beach from the Belmont Pool, a big Olympic swimming pool they have there in Long Beach. I distinctly remember not knowing what to order. I ordered rum and cola and they gave me this huge glass of ice and rum and a splash of cola. It was totally undrinkable. I remember the room with the pool table, wandering in there, and the floor above is where their dance floor was. I remember watching the light over the pool table undulating up and down and up and down from all the dancers upstairs. You think, "Is this thing going to cave in on top of us all." It was the first place I ever had enough courage to go into. I wish I could remember the name of it. There were other places after that, but once I discovered leather bars I was much more comfortable. – Tim Barela

———————▽———————

Chicago, IL (USA)

Berlin in Chicago. I loved every minute of it – reminded of the dance club scene in *Basic Instinct* and I thought I was so urban! – Jim

———————▽———————

What Was the First Gay Bar You Went Into?

Montivideo (Uruguay)

When I was 24 years old, I went to my first gay bar in Montevideo, Uruguay in the '80s. Its name was Arco Iris, it means rainbow in Spanish. It was a narrow, not big place, and without glamour, but it was very important because you can meet people and develop the LGTBIQ that was in the "shadows." – Dr. Eduardo Levaggi Mendoza

—————▽—————

Fort Collins, CO (USA)

The People's Bar. I huddled in a corner clutching a bottle of beer, which I did not drink. The bar burned down in 1986 when someone set fire to its Christmas tree. – Louis Flint Ceci

—————▽—————

Fort Lauderdale, FL (USA)

The Copa, Fort Lauderdale, drove to it at least a dozen times over several months before finally having the nerve to go in. – Robert Hansen

—————▽—————

San Francisco, CA (USA)

My very first bar was an experience that I will never forget. Michael was my very first crush/romantic fling. I didn't know where to meet guys then, so I answered his personal ad in *The Advocate*. I was going to San Francisco for my twenty-first birthday and Mike lived there, perfect for me since I was planning to move there. I didn't, but that's another story.

Mike was stunningly handsome, twenty-three years old and worked for an insurance company in the Financial District on Montgomery Street. We met in the lobby of his office, we went to dinner at an Italian Café in North Beach, we walked around the city after dark, and went for a drink at the bar at the top of the Hyatt Regency San Francisco. Outside the hotel there's a park with walkways lacing underneath a waterfall. This is where I had my first real kiss. It was exciting and romantic with water and lights all around us.

The next couple of days we spent together, going to the movies, shopping, and making love. I also spent my very first night sleeping with a man, it was memorable not only because of the sex, but also because we were together on a twin bed, and I was pinned against the wall and I had to go to the bathroom, but was afraid of waking him up if I moved. I finally got up to go.

Mike took me to Chinatown for my birthday, and after that to Alta Plaza, a well-known bar on Fillmore Street. I had my first drink, a vodka and cranberry that night, and then we spent the night together.

It was on a Sunday, that we had 'the talk'. He told me that he knew I was falling in love with him, but he told me had dreams of his own. He was planning on moving to LA to get into the movies, he already had a job lined up somewhere down there, but if I moved to San Francisco he wouldn't be there, "there will be better men out there for you" he told me.

The last time I saw him was that Sunday evening. He took me with him to visit some friends across the Bay via BART. When we got back to the city, we walked out of the BART station, he kissed me on the lips and walked away. I didn't cry until I got back to Chicago.

I was never able to prove it, but I heard him mention to a friend he was planning on getting into the porn industry.

I never made the move to San Francisco, though I had many opportunities. When I worked for Borders, I interviewed for the store on Union Square, three separate times and the job was offered to me on a veritable 'silver platter', but my mother was sick at the time, and I didn't think it would be the right thing to be so far away. I had to turn it down, and Borders Books closed its doors across the country a year or so later.

I live in Oregon with my husband, Dean, and our soon to be adopted son, there are a lot of ups and downs, but I still think about the 'what ifs'. However, since then I've written five novels, and two of them have been set in San Francisco, so I guess I live there vicariously through the main character. – Jerry S.

———————▽———————

Asbury Park, NJ (USA)

This opens up such a floodgate of memories. I went as a young man of 18 or 19, to a bar called the Odyssey in Asbury Park, New Jersey. I was with a group of people – I was a hairdresser, a straight hairdresser, and everybody I worked with was gay. So when they said they wanted to go out, I said, "Sure, let's go." I was young and fun, and probably on the verge of getting married, or had got married already. I got married early. So it was the first time I went to a gay bar, but I wasn't going to pick anybody up. I was going to dance, drink, and have a good time. So that was my first experience, around '73, '74. – Joseph S.

What Was the First Gay Bar You Went Into?

———————∇———————

South Bend, IN (USA)

The first gay bar I went into was the Seahorse Lounge in South Bend, Indiana. I think it was 1981? It was the only gay bar in the city I grew up in, and was, thus, notorious. It was located on the west side of the city, in an area that had been predominantly Polish and Catholic, but had started to turn when factories started closing. It was small, and dimly lit. Men, mostly older, sat at the bar and around cocktail tables. The police were generally nearby, and I was advised that my license plate was probably already recorded by them. After going there for a few months trying to figure out if this was a place for me, the police started raiding the bar. Pulling us outside, checking ID, and trying to humiliate us for simply being gay, and gathering together. Shortly after that, I moved to Chicago, and never went back there again. I always wonder what happened to it. – Steve K

———————∇———————

Detroit, MI (USA)

It was a place called the Green Door and on weekends they had drag queens in there putting on shows. Although it was a gay bar, there were quite a few straight people that came in to see these shows on the weekends. I found out about it because I had a gay uncle. He said he wanted me to see a gay bar. He said, "I know the guys who own the place and we're going to come in the back door and sit at the end of the bar. So you won't be seen. But I want you to see all this." That was in 1958. – Dan Brazill

———————∇———————

Minneapolis, MN (USA)
Philadelphia, PA (USA)

That was so long ago I've almost forgotten. It was the 90's as in (The Gay 90's) in Minneapolis MN. My then friend Kevin, who has since become a hermit in the wilds of Wisconsin, took me there for my 21st Birthday. We stayed for a grand total of five minutes and relocated to a dive bar on Lake Street near his house. That was the night he wanted to let me know I was being evicted. He was having an affair with the two other roommates in the house and they and I were disagreeing on a bunch of things at the time. It was my first experience with living in a communal setting but not the last. You'd think I would have learned my lesson.

What Was the First Gay Bar You Went Into?

It was only a five minute visit so it doesn't count. The first time I went to a gay bar, and spent any real time there is a tale that's much more fun to tell. Philadelphia, not long after leaving Minneapolis, (the same year as I turned 21) I found a place in a squat in West Philly. Me and my friends, Tim and Leno, stole some bikes from some neighboring squatters and headed to the Bikestop downtown. Three floors of sweaty, beefy dudes, posing and prowling for loose and easy sleaze while guzzling cheap drinks and fucking at the bar. The dance floor was crowded but I stuck it out to watch two studly leather daddies fuck right up at the bar, while the folks around them ordered drinks and watched. I felt at home. And on the way home they introduced me to the cruising park, with guys everywhere and cars in a line down the block. But that's a tale for another time. – Daniel Fisher aka Raid

———————∇———————

Nashville, TN (USA)

The first gay bar I ever went in was the Jungle Lounge & Restaurant in Nashville, TN. Known simply as the Jungle by us locals. – Driveshaft

———————∇———————

Buffalo, NY (USA)

It was called the Hibachi Room and it was down in a basement, red flock wallpaper. I parked six blocks away so no one would see my car. Then I started parking closer and closer. It was a trip. It was the only gay bar in Buffalo. Actually, there were two, but this one was a younger crowd. I had two drinks before I went in the bar to get up my nerve, and I went in and it was a rack. I ended up having a blast. It was 1971, I was only 17 years old and I got in. – Rory

———————∇———————

Fresno, CA (USA)

It was right around Easter 1976. If you're familiar with Fresno, the urban part of Fresno, out on Highway 99, there was a bar called the Hangout. The Hangout had about 500 guys in there. I'd come out to my sister the week before. She was the first one I came out to. I went up to talk to her about being gay, so she brought me to this bar called the Hangout. It was a jeans and white T-shirt kind of bar, it wasn't leather, it was an everybody bar. I like tall guys, I like men to smell like men, like they work in a steel mill all day.

There was this one guy, he was tall, 6' 10" and he was living in a trailer. We went to his trailer. It turned out he was a backup center on one of the NCAA basketball teams. I won't say which one as there's a school named with it. – David

————————▽————————

Norfolk, VA (USA)

The first gay bar I ever walked into, the Oar House, was in March of 1981, located in Norfolk, Va. My high school girlfriend, our friend Chuck, and myself. I was 17yrs old and hadn't graduated high school quite yet. I was surprised, shocked and tripping, literally, all in one. I wouldn't let go of my girlfriend's hand the whole time. I didn't want to go in but they assured me that everything was going to be fine. I went back a couple of weeks later, alone. I have been out ever since. I still keep in touch with my high school girlfriend. If you call playing Words with Friends contact. Our friend Chuck passed away in the early '90s of AIDS. He was definitely a character. – Tripp

————————▽————————

Chicago, IL (USA)

Escapades, mid 1980s, southwest side of Chicago, a dive bar connected to a fried shrimp diner. I overheard my straight guy friends saying they couldn't believe there was a fag bar on the south side by Midway. I stole my parents' car to find it. – Martin Mulcahy

————————▽————————

New York, NY (USA)

Tracks – NYC. We were curious and underage with no jobs or money. People would sneak us in through a side door. – Dale

————————▽————————

San Diego, CA (USA)

The first gay bar was almost anti-climactic. The first experience of meeting other gay men was with the Metropolitan Community Church in San Diego. That was 1970. The only place you could meet outside of the bars was at the MCC rap group. That was scary enough, I went around and around the building several times, before I could get the courage to even go to the porch. I eventually did go in, was nervous the whole time, but felt like I'd found home. So going into a gay bar I do remember. It was called the Caliph and it was a quiet piano bar – I thought it was less threatening than a dance bar. I still sat in the car for a while before I went in. I was only 18 when I went to the rap group, so obviously I couldn't get into the bar, so that had to come later. I was 21. Between those two times, I went off to college and went to the Gay Student Union dances, very early '70s – Bill

—————▽—————

Los Angeles, CA (USA)

It was in my neighborhood. I had to walk by it when I went to school, so it had been there for a while. Later, when I had finally formulated that I was gay, or had tendencies, I was walking by one day and this car was driving into the driveway that would take it to the back of the building where there was parking. What was interesting about this bar is that it was right next to the Fire Station, so there were always these good-looking firemen out there. So, all of a sudden this car is pulling into the parking area and there are a few firemen sitting out front. That was the first time I saw men bold enough to be, not so much wolf-calling, but calling out. I knew – oh my goodness – that this was someplace I might want to go to. Then later I started hearing stories about the bar. So, with a little trepidation, I decided to go there. I walked in and they asked me what I wanted to drink. Well, I didn't know, so the bartender looks at me and says, "I think that you're a rum and Coke person." So, he gave me a rum and Coke. As I was sitting there, I was relaxed. Then I realized they had a show with amateur drag. They were getting up and performing. After I got in there and sat down and relaxed, it was so fun. People seemed to be friendly. That was around 1968. The bar was in what is now considered to be south west Los Angeles. If you drove a few miles you would be in the area of Watts. It was right before the Watts Riots and the complete change of a community overnight. – Kalvin.

—————▽—————

Flint, MI (USA)

The Copa. It was a Sunday night and they were doing a *Let's Make a Deal* game show with a drag queen hosting. Of course, my number got called and I was scared shitless. I chose the box over the envelope and won a smoke alarm. I was so broke, the following Christmas, that I gave my Grandmother the smoke alarm for Christmas which was installed in her entry way. Years after, friends coming over would laugh and point to the ceiling to where the smoke alarm was, my Grandmother having no idea what was going on. – Greg R. Baird

———————∇———————

Long Island, NY (USA)

My brother took me. He's gay. It was a small bar on Long Island, a Disco bar. I had told my brother I was gay two days prior and he took me out with all his friends. It was a nice time, but I went to school in South Dakota and there was a guy there that I always thought was hot. His name was Joel. First time I went in that bar, I look up at the DJ booth, and I said to my brother, "I know him." … "Oh no, that's Brian's lover." He called Brian over and said, "What's your lover's name?" He said, "Joel." I went up to the DJ booth and I said, "Joel!" The reason I was at private school in South Dakota was because I wanted to go somewhere where my parents would never visit. – Ron

———————∇———————

Newport, RI (USA)

David's. The fellow I discovered my sexuality with took me there. I was a little bit apprehensive. I was still living in the marital household and I was in grad school. He was living in his marital household also, but that's another story. I told him I was really nervous about going into the bar as I was in grad school sponsored by the navy. He said, "Well, I'll tell you what, when you walk in everybody is going to turn and look, so just don't worry about it. They just want to see who the fresh meat is." So, I went in and it was really not uncomfortable at all. David's was a mixed-crowd bar, wasn't much leather there. The leather was in Providence. At the weekends the leather boys, the Italian boys, would come down to Newport. Another fellow I got to know later said, "David's patio on a Sunday afternoon ought to be filmed." Well, on Sundays I was with my then family, so I didn't go. That was 1974. – Hal

———————∇———————

London (UK)

In London, in the '50s. It was a bar off St. Martin's Lane, a private bar, can't think of the name of it. There were two of them, and they were private, you had to be members. We paid the police not to raid us. My first boyfriend –

my first gentleman who took care of me, shall we say – he was a member and he took me there. It was very old-fashioned. If you were with a partner and someone fancied you, the waiter would come over with a drink and the man's card with his name on it. It was piss-elegant. It was very grand, not lavish, but it was beautifully furnished. We all wore jackets, shirts and ties. – Bob Brown

──────────▽──────────

Fire Island, NY (USA)

I was just turning 15. And there's a back story to it. I lived in New York, on Long Island. I knew that across from Long Island was Fire Island and I heard about the gay section. I knew there were other people like me out there, but it was a different time. I came out in the '70s. I was post-Stonewall, pre-AIDS. It was an interesting cool time. So I knew I wanted to get out there but I didn't know where. I didn't know where it was, because Fire Island has different sections. So I waited for my mother to leave the house. I decided to call the operator, because in those days in New York, you had an operator that answered. So I picked up the rotary kitchen phone and – I can still see the phone, it was black and had a few dings on it – and I dialed the operator and asked where the gay section of Fire Island was. The funny thing was I had a gay man on the other end. He started to talk to me. It was the whole routine, what are you looking for, where are you looking to go? He told me everything, right down to the schedule of the ferries. It's New York and this is an older man who works for the telephone company and it just happened that he was very nice. It was meant to be. So I was like, "This is great." He gave me all the information I needed. To this day I don't know his name. I wish I did because I would love to thank this man. He changed the whole world for me. In New York at 15, if you're in school or college, you have a driver's license. I had my license, I had a car. I went out to Sayville, which is where the ferries were. I knew that this was the boat that got over there. You're excited, you're nervous, but I was doing this. I was going. I got the ticket for the next ferry. I'm waiting in line with everybody else. It's like it was yesterday, I can still smell the salt water. I got across and I asked somebody, "Where are the bars?" I knew there were bars there, but I didn't know all the details. There was the Ice Palace and the Monster. So one guy said, "Just follow the crowd up to the Ice Palace." I was a kid, but I was six-feet tall and nobody questioned me. It was a different era. I get up there and I'm taking it all in and it was just like my head was unwinding. Seeing so many others that were like me. I'd never seen so many in one spot. I was a kid. I got a deckchair – in those days they charged for a deckchair. The Ice Palace was up there, and the deck was a little further down by the pool, with the hotel across from it. I was just enthralled and nervous to walk into the bar area. I finally watched enough, and I walked into the bar area and I got a Piña Colada. They didn't ID me, nothing. The music was pumping, it was a weekend, it was packed. I didn't know about tea dances back then, I was too freaking young. I was having a ball. This was great. I danced a little bit. I was just feeling good. I went down and sat on a beach chair. I'm just taking everything in because I'm amazed. I was nervous because I was a kid, so you don't know how to address people. Not like that. I was comfortable. But people did start to talk to me because I was a new face. Most of the regulars know who comes and goes. So one of the older men, he worked at the hotel part, the Ice Palace, that whole complex there. His name was Joe, he was so nice. He could tell I was new. He talked to me for a while then he had to go back in. I'm just laying there, and I see a queen coming down the staircase from the hotel area. She looked just like Connie Francis. At first I thought it was, but as she got closer, I realized it wasn't. That was my first interaction with drag. Then they come through and said, "The show is starting, don't miss it." I went up to see the show and I was in the Ice Palace and I was just enthralled with the whole thing. I thought this was just unbelievable. I fell in love with Fire Island. It burned into my brain. When I talk about it, it's like a movie. I can still see some of the people's faces. It just stayed with me. Now I knew I had a place to go to. – Keith Kollinicos aka Missa Distic

————————∇————————

New York, NY (USA)

Most people know me as Lucifers Axe online but that's another story for another time, I guess. The first time I went to a gay bar involves not just me but also my brother, and it also involves my coming-out story. I was late coming-out to my family and friends, I was roughly 23 or 24. At that point I was living on my own, I was in college, I didn't feel that fear of coming-out. My brother was in the Navy at the time and when I was younger we both shared a room. So I always knew that there was something different about my older brother. You could see the signs. I knew about the gay world, the gay life, that was out there, I just never experienced it. I was in college and he was visiting New York and I thought, "Not only am I coming-out to him, we're going to come-out to each other." He didn't know that I knew. So I said to him, "Danny, why don't you meet me for lunch, get something to eat, I want to talk to you about something." So in coming-out to him, I let him know at the same time that I knew about him. It was a double thing that happened. So we both had our emotional moment with each other. After that, it was like now we can hang-out together. He wanted to take me to the first bar that he went to. I thought, "Oh this is interesting." I'm experiencing, through him, going to a gay bar for the first time. I knew where the gay bars were, but I was afraid to go in places by myself. I was shy and quiet that way. It was a small bar on the Lower West Side of Manhattan. I wish I could remember the name of the place, but it was outside of a train station. You came up to street level and the door was right there. It was a circular bar, local place. That was the first gay bar I went to. Now I'm actually doing this, I'm not outside the door anymore. This is my first step. Not only coming out to my brother but going into this environment that is my life. I was just so afraid to step into that. Once I came-out to him and experienced that, I later went to other gay bars. I wanted to experience it all – David Vega aka Lucifers Axe

—————▽—————

Chicago, IL (USA)

It was the Century. It was down the street from the Century building. It was a big oval bar and lots of people and it was frightening. I was more nervous about coming out and somebody seeing me coming out. That would have been late '60s then I went to the Chesterfield. Tillie the old lady performed there. – Laurie Cowall

—————▽—————

Greensboro, NC (USA)

It was in Greensboro, NC. I was 18. I have no memory of the name of the place, which was just a black hole with satin ball, black lights and black-light posters. It was magical. I was approached by a smiling 30 year-old who wore dentures – which means that his effusive smile glowed brilliantly green under the black light. I was slain! He whisked me away on his motorcycle and we made clumsy young love in his daddy's house. His father was the national chaplain for the KKK – I wrote several now-famous poems about the exhilarating juxtaposition! – Gavin Geoffrey Dillard

—————▽—————

Boston, MA (USA)

I'm getting old so I can't remember the name, but it was one of those well-known bars close to Beacon Hill. I was in college in western Massachusetts and I used to hitchhike to Boston at the weekends. This is 1969-'70. I came out intellectually before I had sex. In the dorm that I lived in there was an out queer, it was the beginning of Gay Lib. He told me where the bar was. So, I walked by, walked by, walked by, then I finally went in. Not welcoming, I just felt invisible. Most people are white, and I was not white. Back in those days, even later on, most of the bars were segregated. So, it was predominantly white gay men. I was in college and I didn't dress the way that was acceptable for gay men at the time. I was more hippie-ish. I went in and I maybe went back a couple of times. – Simeon Den

———————▽———————

Sydney (Australia)

The first gay bar I ever went in was in 1979 in Sydney, Australia, it was called Patch's Nightclub and was located on the Oxford Street golden mile during its heydays, before the AIDS outbreak. I was only 17 at the time, but was often mistaken for much younger and the legal age to enter was 18, so I was surprised they let me in. A friend I met asked me if I wanted to go and see a show, I had no idea what kind of show he was going to and had never heard of a drag show or a gay nightclub. I remember being totally freaked out when a really tall drag queen came over to talk to my friend and I thought we were going to be told to leave. It turned out that I had nothing to be concerned about, she was so friendly and welcoming and was just checking that no one was harassing us. It was the most eye-opening experience of my life because I suddenly realized that there are lots of people just like me and so much that I didn't understand about myself started to make sense. – Ian Davies

———————▽———————

Boston, MA (USA)

Sporters on Beacon Hill. At age eighteen, having recently moved to Cambridge, MA, I took the T (subway) into Boston on a Friday October evening. Having no idea when guys went to bars, I figured 8:00 would be a good time. Descending from the elevated T station, I walked up the block to Sporters. … and purposely passed the black glass door. I just couldn't get myself to go in. My stomach was in knots, especially because I'd promised myself, "Tonight's the night," although I couldn't even imagine what kind of wild, orgiastic bacchanals took place in gay bars. "Whatever happens," I vowed to myself, "happens." Up and down the block and all over Beacon Hill until I finally got up the nerve to walk in and sit on the first available bar stool, which was easy to find because the bar was completely empty of patrons at that early hour.

When the bartender asked what I'd like to drink, I panicked – the only alcohol I'd ever tasted up to that point was Manischewitz Extra Heavy Malaga wine we sipped at home during religious ceremonies. (Even though it was a Friday night, the Sabbath, I knew enough not to order *that*.) My mind flashed to a TV beer commercial guaranteeing "This Bud's for you," so I ordered one.

About half an hour later, still nursing my Bud, I grew relaxed enough to remove my light blue wind-breaker. About that time, two men walked in and kissed one another on the lips, deeply and passionately. Men kissing in public? How long had this been going on?! I was so enthralled and aroused, I wanted to cry.

Gradually the bar filled, and some older guy – thirty maybe – from down the bar sent me a beer and raised his bottle to me. Just like in the movies! I went over, we chatted, and after another half hour, he and three friends suggested we go to one of their apartments for some fun. I was terrified, but reminded myself of my vow, "Whatever happens – happens." We walked up the hill, climbed several flights to a tiny attic apartment, sat in a cramped living room with two huge Irish setters loping around and *I Love Lucy* re-runs blasting on TV. Two of the men left after swallowing raw eggs whole – "Mmm," said one of them, "feels just like a gob of cum running down my throat." Really? Was that what a gob of cum felt like?

The remaining two guys passed out. It was already 3:00 AM, and the T had stopped running, so I figured I'd stay a few more hours until the T started up again at dawn. I spent the rest of the night with a big hairy beast lying across my lap on the sofa – one of the Irish setters. This was the wild stuff that went on in gay bars? I could handle it, no problem.

I felt on top of the world. – Daniel M. Jaffe

————————∇————————

Salzburg (Austria)

I was already in my 30s and I was in Salzburg in Austria. I was in a gay relationship and we went into a gay bar and it was extremely full. I saw lots of people who hadn't realized I was gay. It was just wonderful. I just remember thinking, "This is fantastic." I had been very closeted, let's put it that way. That would have been 1995. It wasn't a hidden bar, but it was quite small, dark, and lots of little lighted areas. It was an L-shaped bar and very crowded because there weren't many places that we could all go to. It was mostly gay men in there but some women. The bar was called Zweistein Bar & Cafe – Helen Macfarlane

————————∇————————

What Was the First Gay Bar You Went Into?

Hollywood, CA (USA)

I was just out of high school, about 1970. I think it was Seventh Circle, a lesbian bar in West Hollywood, one of the oldest bars there. It was ghastly. It was very dark, and it smelled like day-old booze. It was all scary women, very butch, and I was just coming into this scene. It was ok, but I felt at home and not at home. When I was in high school, in my senior year, people knew that I was lesbian. I was really into roller-derby and I had pictures of women in my locker. People would see that when they passed by and some of them were "Uggh!" I think I heard about the bar from a newspaper, either a gay paper or one of those free press underground things, or I met somebody … it was so long ago. – Siouxzan Perry

———————▽———————

Washington DC (USA)

I was in the Catholic Seminary studying at the Catholic University in Washington DC. Another seminarian who was gay had a friend coming in to town. I had a car, so I picked him up at the airport. He was a screamer. He asked, "Where are the gay bars?" I only knew of one, the Georgetown Grille, which I'd never gone to. The screamer was curious, so he found this bar called the Plus One in Washington, not too far from the Capital. That's the first bar I went to, and I thought I was in heaven because I could dance with another man. My friend and I used to sneak out of the seminary a couple of times a week to go to the bar. That would have been about 1969, thereabouts. – Marc

———————▽———————

Palmerston North (New Zealand)

I must have been 16 and it was in New Zealand in a small town called Palmerston North. The bar was called Malgra (Manawatu Lesbian and Gay Rights Association). The town was probably 15,000 people. My friend and I grew up in this small rural town of 2,000 people. He was gay as well. And another friend, who was an older man. We were 16 and he was 19 or 20. He told us about it, so one night we drove up there, which was a 30-minute drive. We walked in and they let us in. No ID back then. I remember it was dark, there was a dancefloor, and they had the disco ball. These long rectangular tables, like old-school *Cheers*. There was a mixed bunch of people. From young to old, gay, lesbian. I was totally intimidated. – Gib Maudey

What Was the First Gay Bar You Went Into?

——————▽——————

Baltimore, MD (USA)

I grew up in the '60s and '70s. I was probably 20 or 21 years old and the largest, and only, gay bar that I knew at the time in Baltimore was called the Hippo. It was a big dance club. At the time disco was at its height. I was in college. I had a gay friend or two. I was not out to anybody but myself. Group of us, male and female, went to the Hippo and we danced the night away and drank a lot. It was so eye opening because I just knew that at some point that would be a part of my life. So yeah, it was the Hippo in Baltimore. As a matter of fact, the club was there so long, it just closed two or three years ago. It must have been open for 40 years at least. The Hippo was short for hippopotamus. As a matter of fact, I think they had a neon hippopotamus on the outside, but it was referred to as the Hippo – Cody

——————▽——————

Milwaukee, WI (USA)

There was a bar in Milwaukee called the Baron. It was a hetero disco six days a week, if I recall correctly, and a gay bar on Sundays. If there was another bar in that town then, I didn't know about it. That was my place to be completely me, one night a week. It was mostly gay men, but a few lesbians besides me hung out there, and I fell in love more times than I can count! – Yvonne Zipter

——————▽——————

New Orleans, LA (USA)

I know the date, it was August 14, 1987, and was a day that will live in infamy and it was also the day I lost my virginity. It was a bar called Jewel in New Orleans. I'd found myself in New Orleans because I was corresponding with somebody from Chicago. I was moving to Chicago and we were writing to each other back and forth, with his responses coming to my post office box because I was still living with my parents. This was before email and all of that. You actually had to write letters. Well the correspondence got a little steamy and he said, "I'm going to be in New Orleans, and I'd like to have you come and visit me in my hotel, we'll spend the day together. I took time off work and gave my parents some explanation they accepted, and I met this gentleman who was there with his Hispanic boy-toy in tow. The boy-toy got sent off to enjoy New Orleans on his own. Me, and this older gentleman, who was probably younger than I am now, got to the business of deflowering me. I have to say it happened without a condom because I was too scared and nervous to ask him to put one on. So, we spent the morning together, then we had lunch, and went back to the hotel and had more screwing. And we were going to go to Jewel that night because they were famous for their Full Moon parties and those Full Moon parties always had a theme. The theme for this particular evening was the 75th anniversary of the sinking of the Titanic. The three of us were going to go, plus a friend that we were going to pick up on the way. The boy-toy, I don't even remember his name, decided that he was going to dress up as a pregnant woman and he was going to give birth on the pool table at midnight when the iceberg struck. All very fun.

All four of us went to the bar. I was very nervous. I could feel eyes all over me and clung to my new beau like my life depended on it. Lo and behold midnight came and the boy-toy gave birth and then decided to dance. He took off his little nightie and he was wearing nothing but a body harness. He proceeded to dance. My gentlemen friend and I, his name was Don by the way, had to go back to the hotel and bring the car around and drive him back to the hotel because he can't go walking down the sidewalk looking like that. We went back to the hotel, got the car, we drove in front of the bar and Don said, "I'm going to stay behind the wheel because you really can't park in the French Quarter in front of businesses. You go in and bring him out and we'll go back to the hotel. I went into the bar and he's dancing like crazy on the dancefloor. I'm saying, "We have to go back to the hotel now." … "No, No, No, leave me alone man, I'm having a great time." I said, "No, Don said it's time for us to go back to the hotel." … "No, No, No, leave me alone man, I'm having a great time." So I grabbed him by his body harness and I'm dragging him physically out of the bar. Everybody is watching me drag this half-naked person onto the street. I'm mortified. Then there's a tourist bus that comes by full of people on a midnight tour of New Orleans, flashbulbs are going off all over the place. I lose my grip and he raced back into the bar. I go to the car and tell Don, "I'm not going back in there." Don goes and collects him and we all go back to the hotel.

I was planning to spend the night, or it was assumed I was going to spend the night. The little boy-toy was drunk and belligerent, racing up and down the balcony screaming, and yelling, and laughing. I was freaking out because I think the cops are going to be called. So I collected myself, got my clothes together and left. Got in my car, cried a lot of the way home to Baton Rouge. I got to Baton Rouge around 6 a.m. way too early to appear at my parent's house, so I knew where a classmate lived, and I knocked on her door and she opened it and I pretty much fell to pieces. She kind of collected me and was mortified that I would see this man on the sidewalks of Chicago when I moved, and I did. But I don't think he saw me. It was years later that I found out what his Chicago address was and I wrote him a letter, essentially calling him a monster because he wanted to keep me when he moved back to Chicago, pay my college tuition, and all I had to do was agree to do whatever he told me to do. I delivered the letter and that gave me some closure. But that was the first gay bar I ever walked into. – Michael Wayne

—————▽—————

Chicago, IL (USA)

I can't actually remember, but Cocktail, on the corner of Roscoe and Halsted was the first bar in which I met my formative gay friends. – Chip H.

—————▽—————

London (UK)

It was called Brief Encounter and was in Shaftesbury Avenue. It's not there anymore. It's now an air-conditioning room under a hotel. It had the nickname Encounters in Briefs. I was very nervous. It took me a couple of attempts to go in. I had a college friend who was gay and he came out to me and I came out to him. He was much more "out" than I was at the time. He must have mentioned the pub. I might have gone with him. I went to buy a drink and this nice man behind me rubbed his groin up and down my ass cheek, and I thought, "This is the place where I should be." That was it really. I was in. – Martin

—————▽—————

New York, NY (USA)

Oh, I have to really go back. I know I was in my late 20s because I was married before. It was with my first lover. It was scary to go in because I had no idea, one day I was married, the next day I was living with a man. It's something I haven't really thought about. It was sort of, "I wish I'd done this before." It was very cruisy, that was back in '79-'80. It was a Sunday beer blast and I think it was called … it was on Columbus Avenue between 79th and 78th and it's no longer there but I remember I drank so much I got drunk. I remember now, it was the Works on Columbus Avenue. It was a trip. I met a lot of people. I met a whole bunch of girls who were straight, but they were going there because it was inexpensive. We all became friends. The more often we went, the more people we met. It was a blessing and it was scary at the same time. Scary at the beginning, then you let your hair down and it was OK because everyone was there to enjoy themselves. – Juan-manuel Alonso

What Was the First Gay Bar You Went Into?

—————▽—————

Los Angeles, CA (USA)

I was 18 and I'd just come-out as trans. This is going to sound so fucking bad. I'd just started hormones because I thought I was exclusively into girls before I started T and T totally changed that. I went to a gay bar in West Hollywood and I went as female, because if I'm going to a gay bar I want to look a little more femme. I'm gonna get me a girl. Totally didn't happen. Totally DID NOT HAPPEN. I went bar-hopping in WEHO, to something called Tiger Heat. I was just this awkward gangly queer that couldn't get laid for jack-shit. I was trying so hard. I wanted a girl so bad. My friends were like, "Ok let's go to Denny's, you poor, pathetic, thing you." – Bambi

—————▽—————

Victorville, CA (USA)

It was a bar called Ricky's. Growing up all my friends were older, so they would go there and tell me about it. That was before I could get in. It was my first safe place, I guess. Because it was in the High Desert there wasn't a lot of LGBT people out there, but it was the one area where the few would connect. It was the first time I could feel completely comfortable in my own skin around people, without the judgement. – Hayley

—————▽—————

Riverside, CA (USA)

I was 18 years old. I came out of doing some musical theater practice and some friends said, "Hey! Let's go out to a bar." They didn't tell me it was a gay bar. A lot of my friends at that time were gay and I didn't even think about it. So, I said, "OK." We went out and I remember walking in and then realizing, "Wait a second, this doesn't look like the normal bars I've been to." It was a different experience because it was so lively, upbeat. I was very nervous and very shy, and I didn't know how to react when I first came in, but I didn't feel uncomfortable. I went straight up to the bar and the bartender, who knew me, said, "Did they tell you they were coming here?" I said, "No, they didn't give me a lot of description of it." We ended up going there and it was very different for me because it was the first time I ever had different people hit on me rather than just dating women. It wasn't bad, it was just different. I'm usually open to different experiences. That was the most out of place I felt in a while because I grew up in a very conservative area. The thought of going into a gay bar was never on anyone's mind. That bar was called VIP. – Chloe DeCamp

———————▽———————

New Orleans, LA (USA)

I was married to my ex-husband when I first went into my first gay bar, which was Oz in New Orleans. I was mesmerized. This was back in the '90s, so the age of the Internet had just popped onto the scene. There were chat rooms and I was a member of a chat room that had to do with women who had been sexually abused. I met quite a few women in there and a couple of them were lesbians. They heard my story and I invited them all to come and see me in Mississippi and they were all from northern states, way up there in Washington and all that. They had never been to the south before. I decided to pick them up at the airport in New Orleans because we could go and have a really good time. The night that I picked them up, one of the girls that flew in, she knew about OZ. She was fairly new coming out. She was still with her husband as well. So, we went and stayed in New Orleans, and like I said she found out about OZ. We went in and I remember they were playing *The Barbie Song*. I knew that I was gay and I hadn't figured out how to come out yet. I just started hanging around with some lesbians I met on the Internet. I think I hung out with them to see if this was for me. I've known since I was a kid but when you're growing up in Mississippi you don't have words, nobody gives you those words, gay didn't mean being gay, gay meant happy. It didn't mean what the rest of the United States knew it meant. So, when we went into OZ we were dancing and I watched men have sex for the first time, over in a corner. I was just mesmerized, I wasn't grossed out, or turned on, or anything. It was like a revelation of, "Yes! This is how it's supposed to be for me." It was that kind of "Aha! This is what my world is supposed to look like. Not this straight ticky-tacky live-in-a-box, stay married, have kids." That started my quest for knowledge, which became quite deep. I ended up staying in New Orleans quite a bit. I met a lot of women there. – Jade

———————▽———————

Portland, ME (USA)

The first time I went into a gay bar I was probably 35 in Portland, Maine, with some gay friends of mine. That was my very first experience in a gay bar. It was fun. It didn't feel odd, I didn't feel like … did it give me a warm and fuzzy feeling? No. It was just a fun place to be. Nobody looked at the way you were dancing, or who you were with, and nobody was pointing fingers. Everybody was having a great time. It was funny because I remember it was after a company party. There was about 20 of us and it was half straight/half gay and there were some people who didn't fit into a mold. The bar was around the corner, down the stairs ... now I look back on it, it was like we were going to a back alley. I can remember going in there and some guys are wearing short shorts, no shirts, and girls are holding hands, or kissing, or boys holding hands. I was coming out of a straight relationship and I kind of thought at the time, "How would I feel?" I didn't feel out of place, it was just a good time. – Cathy Melton

———————▽———————

Boston, MA (USA)

I grew up in the South Shore of Boston, in a small town called Weymouth. I worked at a progressive rock radio station called WCOZ, and a lot of the disc jockeys were gay. Men, mostly. There was a guy named Sean, and Sean was a bit of a smartass. Sean and I were party buddies. Sean said to me, "I want to show you me and my world." I said, "OK, I don't know what that means, but let's go to a bar." The first bar I ever went to was called Chaps in Boston. It was a men's bar and I walked in and was completely not welcome. They wouldn't serve me. He got pissed, and he was not a political kind of kid, but he took me somewhere else. I don't remember where the other place was. It was interesting because I was at Chaps just long enough to think, "Oh this is kind of interesting." Although, not welcoming. – Leslie Tisdale

———————▽———————

Dallas, TX (USA)

I had an experience at a bookstore before I went to a gay bar. I guess it took that to open my mind because I had a very difficult time coming out. It was on the street just behind Nieman Marcus – it was the only Nieman Marcus in Dallas. I was looking at the body building magazines. I had so few outlets to explore men. I was looking at this magazine – I was down on my knees – and he walks up and gets into my space, clearly in my space, and he put his briefcase down. I looked up and he motioned for me to follow him. I did. We went out to his car and I gave him a blow job. After that I had enough courage to go to a gay bar. There were a number of discreet ones in Dallas. I went to one. I was very closeted. I would stand over in the corner just observing. Most of the time that's all it was. It was sometime before I left with anyone. But I had to do that to investigate my curiosity of what is this gay thing? And why I am attracted to it. I could not yet define myself as gay. So, my experience was at the bar, watching other men and being a bit envious of them because I would mostly leave alone. I don't remember a defining moment but eventually as I repeated this behavior somebody likely approached me and took me home. – Don Rockwell Coffee

———————∇———————

Detroit, MI (USA)

The Motor City. Menjo's, also known as SDP, the Silver Dance Palace. It was fabulous. I don't know if it's still there. One of the first times I went there I ran into my brother. I knew he was gay. It must have been about 1973. – Jack Farquhar Halbert

———————∇———————

Binghamton, NY (USA)

Oh my gosh, way back. It was either in Schenectady or … probably the most scary one was in Binghamton, New York, only because I was teaching. That was back in the '70s and you'd sneak into it. How did I find out about it? I met somebody who told me about it. I don't remember the name of the bar, but it was beat up and ugly. It was like a beat up sports bar. I was nervous about someone seeing me go in, but once I was in … I had a drink or two. That was probably the only time I was in there. – Paul

———————∇———————

London, (UK)

It was on Clapham Common, or thereabouts, but I can't remember the name of the bar. I didn't go in any gay bars until I met my first partner in 1987. He took me to this bar. I'd never been in a gay bar before. I knew they existed, but I'd never been in one. It was exciting, obviously, to be in a crowd of people like me for a change. Before that I hadn't been out to many people, I'd been fairly closeted. So, I walk in this bar and there's all these men there. I was clueless, and I distinctly remember being with Gary, my partner at the time, and we'd been standing drinking for a few minutes, and he said, "That guy over there is cruising you." And I said, "What guy? Where? And what does 'cruising' mean?" It was quite an awakening for me to realize there were so many other people. I'd actually been involved in gay politics before that but as a supporter. – Tess Tickles

What Was the First Gay Bar You Went Into?

—————∇—————

Albuquerque, NM (USA)

Rear Entry in Albuquerque. – Allan Hunter

—————∇—————

Columbus, OH (USA)

The bar no longer exists at the original location, but it was called Union Station. I went when I was 19 years old in 2002 with a college friend named Aaron for burgers. I was not out yet and only remember being scared to death. – Mike Gifford

—————∇—————

Asunción (Paraguay)

Actually, I didn't know it was a gay bar. I went on a school trip and there was this bar across the street, and we all went. And then I noticed there were a lot of dudes. So I was in another country with all my high school friends, classmates and teachers. There were guys there and they were touching. I was fascinated by that. I was 17 years old. – Ives

—————∇—————

Chicago, IL (USA)

The Glory Hole. I went there for a drink in the afternoon after visiting the Bijou Theater. We took the *Chicago Tribune* at home, which carried daily ads for the Newberry and Bijou gay porn theaters, and I went there before I ever went to a bar. – Anonymous

—————∇—————

New York City, NY (USA)

1981 - Uncle Charlie's East. We had all just been to see *Mommie Dearest*, so for me, just out, the whole thing was getting a bit too stereotypically gay! In the bar we kept to ourselves. I was too nervous at that point to start going up to strangers. I thought guys in bars would be insincere or judgmental. – David Pratt

—————▽—————

Bath (UK)

The Garrick's Head pub in Bath Spa. It was a theatre bar, all plush velvet, carpet, and photos of celebrity thesps. The other bar in the same pub was straight and never the twain would meet – or seldom, anyway. I was 19, with my 31-year-old partner of the time, and quite nervous. I was wearing a woolly sweater my Nan had knitted for me, and in the crush, it got caught on the belt-buckle of a much older "Uncle Monty" type. I was frozen with fear as he pulled away and my sweater started to unravel. The Uncle Monty type became an occasional drinking pal, subsequently, and this bar was the first place I felt desirable to other men. – Diesel Balaam

—————▽—————

Akron, OH (USA)

Robin Hood. I went with a new boyfriend who was to become my first partner. I was nervous. When a cop in uniform walked in, I was sure it was a raid. But someone told me he was probably the bagman. – Alex Gildzen

—————▽—————

Chicago, IL (USA)

The Normandy, which was located near Clark and Roscoe Streets in Chicago is the first bar I remember going to. I was so nervous and felt so out of place that I kept drinking bottles of beer while focusing my attention on playing a video game which was either Ms. PAC Man or Galaga. There was also a Latina lesbian bar in Logan Square called El Gran Caribe that I used to frequent with my friend Steve, and I would shoot pool there and listen to the juke box. He is the one that took me to Normandy and later introduced me to my favorite gay bar of all time, Bistro Too on Clark and Winnemac on Chicago's North Side. I spent many nights dancing the night away there. Sadly, the building which housed Bistro Too (and later Man's Country and The Eagle) was recently demolished. – Robert Castillo

—————▽—————

What Was the First Gay Bar You Went Into?

Guadalajara (Mexico)

That was in 2008. It was called Monica's. Even though I was older, I couldn't go before, back home. I'm from Venezuela. It's not that I couldn't but I didn't want anyone to see me doing that. Yes, I went to the gay bar and it was all new for me. I was kind of scared but as I overcame – the scariness, I guess – I just started to have fun and realize that I was missing something I like. That's when I figured that my life had changed forever. It was also in Guadalajara that I first went to bathhouses. It was awesome as well. I was frightened, I was terrified, I was shaking. – Carlos

—————∇—————

New York, NY (USA)

Too bad the question isn't, "What is the first Gay place I went into?" because that would have been the GAA (Gay Activists Alliance) Firehouse on Wooster Street in SoHo in New York. I was 17, and took the subway, the D Train, into Manhattan the night of July 20, 1973. GAA had dances every night at their firehouse, their headquarters. They set up the dances so Gay people would have an alternative to the Mafia run bars. It was only $1 to get in. I went there with my friend Milton, who also thought he was Gay. I was scared shitless, because this was a big step for me, you know, going to a real Gay place. At the time, my naive 17-year old self thought that if nobody picked me up, that would mean I wasn't Gay. I never said I was a very logical 17-year old. But I was a very gutsy one.

The firehouse was PACKED. I had never been with other Gay people before then and it was a very diverse crowd. Young guys, older guys, lesbians, drag queens. It was all brand new to me.

I did get picked up there by an older guy (he was 27) who was also a rabbi. Well, a reformed rabbi who told me his name was Barry Shapiro (it turned out it wasn't, but then many people used false names back then on the Gay scene). He asked me if I wanted to go to the beach with him the next day, Sunday, and if I would give him my phone number. I was so paranoid that Milton would see me giving out my phone number that I made the rabbi memorize the number. I did meet him the next day and lost my virginity on July 21, 1973. I found out that a little red bathing suit was not quite a suit of armor. But that's another story.

My first Gay bar is far less interesting. The rabbi introduced me to Gay life and took me to the Village and the first bar we went into was the Roadhouse. I think it was on Hudson Street. I had never been in a bar before, let alone a Gay bar. I remember that it was very smoky and that it was full of older men (they were probably in their 20s). – Ian H

149

What Was the First Gay Bar You Went Into?

―――――――∇―――――――

Chicago, IL (USA)

I was in high school (Notre Dame High School, Niles Illinois) and a gay friend and I drove down to the city and visited Piggin's Pub at Clark and Diversey. I remember ordering a cheeseburger and we did the Century Mall. My second gay bar was, I was dating Jim (I think he was in his 30's – we met at Schiller Woods, I was 18) he took me to the Glory Hole and a couple weeks later he took me to the Gold Coast. – David Plambeck

―――――――∇―――――――

Pomona, CA (USA)

I went with a friend of mine from high school, who also worked with me. He liked me, not as a lover or anything like that. He was very Christian, he believed in the Lord. It was hard to get along with him at first, but we became best friends. And then he realized he was gay, and he said, "I've always wanted to go to this bar. I'm scared to go on my own, would you go with me?" So, I said, "Sure, I know where it's at." It was called the Alibi East, at the time there was also an Alibi West. That first time he had to sneak me in. We climbed in over the fence, barbed wire, and everything. Then it turned out the guy working the door was a friend of my friend, so I didn't have to sneak over the fence after that. As soon as we found out he was the doorman, my friend and I started going there together more frequently. Then I started going by myself. – Felix

―――――――∇―――――――

Seattle, WA (USA)

It was the Brass Connection on Capitol Hill which is the gay ghetto for Seattle. I remember going in and you had to show ID. This was when I was in my early 20s. It was one of those moments when you say, "Oh my heavens, all these gay men." It was like being in a candy store. I had to look at every single one of them. I was with a friend. He knew about the bar and I'd seen an ad for it in the *Seattle Gay News*. I was married at the time to a woman. I was in Seattle for a conference. I talked to one of my gay friends at the conference and he said, "Well, do you want to see what that's like?" I said "Sure." So, we went, loud music – too loud for me – but the eye candy was amazing. And, it turned out that I saw someone there that had been in some

activities with me at high school. I said to him, "Ron," and he said, "——,"
and I said, "So you come here too." And he said, "I'm the manager." – OT

—————∇—————

WHERE IS THE WILDEST PLACE YOU EVER HAD SEX?

Parker, CO (USA)
Chicago, IL (USA)
St Louis, MO (USA)

What qualifies as wildest place you've ever had sex in a lifetime of being adventurous, especially when unique places kind of turn you on.

Do I claim the out-door trampoline in Parker, Colorado when I was 16? The house was very remote, and it was with a girl.

Can I claim an open garage in an alley behind a sleazy gay bar in Chicago, Illinois? Giving head to a friend with benefits 20 feet away from men doing much more scandalous acts behind a wooden fence at a late hour seems safe. My knees and jeans were covered in dust. I took a pic on the way home on the CTA, joking "My heels didn't get round from walking."

Again in Chicago, Illinois, I went on a date with a leasing agent in River North. We went to a 33rd floor balcony. When he went down on me, I looked out at the skyline and Chicago River and thought, "I will remember this."

I'm not completely slutaceous. On a road trip to St Louis, Missouri, I turned down a friend with benefits who wanted a hummer in a rest area bathroom stall. I have standards.

Does giving road head qualify as wild? It was a 16 hour drive from New Orleans to Chicago. I had to pass the time somehow.

After discussing with a friend with benefits, I decided on the pier at Hollywood Beach in Chicago was the wildest place. It was around 2 a.m., we had hung out most of the night, and when I proposed the idea, it was partially a joke. However, he was game, and we were on the other side of the light house in the dark. No one was around. When he came in my mouth, he moaned and we heard a startled "Oh!" Someone was out for a late night walk and was on the other side of the light house! We had been caught, at least audibly. If he came a little later, the person could have walked around and visibly caught us! I just give credit to my innate timing. The person quickly walked away, never exploring further. My friend and I laughed about it on the way home. – Thomas Bottoms

—————∇—————

Chicago, IL (USA)

The last long seat at the back of the CTA bus from Halsted to Cumberland and back to Halsted ... Bus driver did not say a thing ... made no stops and just said ... wow!!! when we departed the bus. – Don Strzepek

—————∇—————

Los Angeles, CA (USA)

I used to go to Griffs. It was my favorite bar up in LA. It was on Melrose and Gower. I even talk about it in my comic strip, it's where Leonard & Larry met for the first time, at a beer bust at Griffs that they had every Sunday afternoon. It was just a small bar, but they had a parking lot and they strung a cable between two buildings, hung a tarp from a cable. That's where their temporary patio was. Oh god, it was great, all these men in leather, all the motorcycles parked out front. I'll tell you, the thing about Griffs is that it was right across the street from Paramount Studios and it was right across the street from the two studios that could accomodate audiences, right there on Melrose Avenue. They had marquees because that part of Paramount used to be the old RKO studios and they used to do radio programs there but at that time, in one of the studios, they did *Happy Days* and the one next door they did *Laverne & Shirley*. Audience members would be lined up on Melrose, around the corner down Gower, waiting to get in to see the taping of these TV shows on Friday night. There would be all these people from the suburbs and their relatives from who-knows-where, the Midwest, coming to LA to see a TV show they had only seen on television, to see a live taping. They would be lined up down Gower and they would have a view of Griffs on a Friday night when it was just buzzing, hopping with gay men in leather.

This was before I ever got up the courage to go in there. I would just ride by on my motorcyle, and these people waiting to get in to the taping had ringside seats to the show going on across the street. One night there was a white stretch-limo pulled up in front and disgorged all these men in black leather and there were all these tourists standing there watching it all. It was great. Griffs became my favorite bar. I used to be there religiously every Sunday afternoon for their beer bust. One day, I rode up there on my motorcycle, one drizzly afternoon in the winter. It wasn't raining so much that I couldn't ride my motorcycle up there, and besides I never missed their beer busts if I could help it. There weren't too many people there, it was wet, drizzly, gray and late in the afternoon. There was one guy there and we became very good friends. It was so many years ago, I don't even remember his name. I think his name was Martin. I believe he was an aerospace engineer working on some project up in the Mojave desert for the government. He was from the South East somewhere, he had a twangy southern accent. He was kind of kinky. He came into LA every weekend and he liked to go to Griffs. He was all in leather, leather daddy cap and his jacket and his chaps and he had big rubber hip waders over his chaps. I had to go say something to him, "Those are great boots. I like your boots." I got a terrible boot fetish. We started talking and we had to go out to his truck, parked on Melrose. His truck had a camper shell on it and the back of his truck was full of hip boots. He never went anywhere withought hip boots. That was his big thing. He had me try on a pair of hip boots. I was wearing these big cowboy boots, extra tall cowboy boots, and he insisted on pulling them off for me. He didn't expect them to be that tall and I'll never forget him pulling on my boot and it just kept coming and coming out of my pant leg. He was looking at it, going "Wow!" They're buckaroo style, that's what they're called. Anyway, he had me try on a pair of his hip boots, he wanted to see what I looked like in them, so he had me stand outside on the sidewalk with the truck door open. He got so turned on. We had to do something about it so we were driving around looking for a place and where are you going to go on a rainy Sunday night. We ended up in the parking lot of the John Anson Ford Theatre, across the Hollywood Freeway, right up against the slope of Mount Cahuenga where the Hollywood Sign is. It was a Sunday night, but there were no cars in the parking lot. We parked up against the cliff. I got behind his truck, up against the rock face. He got down on his knees, and there I was standing in his hip boots. That's a very fond memory. We were good friends and we did stuff together a lot after that. He was a nice guy. He moved back to the east somewhere and we lost touch. – Tim Barela

––––––––––∇––––––––––

Provincetown, MA (USA)
Fire Island, NY (USA)

Outside. Truly such a freeing feeling in the summer moonlight. – Jim

––––––––––∇––––––––––

Where is the Wildest Place You Ever Had Sex?

Aguas Dulces, (Uruguay)

It was in an empty and wild beach on the Atlantic Uruguayan coast at Aguas Dulces, with a wild forest behind. You can walk naked, so I met a top and we fucked in that fantastic environment. – Dr. Eduardo Levaggi Mendoza

————————▽————————

Lombard, IL (USA)

The wildest and also the most embarrassing was a fitting room in Carson's Department Store in Lombard, Illinois. I was on break from work, and a guy cruised me in the mall. We didn't want to go into the restrooms, because mall security was cracking down on sex in the restrooms, so we went into a fitting room. I made a mess of my shirt and tie and had to return to work. I made something up instead of announcing to my co-workers that I had sex in a fitting room. I poured cold coffee down the front of my shirt and tie, it was cold, and I had to buy a new shirt and tie, but it was memorable. – Jerry S.

————————▽————————

Chicago, IL (USA)

In the mid '80s I used to date (mostly just a sex buddy) a man in northwest suburban Chicago who owned a cleaning business, because of roommates we couldn't meet at either of our places, so I'd always meet him at the places he was cleaning, so behind the teller stations in a bank, on a booth in a restaurant, and on a chiropractors patient table. – Robert Hansen

————————▽————————

Middletown, NJ (USA)

I owned my own business most of my life. Probably one of the first people I had gay sex with worked for me. At this point in time that would not have been a nice thing to do … ok. He was much younger than me. He was enamored by me and I was very turned on by him. He was the first man I ever kissed. The wildest place was in the storeroom of my store. I was sitting on top of the dryer, dressed up for work. It was the end of the night, everybody was going, saying goodbye, and I was doing last minute shit like cleaning up the place or putting paperwork together. He was my assistant. He came in and started talking to me. Next thing I know he's all over me. I

155

said, "What are you doing?" He said, "I really want you." I said, "Then take me already, I'm yours." That went on for quite some time. It was wild. We fucked on the dryer in the storeroom of my business. I think back on that, and I was shamed by it for a long time. What's wrong with you, you have a wife and kids? Fucking this boy. – Joseph S

───────────▽───────────

Ventana Wilderness, CA (USA)

Los Padres National Forest, in an icy pool beneath a waterfall overlooking the Big Sur coast. – Louis Flint Ceci

───────────▽───────────

Atlanta, GA (USA)

I was in Atlanta, it must have been 1983 or '84? I was there for some conference or event. I was walking through a hotel late at night – it may have been the Omni – when I met eyes with a sandy haired man in tight white jeans and black ankle boots. We cruised each other a bit and introduced ourselves. He was Luke. He was from San Diego. In one of the hallways off the lobby we started kissing and grabbing each other. Soon, we decided we needed to get somewhere more private, quickly. He had a room near the top of the hotel, so we decided to go up, and fuck. When we stepped into the glass elevator and as the door closed, he roughly grabbed me and pinched my nipple, and that was it. I immediately dropped to my knees and yanked his jeans down and began sucking him. I sucked that beautiful cock of his for at least 15 floors in the glass elevator. When we got to his floor, he pushed the lobby button, and we decided to continue in the elevator. – Steve K

───────────▽───────────

Chicago, IL (USA)

In one of the bathrooms at O'Hare airport. I was waiting for my plane. I got the ticket and everything and the plane was delayed. This guy, we were looking at one another, he got up and took his briefcase with him, and said, "Have you got a few minutes?" I said, "Sure." We walked into the end stall and I fucked him. – Dan Brazill

───────────▽───────────

156

Where is the Wildest Place You Ever Had Sex?

Chicago, IL (USA)

Behind a statue across the street from Lincoln Park or in the bushes around the Lincoln Park Lagoon. Orgy room at Man's Country was always very interesting also. – Kbro

———————▽———————

New York, NY (USA)

The Mine Shaft ... Unbelievable! – Gary Chichester

———————▽———————

(USA)

On a softball diamond in a public park in broad daylight. – Driveshaft

———————▽———————

San Francisco (CA (USA)

That's another one that is difficult to answer. I've pretty much had sex everywhere with the exception of a viewing platform on the top of a skyscraper. And obviously countries where I haven't been as yet able to travel. The BART Platform in San Francisco Mission Park stop at 6:08 am on a Friday morning stands out. I'm sure it was memorable to the morning commuters as well. My knees were on the platform along with the guy behind me, he held on by the belt around my neck. You can imagine the details, however, I will state I'm very glad my hands didn't get torn up from the gravel on the tracks. – Daniel Fisher AKA Raid

———————▽———————

Seattle, WA (USA)

The wildest or the most extraordinary? The most extraordinary was out in nature. I'm a nature lover. I was with a friend and we both said, "We've got to do this out in the sunlight, in sunshine, on the earth." The wildest was at a sex club in Seattle called The Institute for Sex Positive Culture, which is more than a sex club, it's educational, all kinds of things. They would have certain nights where on demo-nights you came in and explored different things. This was about 5 or 6 years ago. I had some extraordinary experiences with some people who were very experienced in what they did. So I really learned a lot, I'm talking about kinky things. When you're with someone who really knows what they're doing, a whole new part of you comes alive. That was wild. One example, one night we were learning about oil wrestling, getting naked with various types of vegetable oil, learning how to slip and slide all over each other. It's almost like erotic massage. It was extraordinary and it was wild, and it was wonderful. – Bill

———————▽———————

(USA)

In a bathroom at Denny's. I got the grand slam. – Rory

———————▽———————

Chicago, IL (USA)

Not even sure if this is even wild anymore. In an alley with a stranger and it was good. – Dale

———————▽———————

Falls Village, MA (USA)

On the rocks below a vacated waterfall in Falls Village, MA. I was working at a summer camp and my boyfriend had gone out with me. We were out sitting on the rocks, looking over the edge and the full moon in the sky and made lust, I mean love, on the rocks. – Greg R. Baird

———————▽———————

San Onofre Beach, CA (USA)

That was at Camp Pendleton. There is a gay beach that is also a surfing beach. It's on the other side of the nuclear power plant. It's called San Onofre Beach. It's difficult to get down there, you have to do a lot of walking. At one point it was a quite popular place to go. This is a little bit later when a lot of the gay activity had stopped. There was still that freedom to be unclothed, run around naked and really feel part of nature. I liked that which is a sensuous feeling. It was a place where one could express their sensuality. For me that's more important than the sex act itself … so quick, you know. The reason this place stands in mind is because one day I was there, naked as a jay bird, on the beach, close to the water. Laying there and contemplating my thoughts, when out of the water comes all of these men in wetsuits running past me. As I said, this is on a military base, so it was on one of the days when they were doing military maneuvers. – Kalvin

———————▽———————

New York, NY (USA)

In the Mineshaft in New York. It was an incredible place, there were people sitting in bathtubs, getting peed on all night. People crawling around on the floor, masters with their slaves walking around. Crawling in chains behind … it was wild. I still have two original posters from there. – Ron

———————▽———————

San Diego, CA (USA)

In the wild. I had a fellow in San Francisco who wanted to come and spend Thanksgiving with me. I was living in the mountains east of San Diego. It had a 4,000 feet elevation, and at 4,500 feet there was a trail that lead down to a stream which was active. His dream was to be fisted in the open next to a running brook. Perfect! So that was wild in many ways. – Hal

———————▽———————

London (UK)

In the late-'50s I was with two agents, one for acting, one for modelling. This agent, I would periodically go and do a photo session for him somewhere. He would send me off. He invited me to a party, and he said, "It's a private party." And I said, "What do you mean by private?" He said, "You can't bring your boyfriend. This is a special evening I'm giving." So I said, "OK." So I said to Bob Robinson, "I'm going to a party next Saturday and I can't take you because it's a sort of business thing." So on the Saturday night I went to the guy's apartment in Knightsbridge. I rang the bell and the door opened. I stepped in and there was a guy standing there and he said, "I'll take your clothes." So I said, "What do you mean, you'll take my clothes?" He said, "You have to be naked before I let you into the room." So, I said, "OK." So I stripped off, walked into this room stark naked, and there must have been about 15-20 guys. We were all the same age almost, we looked the same, and the floor, which was fully carpeted, had been covered wall-to-wall with plastic sheeting. I thought, "This is crazy." It was like looking into a mirror, we were

159

all 20-24 years of age, blond hair. The host, our agent, started giving glasses of punch around. Well, there was something in that punch, which was unbelievable because in about 20 minutes we were all rolling around fucking each other on this plastic sheeting. – Bob Brown

———————▽———————

Chicago, IL (USA)

I would say in the Manhandler, because I was chubby and had a very bad body image, I wouldn't go to the baths or anywhere where you took off your clothes, which is why I'm alive. I wasn't going out and having anonymous anal sex in the years when everybody else did, because of my inhibitions. Had I had a fabulous body, I wouldn't be here. I think sometimes that God made me fat. – Laurie Cowall

———————▽———————

Hempstead, NY (USA)

In a Greek church in Hempstead, New York. I had a cousin getting married. Already at that age, I was older, I was out, but I was still young. And the family, whenever we got invitations, my mother would get the phone call following the invitation to make sure I was kept under control. "No stunts! No stunts!" That's what I was hearing for weeks before the frigging wedding, so I already knew. They have very long services at the Greek Orthodox Church. My father was Greek Orthodox, his side of the family is all Greek Orthodox. So they have these long masses and long weddings. It's a major ritual and they really frown on people like me. Wedding day came. I said to my mother, "I'll meet you over there." … "No, we'll go in one car." I said, "No, I'll meet you over there." She left. I went and got dressed in purple pants … oh yeah. I looked like a real gay blade. I walked in and everybody turned, everything stopped. My mother says to me, "Not one time, you have to embarrass me." I said, "You better fasten your seat belt because it's going to be bumpy." I took one look at that priest that was doing the service and I just … I have a cousin that I grew up with and she's the polar opposite of what I am. I knew in four languages by the time I was in grade school, derogatory names for gays. What they would say would cut me like a knife. My cousin and I were talking, and I said, "The priest is gay." She said, "No, you think the world is gay." I said, "I'll prove to you he's gay." … "How are you going to do that?" I said, "You'll find out." They're going on with the service. And they have other ones that come out. It's not just one, there's more than one. They're doing the whole service, and I said, "I've got to pee."

I went out the back, I came around, I came up in the back … because I knew as a kid the ins and outs of that church because my father belonged there, it was St Paul's. I wound up hooking up with the priest in the back while everybody was still in the pews. I got him good, because I was always a little pig. Whatever was in my head as a fantasy I've lived out. I was going to do him, and I was going to make sure my cousin knew I did him. I did him. I did him right there when the church was filled with the whole family. They have a couple of steps up to the altar with the table where the bride and groom go around three times and behind all these pictures of icons which are doors. Behind there, I banged his brains out. And I got cum on me. Then I went back around, and my cousin said, "What took you so long? Oh my god, that's so disrespectful." I said, "Look, you wanted to know, here's the proof. Here's his jizz." It was all over. I had a huge glob on the purple pants. I was laughing my ass off. By the time we got to the reception everyone knew. I was proud. – Keith Kollinicos aka Missa Distic

—————▽—————

New York, NY (USA)
Venice, FL (USA)

I was recently coming-out of the closet. I was letting all my friends know. There was one particular friend in college and we were very close. He was the first person I came-out to. I knew he was gay and so did everyone else. But now we were hanging out together they were automatically assuming we were a couple. But we were just friends. But he started taking me around to all the gay bars, saying, "I want to show you around town, I want to show you around the city." He showed me the gambit of what was out there when it came to gay bars, from the drag bars, to the Asian bars, to the black bars … meaning all-Asian people, all-black people … even in the gay community we're very segregated within ourselves. So he showed me all these places, because everyone's into something different. He took me to this place called the Vault., two stories, the lower level was men and women, and the upper level was men only. Little did I know that this was a sex club. He said, "David, you've got to check this place out. You don't have to do anything if you don't want to, but I want you see what this place is like." So we go upstairs and I'm thinking to myself, "Is this what I think it is going on in here?" I'd never been to a place like that before, but I knew they existed. It was one of those things where it was the most wild because it was out in the open. You got to the top of the stairs and it was a fake-theater kind of room with benches and they were playing dirty movies. You went around the corner there was a clothes-check. The further in you went, it became more … like hallways and rooms, an apartment almost but bigger. A giant loft. It was in the meat-packing

161

district and one of the rooms had the metal hooks for meat and it was the first time I experienced the darker, seedier side of the gay world. The S&M community, that kind of thing, because that was what was happening there, geared toward that. That was probably the wildest place. It was the first time I'd seen it happening in front of me. Guys having sex in front of me. Mind you, this is in the mid-to-late '80s that this was going on. So I already knew there were diseases and sicknesses out there, but when you're young and you're first coming-out, and you're experiencing all this for the first time, you don't care about that. You put it to the side of your brain over here and you say, "Ok now I'm going to live the side that I want to live, that I want to experience." Now that was the wildest place. As far as the most heart-racing experience sexually for me would be one of three places: it was the docks in New York City, Central Park, or the beach, because you could get caught. Your adrenalin is rushing, so it wasn't that there was a wild scene, it was just where it was happening. I had a jack-off session with somebody on the docks, people passing. It was, "Holy fuck, I can't believe this is happening out in the open. I think Central Park and the beach was the most fun. The gay beach in Venice, Florida. Caspersen was the name of the beach. We used to hang out there all the time. – David Vega aka Lucifers Axe

—————∇—————

Sydney (Australia)

The wildest place would have been in the tall grass underneath the Sydney harbour bridge (north side) while busloads of tourists could hear us, but could not see us. They knew what was happening, but had no idea it was two guys going at it. – Ian Davies

—————∇—————

West Hollywood, CA (USA)

On a butcher's block. This was 1975 maybe. WEHO was changing then, gays started buying up properties and it was starting to look like a nice neighborhood again. I used to walk past, on my way to the gym, or dance class, a boutique butcher – it was a gay neighborhood, so it was very out-front chichi looking. There was sawdust on the floor. I went in and he fucked me over the butcher's block. The smell of meat and the sawdust and his hands … oh yeah! … oh yeah! – Simeon Den

—————∇—————

Where is the Wildest Place You Ever Had Sex?

Washington State (USA)

Somewhere east of Seattle off the Interstate in the woods with a guy who passed me up in his car, and I passed him up, and we exchanged glances, and we did a bit of a dance with our cars, and we took an off ramp, and I followed him into the woods. – Mark Zubro

———————∇———————

Yucatan (Mexico)

I've had sex in most of the Mayan pyramids in the Yucatan. With Leonardo. During the monsoons. It was positively mystical. – Gavin Geoffrey Dillard

———————∇———————

Santa Barbara, CA (USA)

In my imagination. I don't say this to be cute, but to be sincere: nothing beats the wild sex I have in my fantasies. Oh, the places I go, the things I do, the men I ravish. – Daniel M. Jaffe

———————∇———————

Palm Springs, CA (USA)

I'd say my open gay life started here. For me the wildest place was in our swimming pool. It was quite a wild afternoon. I let my hair down. – Helen Macfarlane

———————∇———————

Auckland (New Zealand)
Amsterdam (Netherlands)
Sydney (Australia)

Something that sticks with me is in Auckland, a guy and I were getting it on, on the dancefloor. Then we went upstairs and got it on big time. But Amsterdam was the wildest place for me. I think it was called the Cock Ring, down in the dungeon was like full-on ... oh my God. They treated me like I was a smorgasbord. Even in Sydney, when I was 17 years old and moved to Sydney with my best friend who was gay. We used to have wild sex in a toilet at a place called Capriccio's, a gay nightclub. It was wild, you'd walk into the bathroom ... black, and it was full-on, you couldn't see. There have been many places ... in a paddock, but then that's not wild, outside in a paddock. Cars ... that's not wild. – Gib Maudey

———————∇———————

Mid-air
Anaheim, CA (USA)

Two places. On an airplane. In the seats under a blanket. You can do that if you're girls. And the railroad train at DisneyLand. – Siouxzan Perry

———————∇———————

San Francisco, CA (USA)

The back of the No 8 Market bus in San Francisco. The buses didn't have regular schedules, so people were trying to get to work, the buses were so crowded. When they started at Market and Castro it was fairly empty, so we moved to the back. – Marc

———————∇———————

Santa Barbara, CA (USA)

Nothing terribly wild. Out in the open on the beach, up in the Santa Barbara area. It was during the week, I had the day off work. I was just laying out there and it was an unofficial nude beach. I was laying there and this young guy – he must have been a college student. I was at least 10 years older – just came up and asked me what time it was. I was obviously aroused. He asked me what time it was, and I told him, and he said "Thanks" and walked away. I stared down the beach and I see him jerking off. All of a sudden, I got up and we sucked each other off on the beach. I didn't even give a shit if there was anyone there or not. And there wasn't, to my knowledge. I'd say that's probably the wildest. – Cody

———————∇———————

(USA)

I'm pretty tame. Depends on what you call sex. I didn't get off, but I gave someone a hand-job in the back room of a bar. But that's about it. I did blow somebody in his parked car. – Mike Wayne

Where is the Wildest Place You Ever Had Sex?

——————▽——————

Chicago, IL (USA)

Compared to some, I'm probably rather tame. I can't say if it's the wildest place I've ever had sex, but I had sex behind a dumpster behind Crowbar, in Chicago. I'd gone there with my boyfriend at the time and spent hours on the dance floor with him and a drag queen, after excusing ourselves, we went to find a "discreet" place to kiss, and the dumpster was just far enough back from the street and any doors likely to open. It was pushed out at just enough of an angle for a bit more than kissing. – Chip H.

——————▽——————

London (UK)

I quite like straight S&M clubs and having gay sex with my boys tied up and various things with 200-300 straight people watching. Performance art sex thing. It's strange because the women really get off on watching gay men having sex, straight men get very nervous and clutch onto their girlfriends. I think it's like straight men enjoying lesbian sex, watching hetero-lesbian porn, the straight women enjoy gay men having sex in the public arena. So, the wildest is having gay sex in straight clubs. – Martin

——————▽——————

In mid-air

The belly of a plane, a Jumbo 747 with a steward. He said, "Do you want to go and smoke a joint?" I said, "Sure." Then we went down into the belly of the plane and had sex. – Juan-manuel Alonso

——————▽——————

Victorville, CA (USA)

I was fairly rebellious in my teen years. I would say the wildest place – oh my god, this isn't me today – I grew up in the Victorville/Hesperia area and there were these aqueducts, water things that flowed through the city. Some of them had little bridges and I hooked up with a guy under one of the bridges. Yes, dark days. – Hayley

Where is the Wildest Place You Ever Had Sex?

——————▽——————

Anaheim, CA (USA)

DisneyLand parking lot. This was when I was working at DisneyLand. I was a cast member. I was with my fiancée, we did about six dabs each, so we were super high, and we took towels and blankets, then we rolled the windows down, put them over, rolled them up so we had privacy. We totally fucked in the DisneyLand parking lot in Downtown Disney. I've had a lot of sex in DisneyLand and on my way to and from DisneyLand. The happiest place on Earth, what can I say? – Bambi

——————▽——————

Riverside, CA (USA)

We were at a public pool. It was at night, so it was kind of dark. There were other people swimming around and me and this girl had been fooling around. Then we moved it over into the jacuzzi where the bubbles were hiding certain thing. Things escalated from there. While everyone was swimming in the pool. It was a little different, definitely. It was very, "Oh my God what if someone catches me? What if someone gets into the jacuzzi? Do we act normal? How do you act normal?" – Chloe DeCamp

——————▽——————

New Orleans, LA (USA)

It the dressing room in Dillard's department store. I had flown into New Orleans. I was visiting my parents and my first girlfriend came and picked me up. We were staying in New Orleans and I needed something at the mall, and we went to the mall and we were in Dillard's and we hadn't seen each other … and that's just the way it happened. Young, didn't care. – Jade

——————▽——————

Palm Springs, CA (USA)

In a busy parking lot in a car. I've had sex in cars frequently, always in the daytime. I didn't care. But I have to tell you, that was probably the best sex I've ever had. I wasn't ashamed. It was good hot sex. – Cathy Melton

Where is the Wildest Place You Ever Had Sex?

————————▽————————

Provincetown, MA (USA)

I think probably a churchyard in Provincetown. I lost my wallet. The church attendant, the church maintenance guy, or whatever he's called … this guy found my wallet the next day. I woke up with a hangover to beat the band and a blackout. How did it happen? It happened that I was drinking Harbor Lights, and we were having a Harbor Light contest and I can remember ten of them. They were in rocks glasses, and there were three different kinds of alcohol, and you set the top on fire. – Leslie Tisdale

————————▽————————

Melbourne, Victoria (Australia)

It's 2005. The music practice rooms under the student union of Monash University Clayton. They're sound proofed and a popular spot with students. I go there with my then girlfriend. I remember sitting on the piano stool and coming. – Anita Morris

————————▽————————

(USA)

Three-way tie between a) a couch in the graduate student office I shared with four other grad students, with no way to lock the door; b) in the alley by the exit door from a movie theatre, perched on one of those fire department water-sprinkler fire-hose attachment thingies; and c) standing up, in the Atlantic Ocean on a public beach, underwater from navel-level on down. – Allan Hunter

————————▽————————

Istanbul (Turkey)
Palm Springs, CA (USA)

It was in a bathhouse. Everyone there was a tourist, so it was very free and open – don't ask me any questions, just about sex. It was so delightful because there were men who were different–there were Algerians, Turks, a wide variety of people. And when I went, I did not expect it to be a gay bathhouse. I went thinking it was a Turkish Bath. I was directed to it, took the train and took some time, then I had to walk several blocks. When I went in, I paid my money and then I realized it wasn't what I thought it was, what I expected it to be. So my mind was transformed into, let's go with this, I've already paid my money, I've taken the time, let's see what it's all about. That was probably the most uninhibited time. There have been many, even in Palm Springs. Years ago, I went to Camp of Palm Springs frequently. I found it to be my favorite of the gay motels. – Don Rockwell Coffee

—————▽—————

San Mateo, CA (USA)

Bay Meadows Racetrack, jerking off in the bathroom. I was a manager there. – Jack Farquhar Halbert

—————▽—————

San Francisco, CA (USA)

At the back of Powerhouse. It was a leather bar and far back there was a door that opened up and it was like an alley, but it was enclosed. It was originally out there for people to smoke, but it got to a point where people were out there to smoke and have sex. It got really packed, cramped space. There was a lot of sex going on back there. One time I went home with eight people and we were around the dining room table and we were going around and around. Is that wild? I think that's wild. – Paul

—————▽—————

Chicago, IL (USA)

For this I have two locations of equal merit and I should note I was sober for both instances.

In a stopped elevator car in a building that housed a very sketchy hipster after hours club on Division a few blocks west of Ashland.

The other would be the alley next to the former Essanay Studio building while leaning on the wall of the Catholic cemetery on Clark Street.

My favorite is a place I did not have sex. I co-wrote and directed the bawdy production of *Steamworks the Musical* and so I was invited to go to Steamworks Baths for free. I went with a group of my cast one Friday night for the first time as a guest but I'm a prude by nature. So after walking around the place and witnessing the debauchery I went into my room, locked the door and just took a 4 hour nap because I was so tired then woke up and went home. I really needed the sleep. – Mike Gifford

Where is the Wildest Place You Ever Had Sex?

———————∇———————

London (UK)

There was a leather bar in the Mile End Road where I only went in there for a drink and ended up doing a show in front of the entire bar with a guy. I wasn't into leather at the time but a friend of mine had said, "This is a really great bar," so I walked in and there was a guy in a cage in one corner and all these leather queens about. I'm just standing there having a drink and this guy comes over and drops his trousers and presents me with his butt. It would have been rude to say no. – Tess Tickles

———————∇———————

Santiago (Chile)

I was seeing this married guy who had his own business, a bakery. He had a truck and we had sex in the parking lot of the mall. – Ives

———————∇———————

Chicago, IL (USA)

In the alley behind the Loading Dock. – Anonymous

———————∇———————

New York City, NY (USA)

Outdoors a few times, no place more or less outrageous than any other. – David Pratt

———————∇———————

Milwaukee, WI (USA)

In a DJ booth with a bartender while the DJ watched us. He made sure to put a VERY long song on the turntable. – Anonymous

———————∇———————

Where is the Wildest Place You Ever Had Sex?

Chicago, IL (USA)

Tea rooms. The Sears Towers 3rd floor or down on their cafeteria level, very festive around lunch time. Also, the Bismarck Hotel after work. And Marshall Fields. Once when I was there, I met someone. He was deaf and took me across the street to an office building, he knew all the codes to get into THAT bathroom and we had sex there. – David Plambeck.

——————▽——————

(UK)

I'm not that wild a person by gay standards, and naturally cautious. Sex al fresco is as racy as it ever got. – Diesel Balaam

——————▽——————

Chicago, IL (USA)

Bathroom of the Metro. It happened. – Terry Gaskins

——————▽——————

Venice (Italy)

Beside a statue or monument (it was many years ago and I was drunk), near the canal just off the plaza. – Alex Gildzen

——————▽——————

Seattle, WA (USA)

In high school on a church outing to Salt Water State Park near Seattle. Up in the woods with a guy that I went to high school with and that was surprising to me. The other interesting story was when another high school student, when I was a senior, invited me to come to his grandmother's apartment building on a weekend, just to hang out and visit. He took me down to the washing machine room for the apartment complex and he pulled out a massage vibrator and asked me to pull out my penis so he could show me how fabulous this felt. I just ran out of the room, down the hall, out the door and took a bus home. He ended up in prison and passed away. – OT

Where is the Wildest Place You Ever Had Sex?

—————▽—————

Chicago, IL (USA)

He knows where it was, and it will remain our secret, plus a girl doesn't kiss and tell. – Robert Castillo

—————▽—————

New York, NY (USA)
Chicago, IL (USA)

Wild or odd? There's a lot of competition for wild, but that was probably the trucks in New York with a guy who was visiting from Spain. Odd, it's a toss-up, it's either inside an Episcopal seminary or on the floor of a pastor's office in a Seventh-Day Adventist Church. – Ian H

—————▽—————

WERE YOU BULLIED IN SCHOOL AND IF SO, WHAT FORM DID IT TAKE?

Rural Iowa, (USA)

I went to high school in the mid-1970s in rural Iowa. I was one of the bigger guys, muscular, physically designed to be a football player or wrestler and my Algebra teacher was the football coach and continually harassed me to sign up for football. I liked chorus and theater and English, and while I crushed on many of the boys in my class, in that time, in that place, you tried to hide something like this. The coach's constant urging in class, and my obvious discomfort in my quiet refusals set me up to be called "faggot" or "homo" by those very boys who did play football or wrestled. My saving grace was probably my popularity with teachers and all the girls in school, and the fact that I had a natural sense of humor and was often the class cut-up, and (I'm not bragging here) but I was good-looking and broad-shouldered and none of the bullying went beyond name-calling. – Timothy Juhl

———————▽———————

Temecula, CA (USA)

I was bullied by my older brother, bullied by other kids. I was a pretty non-conformist, non-conventional type of person. It went on throughout my whole school experience, right through high school. It was just par for the course, as they say. It was something that I had to put up with. – Tim Barela

———————▽———————

Were You Bullied in School and if so, What Form Did it Take?

Indianapolis, IN (USA)
Parker, CO (USA)

Was I bullied in school? Is the pope Catholic?

My first time really being bullied was in the third grade, when I attended Crestview Elementary in Indianapolis Indiana. Two kids in another class decided that they would pass time at recess tormenting me. They mostly threw things, because when they got close, I was stronger and far more aggressive. They both stopped after third grade, with one of them aiming for friendship in fifth grade. My memory was too good and my family was ready to move again.

When I lived in Country Lake Apartments off Post Road in Indianapolis, a really tall kid liked to call me homophobic slurs and jumped me once. He was bigger, taller and stronger. Since I was living in the ghetto, I learned to focus on my education and not running the streets.

My worst round of bullying came when my family moved to Parker, Colorado. Being born in a foreign country to an immigrant family, I was different. Living for a year on the Navajo Nation and years in the Indianapolis ghettos, Parker was my first introduction to an all white town. (Okay, there was one black kid and he was my friend.) They were mountain folk merged with new money, and horribly narrow minded. They were part of the 5%. My being a punk didn't help. Within a week, I got in a fight on the bus (I won) and was suspended from the bus for a week (the other kid received no punishment.) Things, unfortunately, went down hill from there. Do I call out the people who called me homophobic slurs and threw things at me? Do I call out the faculty who allowed the treatment? Do I call out the Jewish teacher who felt she wasn't protected under hate crime laws and was pro-Amendment 2? Do I call out the sociology teacher who complained about *Heather Has Two Mommies* and *Daddy's Roommate* being introduced in New York City elementary schools and how wrong that was? (Please note its good for anyone pursuing sociology to go in with a closed, judgmental mind.) Do I blame the theater teacher who stood behind her bible, condemning abortion and "queers" with charismatic venom? Do I hold contempt to the speech teacher who called me a "son of a bitch" to my face? Do I hold on to a specific hatred for the kid who threw my jean jacket in the sewer on the day of my youngest brother's memorial service, a baby who died at 15 months of age?

Years later, while in therapy, my therapist said, "What did you expect being a punk?" I said, "I didn't expect to be bullied three years for a hairstyle I had for less than three months; and thanks for saying I asked for it."

Decades later, with the power of Facebook, I learned a fellow gay comedian was friends with one of my high school bullies. I reached out to him to make him aware. They had become friends in Boulder Colorado in college. He asked what the bullying was like. I stated, "calling me 'fag' in class, chasing me out of classrooms, getting two friends to help beat me up in the school parking lot." He was shocked to hear the bullying was that bad. He attempted to console me by telling me the story when the bully's girlfriend got drunk at a party and admitted the bully liked to have anal sex with her. She didn't mind. His dick was small. The story made me feel better.

As the years have gone on, former classmates have passed. While I don't dance for joy, I remind people who bring me the news that they need to shop for empathy elsewhere.

To this day I still fear being surrounded by white people. I am exploring therapy.

I transferred my senior year of high school. I got my diploma. I got a scholarship for college for low income kids with GPAs. Even after another brother's death, I did get my college degree.

When I transferred my senior year, people said, "You will miss at the reunions." I now joke, "Not if I keep practicing with my rifle."

Unique tidbit, Parker Colorado ranks fourth in teenage suicide. – Thomas Bottoms

———————▽———————

Chicago, IL (USA)

Yes, very much so in grade school with 6th grade through 8th grade being the absolute worst. Never by people in my own grade as they knew me the best but definitely by the older classes. It was name calling, pushing/shoving and more – but nothing near what others have experienced. – Jim

———————▽———————

Chicago, IL (USA)

I was called a "Fem" and "Faggot" on occasion and was threatened with a beating up after school two or three times. – Robert Hansen

———————▽———————

Gainesville, FL (USA)

I was terribly bullied. My homosexuality was not a secret (I never made it one) and was presumed before any announcing. I got names hurled at me. I got phone calls threatening to kill me (to which the police did nothing) before caller ID. I was physically abused (shoving, punching, pushing, thrown into lockers) not only by students, but also one or two teachers. It happened every day from about March 1983 until graduation (and beyond) in June 1985. I was nominated for Homecoming Queen (not by choice) three years in a row. I was consistently asked if I wanted to wear a tux or a dress in Yearbook photos. Homecoming week of Junior year, outside my Home Room, a poster was printed and hung on the wall: "Vote Eric Katz Homecoming Queen! Get VD! Kissy Kissy. Love your boyfriend James!" (I had no boyfriend named James at the time and had yet to date one) For my senior year I decided to accept the nomination (to make a point) and would have won, but was disqualified when the Homecoming King refused to accept the position with me. In the "Senior Wills" of graduating students, I was left (in three different individual testimonies) cases of AIDS, and on my own Senior Will, the school paper changed my byline name to "Gay Talese." The student editor let it be printed since the sponsoring teacher was the one to suggest it. On graduation, people yelled out "faggot" as I was accepting my diploma – this was at the graduating ceremony in front of their parents and mine. DESPITE IT BEING BROUGHT TO THE PRINCIPAL'S ATTENTION SEVERAL TIMES OVER THE YEARS, NOT ONCE WAS ANY KIND OF HELP OFFERED! – Eric Andrews-Katz

———————▽———————

Chicago, IL (USA)

Omg ... yes ... in elementary school ... non-stop ... put into a garbage can almost daily ... my sister would tip the tall metal can and I would crawl out. – Don Strzepek

———————▽———————

Greenwich, CT (USA)

It's unbelievable to imagine but from the first moment I went to kindergarten I was rejected by all the other kids. I remember the ringing in my ears and the taste of blood in my mouth. I clearly remember playing with all the girl toys and not the boy toys. There was a play kitchen I went right to, and all the other girls walked away from it when I was playing with it. From 1st grade until high school graduation I was verbally, emotionally, physically, socially, abused. The nightmares I had as a small child were terrifying (I still have them from time to time). I used to hide in the hallways when school was over so I wouldn't run into anyone who would beat me up. I went home in many different ways because there was always someone waiting for me on my direct route. I took a deep sigh in class one day and looked over to see one kid give me the most evil look as he pounded his fist into his other hand, after school that day he got me by the bike racks and said I was not allowed to breath the same air as all the other kids and he beat me so bad I was black and blue. Kids used to call my house and invite me to a ballgame, I went the first time and they beat the hell out of me. By the third or fourth grade they put me into Special Ed class (if I wasn't visible I wasn't a problem) it did help a bit but at the same time it just reaffirmed that I was different, the staff couldn't fathom acknowledging me as gay because that would mean sexualizing a child. The more kids learned the more they learned to hate, middle school was the worst, the kids were stronger, and the beatings hurt so much more and the psychological ridicule and torture had so much more meaning. Things were better in high school as far as the physical, I had friends but the personal struggle was hard for me. I dated a girl on and off for a while for the sole purpose of getting everyone off my back. On the off time I had friends who knew I was gay, my education suffered so much because of it all, I never went to college, never learned a skill and could only do rudimentary work. – Thomas Autumn

———————▽———————

Milwaukee, WI (USA)

Yes. I attended St. Albert's Catholic grade school through fifth grade. I was frequently the target of a prank called "nigger pile," where one person would be designated the "nigger," get thrown to the ground, and everyone nearby would pile on top of him. These pranks were never broken up by the supervising teachers or nuns, nor was anyone ever scolded for using the word "nigger." There were no people of color at St. Albert's or anywhere in our neighborhood. – Louis Flint Ceci

———————▽———————

St. Louis, MO (USA)

I was indeed bullied, starting back in elementary school. Not constantly, but when it did happen it dragged out for some weeks at a time. Back in the 1970s in the U.S. Midwest in St. Louis, attitudes were a bit Republican and religious. Even though no one knew that I already knew I was gay, I was a very bony, skinny kid. That was a sign of weakness to them, and that equated to being gay because you were weak. Although the big word was QUEER then and it was thrown around generously. I didn't care if it was called snitching, I put an end to it by telling a teacher. When I got into junior high (7th and 8th grades), I finally got tired of being pushed around. One guy bothered me so much I just turned around and punched him, then pulled his long hair. A girl that came up behind me and started smacking my back with her sharply bristled brush, I did the same thing. In high school around 10th grade, the boy sitting behind me in algebra class got a punch in the face after I got sick of his insults and I knocked him out of his desk. Yeah, I know, violence is not the answer. But it was the 1970s and no one really reached out to protect you. I was finally left alone when others realized I wouldn't take it anymore, particularly when I became the school band's first drum major. I had won the spot over about five other guys who only tried for the spot because they just didn't want me to have it. It would have meant they had to go by my commands. My first experience in domination, I'd say! – Todd Jaeger

———————∇———————

San Diego, CA (USA)

Not really, because I was always the big kid. In college I was more bullied because I allowed more of my feminine side to come out. I had long hair, I had my ear pierced … in the 1970s there were not that many men with an earring on. And I didn't wear a little simple earring. I had a huge honking gold hoop in my ear. My pirate earring. One time this guy followed me around campus and I finally turned around and said, "What's the problem, do you want to suck my dick?" I said it in front of a whole group of his friends. About two days later he cornered me and says, "Were you trying to make me come-out?" I said, "Do you want to?" That's the biggest incidence of bullying I had. I mean, I was bullied as a kid for not being good at certain sports, but that's because I was so blind. I've worn glasses since second grade. I couldn't see the end of my nose. I couldn't play baseball because when I turned sideways, I couldn't see. They picked on me about that but by the time I was junior high school, I was wearing contact lenses. I played soccer, baseball, gymnastics. I didn't fit any of the molds. – Art Healey

———————∇———————

(USA)

Seriously so. We lived in some very, very tough neighborhoods when I was a kid. To give you an idea, from high school to college we lived in 39 different places. This is a kid going on 19 years old. Many of the places we moved, we didn't find out until the day before. It wasn't like moving from Seattle to Oklahoma, from Oklahoma to California. It was often maybe in the same urban area but always different schools, so we didn't know where we were going to be. In some of those schools, the bullying was pretty intense. And was it anti-gay bullying? I think some kids saw a difference. Because I didn't realize I was different, I would do a lot of things just assuming it was normal. If kids see a difference, they'll pick on it, they'll attack it. People don't understand something, they'll try to learn about it or they'll react negatively to it. I got beat up on the way to school, at school and after school. It was like Germany bombing London basically. Everyday. In some cases, guns were involved. Some nasty stuff. In third grade a kid got shot and killed in a classroom. I didn't get shot at, I had another attempt on me with a gun, but that wasn't because I was gay. I just happened to be the person who was there. This guy, he had a history, he lived down the other end of the block from us and he had taken a cat and stuffed it in a corner mailbox and poured gasoline in it and lit it. This was two weeks before he stuffed a gun in my mouth and pulled the trigger and went "bang, bang, bang." It wouldn't go off, he was trying to fire the thing, well he didn't have the safety off it. It was a Navy pistol, ten rounds. Well, I grabbed it from him, and I fired ten rounds and then stuck the thing in his chest. I tried to tell my dad about it but he couldn't get his head buried out of a newspaper – this is when someone tried to murder your son, you heard ten rounds a half a block from the house, and this was a Navy pistol which was loud. It's not a .38, it was a loud gun. Couldn't get his eyes out of the paper. That's how he didn't want to deal with things. So, the bullying and the reaction to it and the defense against it. You have to defend yourself and get involved with defense things. – Dave

————∇————

Trinidad (West Indies)

Oh yes. I was called every derogatory name and was accused of some horrible actions that were so untrue. – Dale

————∇————

Hoboken, NJ (USA)

I went to a parochial school, K-8. I was different. I was a softer kind of kid and I was pretty, so people used to pick on me. I had a bully in school. In 6th or 7th grade, just before I graduated. He used to beat me up and threaten me in front of people. I remember most of my friends stuck up for me, but he was a pushy kind of guy. He used to call me fag and say all kinds of things when I was a little boy. I used to say to him, "It must be because you want me. Or you wouldn't say something like that. I don't want you. Are you angry because you want me, or because I don't want you?" He would be furious, kids don't understand that stuff, but I put it back on him every time he would do something. My friends, which were mostly girls, they would say, "Don't put up with any crap from him. We'll beat the shit out of him if he comes over here and starts picking on you again." The girls were coming to my rescue. It was the coolest thing. I think back and it was terrible at the time. I remember thinking what a failure I was as a young man. I wasn't violent. I wouldn't even reach out and protect myself. The whole bullying, threatening, thing was a big deal and I don't think I've had a fight in my entire life where I've had to physically hit somebody. Later on in my life, I did, but at that point I did not. – Joseph S

————————▽————————

Chicago, IL (USA)

Bullied relentlessly in junior high school. Called "sissy," "faggot," all the usual stuff because I was small and underweight. I was totally out as a bisexual in high school because everyone had already called me "faggot" and I might as well enjoy all that faggot stuff as long as I was being harassed. I was bisexual, and getting all the dick I could handle, and more pussy than just about anyone, so the joke was on them anyway.

My children's experience was totally different.

My son was often harassed for being a "fag," but he would just turn it on its head and say, "I'm not a fag, I'm a top! Bend over and I'll show you!" He got into some fistfights over this and always won them. He too was bisexual and this reputation, as being the bad-ass fag, actually made him more attractive to girls. He would go to meetings of the gay/straight alliance just to pick up free condoms to fuck girls. He always bare-backed the boys.

nineMy little girl was also bisexual and not much interested in boys when she was in high school (they were too immature). She was dominant and aggressive and could pretty much have her pick of the lesbian girls, but she also dressed very femininely (dresses and stockings), so no one ever thought of her as a "dyke," so she ended up defending a lot of her girlfriends against harassment. – R.M. Schultz

————————▽————————

Indiana (USA)

I grew up in central Indiana in a community that had Sundown Laws until 1975. Yeah, I was bullied a bit. However, with so many things to choose from, the bullies were all over the place. I was a vegetarian at the age of nine, the fat kid, the poor kid, the kid who came from the white trash family. Had to wear old clothes, take showers at school when the heat was out, got the government cheese. That sort of thing.

Plus, I was the kid who refused to dissect the frogs, stand for the pledge of allegiance and questioned the Christians when they'd do their propaganda tours masquerading as anti-drug rallies. (The whole rock music is devil music crap) So I had a bit of a target on my fat ass.

My two older brothers were also the local pot dealers, so that gave me some protection. Most of the physical stuff came from within the family. My dad, and my middle brother, who became a bully. He'd beat me up almost daily, so the kids at school or in the neighborhood were nothing. By the time I was in high school I'd been threatened with violence so many times I lost count. Finally, simply because I was tired of hearing how the football team was going to "fuck me up" because I disagreed with the quarterback in social studies (he was a dumbass, and a bigot) I threw a desk at him. Like most bullies he backed the fuck down thinking I was crazy. Which I'm glad for, because he shot someone before graduation because they disagreed with him. He did give me his tie at graduation, so that was nice considering he couldn't graduate. – Daniel Fisher aka Raid

—————▽—————

Los Angeles, CA (USA)

Oh yes. Like I said, labels like "gay" and "straight" don't really mean anything to me as much as whether I am going to have a relationship with someone. And what kind of relationship I'm going to have with them. I think a part of that was the way I was brought up. First, I was bullied because I grew up in a predominantly Afro-American black community and I didn't play ball, I didn't have the jive language down. Then because my father and the type of work that he did, we were able to move into a solid middle-class neighborhood of all-whites. So there you go. At that point there's a situation going on where in this all-white neighborhood and my mother – bless her heart – was a small thing, 5' 4". Very petite, never weighed more than 110lbs. She was always a tom boy, so she wasn't going to put up with shit. People in the neighborhood we moved to were aghast. So I was bullied there. Then the bad boys of the school get involved and they want to beat you up. Not so much because you're of a different color, but because you don't play ball and you seem to be a target. Then the terror begins because all of a sudden people go into puberty. So there's already a power-trip going on. So now they no longer want to chase you down and beat you up, now they want to chase you down, have you suck their cock, then beat you up. There was a piece of mail that came to our house and the bully lived on the next block over. It was supposed to have gone to his address. It was a day off from school. So my mother wanted to me to deliver the mail to the bully's house. I said, "No, I don't want to do it." Of course, I did. I took it over there. Stupid me, there was no car in the driveway, so I should have just dumped it in the mail slot but I didn't. I rang the doorbell. All of a sudden I heard all this scurrying going on. I ring the doorbell again. Then the door opened, and I'm pulled inside the place. I'm trying to adjust to the darkness there and I see is all these lily white bodies all around. Then it dawns on me that they all have their pants down and they're having a circle jerk. The ones that are in the room are the bullies, the football players, and all of the ones of that ilk. All of a sudden the one who's house it is, he comes over, punches me, and said, "Get that fucking faggot out of here." So for years I was confused over what a faggot was. I thought that meant that you were more feminine than somebody else. – Kalvin

———————▽———————

Chicago, IL (USA)

I felt bullied simply by being ignored, not fitting in with any group. – Martin Mulcahy

———————▽———————

San Diego, CA (USA)

No. I was very careful to stay out of harm's way. I would walk on the other side of the street if I thought there might be trouble. So no, I wasn't. – Bill

———————▽———————

New York, NY (USA)

I was smart as a kid. I probably put myself in this position a lot of times. I used to sit in the front row and I tried to answer every question. So my hand was always up. The hoodlums would sit in the back and throw spitballs at me. Years later, my nephew had a business and he hired one of the kids that used to bully me. They said to him, "That's your uncle." My nephew said, "Yes." ... They said, "Oh he was such a smart aleck, he had to answer every question." I used to think it was because I was ugly and stupid. It turned out they thought I was a smart aleck so they bullied me. I also knew I was gay and that they had to have figured it out. – Ron

———————▽———————

Were You Bullied in School and if so, What Form Did it Take?

Imlay City, MI (USA)

My brother was my bully and beat me. Much of my bullying was in the form of body image shaming. It came from my parents also. My mom used to cut the male model out of the Sears catalog and cut his head off. My mom then would attach my head and tape it to the body, then place it on the front of the refrigerator and say, "This is the son that I want." – Greg R. Baird

——————▽——————

Amersham (UK)

The boys would bully me. In particular I was good with the English classes, but arithmetic – as we called it those days – I was dreadful. I took a step down in class and I think some of the boys realized I was gay or something different, and they used to take the piss out of me when I couldn't answer the questions. But physically, sometimes I would get into fights. But I was very lucky at school because I had a boy who looked after me, Tony _____. He used to come and protect me. We had our first sex together when I was 13. – Bob Brown

——————▽——————

Honolulu, Hawaii (USA)

No, because I was always the friend of the team captain. I look back and whoever was the alpha male in school, either the team captain or there was a junior police officer organization, I was the best friend of the captain. So normally if you kind of choose teams I would have been one of the last but I was always picked first because I was the best friend of the alpha male. That was so unconscious. When I think back I realized that. – Simeon Den

——————▽——————

New York, NY (USA)

Oh yes, not just verbally, but physically too. I could run fast which is why I'm still alive, and I'm not kidding. It's not one of those snappy one-liners I usually pop out with. The kids were brutal, and I was out. I knew the fastest way to get out of the school, across the field, and either over the fence, and I could get away. Elementary school, it was bad. Junior high it got physical. Junior high it was … I was going to get killed, and I had a mouth. So I wasn't the type of queen … back in that era you have to realize, I was six feet tall and I had an Afro bigger than any other kid in school because my hair was down to my behind. You could tell I was not like anybody. I was very feminine and if you said something to me, I went right back at you. High school came along and I knew I wanted out because I could not take it anymore. I had to think of a plan everyday, how I was going to get back home from school without getting the shit knocked out of me. And going in the morning … we had a school bus stop a block from the house. Everyday I came in, "Ma, I missed it." So she had to drive me because getting on the bus was not an option. I got it that badly. I can remember all the kids and their names. Finally, by high school I had had it to my back teeth with this shit. I don't know what came over me. One of the kids was bullying me. He was going along with all the other ones, and this wasn't a kid who usually chimed in with them. He was now in front. He cornered me in a way where I felt really threatened and trapped. Mind you, this is in a classroom with the teacher sitting on her ass doing nothing. I picked a pencil up from the desk and I stabbed him with it. I stabbed him and it went in so deep that to this day he has a scar. And the reason I know, I went back to my 35 year school reunion. I had never gone to any of them, never had any desire. All through school I had three friends, and to the rest of them I figured I was a ghost. I go back to the reunion in Freeport, Long Island. There were quite a few from the class, I was surprised to see how many turned out. Some I recognized, some I didn't recognize. Nobody recognized me. They thought my partner, David, was in their class. Until they looked at my nametag, because I have a very long, very Greek last name. The first person that realized it was me, "Oh my God, you're Keith!" because they looked at the nametag. "I can't believe you're living, I thought you would have committed suicide." Right to my face, I thought you'd be dead by now. I looked at them and said, "Really! Going to school with you kids was basic training for life. I got real thick skin. I'm not like I used to be. A couple more came up, like they forgot everything they did. I don't know why I was like this, but a lot of them came up and were talking like we were good friends, we weren't good friends. I was thinking, "You used to try to beat the shit out of me, torture me, chase me, put gum in my hair" but I let it go. It came over that they did not realize what the hell they were doing. They really didn't. They moved on, and I moved on in a different way. I remember everything in detail. By the end of the night, and it was a long night because we got there early at 7 o'clock and we did not leave until after 2:00 in the morning. But before we left there was a man there I went to school with and I recognized him. He did not come near me. He stayed far away. He stayed by the bar until he had enough to drink and then he came over to introduce himself. I didn't get a word out before my husband said, "You're the man Keith stabbed, I know exactly who you are." His face froze. I said, "I never forgot you. David knows all the details." He said, "I have to apologize to you. I am so sorry. I never bullied anyone again, ever. I never forgot about you." Every day that man looks in the mirror he sees a scar that never went away. He remembers vividly what went on. I did too. I was just so taken off guard, 30 years later he came over and apologized. It was a surreal feeling. I can get past things, but I never forget things. Never. Especially traumatic, imprinted experiences. Yes, I was bullied relentlessly in school. – Keith Kollinicos aka Missa Distic

—————▽—————

Spring Valley, CA (USA)

A little bit, not much. I was small for my age, frail looking. I didn't start to grow and fill out until I was 17 at junior high school. I went to a K-8 elementary school when we moved from San Diego to east of San Diego, in a place called Spring Valley. It was a La Mesa grammar school and it was K-8. It was the last half of my 6th grade when we moved there, and it was a whole different scene. It was a school bus ride from our rural farm into La Mesa. There were some natural bullies on that bus. I didn't get a whole lot of flak from them, but going home we had to change buses at a certain point, and there were two or three boys older than myself who started harassing me. One boy, he stepped in and said, "Leave him alone." They never bothered me again. To this day I don't remember his name. But he stood up, not easy ... he was a bit larger, filled out. – Hal

—————▽—————

New York, NY (USA)

Unfortunately, yes. For me it started in the 5th or 6th grade because that's when puberty kicked in and my body changed rapidly. I was always the big tall hairy guy at the back of the room. Even back then, I was the biggest kid, the heaviest kid. Sideburns grew in, so I left them and I had these bushes on the side of my face. I was always the fat kid they picked on. Eventually I had my breaking point, somewhere in the 5th grade. During lunchtime you go out into the school yard and everyone breaks out into their factions. This group plays over here, this group plays over there. You can't go to that side of the park because that's their side. So I had to make my way over the field so that I can be left the fuck alone. The fat, tortured, kid can't run. They would egg me on then run away, and I couldn't run after them because I was very heavy at the time. Finally, I got my chance to get you. I made sure I kept rocks and bricks next to me on the floor, and I would throw rocks at them because I didn't know what else to do. Eventually it escalated. It went on through junior high school, high school. Finally, in high school, I stop myself from retaliating back because I thought to myself, "Eventually I'm going to go to prison. If I allow them to do this to me." I never got to the point of stabbing anyone. I threw bricks at people. – David Vega aka Lucifers Axe

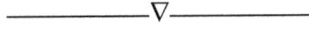

————————∇————————

North Carolina (USA)

Always. But I was also the first hippie kid in my hometown and thus bullied for having the longest hair and wearing the first bell-bottoms. I got along better with black kids than white, and was sort of the hero and bodyguard to some of the more timid and fey kids. I remember getting chased off the school grounds the last day of junior high by a gaggle of jocks with hedge-clippers (but I was also a track star and could run like the wind). – Gavin Geoffrey Dillard

————————∇————————

Chicago, IL, (USA)

Yes. And although I don't recall the names of my two primary tormenters, I can still conjure their horrible faces when they shoved me into lockers or grabbed my books because I chose to carry them "like a girl," in front of my chest, instead of under my arm at the side, the way the other boys did. There wasn't much room for gender non-conformity in south suburban Chicago in the '60s, but that was all about to change. And in a big way, especially after Stonewall. – David Cee

————————∇————————

East Randolph, NY

More than bullied, I think I was ostracized. I was a gay kid in a small farming town in Western New York and while there was something obviously different about me, I was a handsome kid and not overly effeminate. In other words, for the most part, I passed for straight … even though many of my peers seemed to guess that I wasn't. Thus, there definitely was an issue of avoidance – the popular kids wouldn't talk to me and I wasn't about to win Prom King anytime soon. I had begun doing summer stock and arts programs during the summer and took inspiration and hope from the cool, arty kids from the bigger cities. I remember I broke a shoelace on one of my High Top sneakers right before rehearsal for my senior graduation. So, I took a red lace from a winter boot and looped that in … it was something I saw someone do at some camp I had been at. I was feeling really cool, thinking it looked awesome, but the girl who was paired with me took one look at what I had done and blanched like I was Satan in the flesh. She refused to walk down the aisle with me. So, my final moments in high school kind of reflected my experience as a whole – me walking alone, with scornful glances thrown my way, as I beat, tentatively, to my own drum. – Brian Kirst

―――――∇―――――

Sydney (Australia)

I wasn't bullied at school for being gay because no one knew, I wasn't fully aware myself at the time. I had the general bullying for being very small for my age, which was more because it made me an easy target. I also had a lot of bullying for being the new kid, because of my family situation I attended nine different schools. It never lasted more than a few months and I learned pretty quickly how to handle those situations, so I don't think it was any worse than most kids. The general homophobic banter at school was never really more than teasing someone to piss them off, not the hateful violence I experienced as an "out" adult. – Ian Davies

―――――∇―――――

Cherry Hill, NJ (USA)

In junior high school and the beginning of high school, I was bullied as one of the smart boys who was lousy at sports. A group of boys would knock books out of my hands, shove me, call me names. Once, but only once, I was teased for being Jewish. After one bully grabbed my glasses, held them out the bus's open window, and threatened to drop them, I stopped taking the bus to school so that I'd never again feel captive. Instead, I hitched a ride with Dad on his way to work, or I walked the mile to school each way, regardless of rain or sleet or snow. (I should have become a mail-carrier.)

Some of the bullies were friends with a kid up the block, who was pleasant to me when alone, but who joined in the taunting when others were around. I stopped going to our neighborhood swimming pool in summer for fear of being harassed. Before going out to play with my dog on the front lawn or mow, I'd look out the window to check that none of the bullies were on the block.

Finally, I sought advice from a Guidance Counselor, who convinced me to fight back. After I started returning their shoves and book knockings, those boys gradually stopped bothering me. Fascinating, but nevertheless scarring. – Daniel M. Jaffe

Were You Bullied in School and if so, What Form Did it Take?

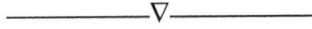

———————∇———————

(UK)

Sometimes, but it was more that my father was a teacher and my parents were getting divorced. It was an extremely traumatic time. Personally, for being gay or anything like that, I rarely had a problem. But we did experience physical violence because of kids who listened to the gossip of their parents. One of which ended up being thrown over the hood/bonnet of his car by my mother in a final attempt to persuade him to tell his son to lay off our brother. It worked. – Helen Macfarlane

———————∇———————

Manhattan Beach, CA (USA)

I was bullied because I was shy. I just kept to myself. I had a couple of friends. During my later years of high school, I would fill my thermos with vodka and orange juice, and I would sit under a tree with my friends, who were also very shy, I hung with the theater people, the art people. I just didn't fit in. I wasn't popular, I didn't go in for any of the clubs, I went out and did art, that's it. Art, art, art. I got bullied and pushed and I remember one girl who was bigger than me, kicked me right in the crotch. I remember her. I don't even know why I was being bullied. I just didn't fit in. I didn't hang with the right people. – Siouxzan Perry

———————∇———————

South Bend, IN (USA)

I went to a Catholic grade school and I was the nun's favorite so no-one dared touch me, because they would get whacked with a ruler. In high school I was in the clique of nerds, so we kept to ourselves. – Marc.

———————∇———————

Shannon, Northern Island (New Zealand)

I used to get freckle-face, redhead, carrot top, fly shit-face. They used to call me moldy because my last name is pronounced MolDAY but they pronounced it MolDEE. The spelling of my last name has been changed five times since the 15th century on my father's side. So I changed it from M-o-u-l-d-e-y to M-A-U-D-E-Y. I got moldy bread, moldy crust … got all that. I hated it, I thought, "You fuckers are cruel."– Gib Maudey

——————▽——————

(USA)

I was bullied a little bit, but it wasn't bad. I mean, I had my Cheryl Ladd shirt when I was 11. That was a little unusual for a boy. I would say in high school no I wasn't bullied, but when I was younger I was. In High School I had a girlfriend and I had a boyfriend. I was having sex with both. The girlfriend, luckily her brother was the school Jethro, he was really too old to be there. He was a big man. So nobody messed with him. Everybody got out of his way in the halls. So that helped me greatly. – Bart

——————▽——————

Baton Rouge, LA (USA)

Name-calling, somebody spit on my jacket one time. The 5th grade class collectively came at me and started throwing rocks at me during recess. It started as this mob action and people just joined in. It was like *Suddenly Last Summer* when all those native children mob poor Sebastian. Then in Junior high and high school – Junior high wasn't too bad because I was on the football team, so then I was one of the guys. Then when I got into high school and I went into choir and drama and didn't play football, then suddenly the friends I had weren't my friends anymore. But it was just name-calling, never anything to my face, just whispered … it certainly wasn't anything like it is now. – Michael Wayne

——————▽——————

Chicago, IL (USA)

I didn't receive any unusual or even pronounced bullying from peers; I had playground and after-school scuffles, but let's face it, hit a straight guy and he's your friend later on. Adults, however, were far less mature. The largest, most damaging form of bullying I received was from adults, primarily Born Again Christians in the African American community of Chicago's far south side. During the formative years of my sexual life (puberty) I endured sermons in "Chapel" a period of the school-day reserved for … well … church-like sermons in the school auditorium. During these times, the whole student body was lectured on the evils of those *"homasexes"* … apparently, a

188

particular Born Again Christian term for "homosexuals." The bullying transferred to my home, in which case it came from my mother and stepfather in the classic pattern of Fundamentalist Christian psychosis. Now, things are cooled down between my parents and I, but within a year, there will be no parent/child relationship as I'm in the slow process of breaking all familial ties. – Chip H

————▽————

Southend-on-Sea (UK)

No. I was very good at avoiding people. I think my intelligence level was much higher than those around me at school and I could negotiate my way out of any incident. But I took part in clubs. I was a member of the chess club, didn't really like it but it got me out of the school playground. I was in the school choir but I couldn't sing at all but I pretended I could – got me out of the playground again. I looked after the science block's rats and guinea pigs for a while. It just moved me out of the danger zone. It was quite a violent school. It wasn't a nice school at all. It was a comprehensive in quite a rough area. My brother got bullied much more than I did. I just used the power of negotiation to avoid them. – Martin

————▽————

Chicago, IL (USA)

Yes, I was bullied in school, both verbally and physically.

It went on from grade school through high school. I graduated a semester early from high school so that I could get away from the bullying.

Interestingly enough, years later, through Facebook, I have actually become friends with a few of the former school bullies. Some have even acknowledged the bullying and offered apologies. – Gregg Shapiro

————▽————

Havana (Cuba)

Oh yes, I was beaten up by other guys. I had a girlfriend. All the guys had girlfriends. We would all get together but there was sometimes when my girlfriend was not there, some of the other guys, two Cuban guys especially, would beat me up and call me faggot. I remember on the train going home from school that the girls would defend me. They would tell them to leave me alone, that I was not what they were calling me. In horsemanship, the

189

other kids would call me la java de la jaba which means 'the girl with the shopping bag' because I would not go dressed in my riding boots and clothes. I would go with my regular clothes and change once we got to the riding school. The reason was I had a whole bag with all my clothes in. The reason I had a bag of clothes and I was always dressed nice, so they called me the girl with the shopping bag. It was very upsetting. They would do things to me, but I'd always get back. Someone did something nasty to me and, in a competition, I put Coca-Cola bottles on the cinch, so on the third jump he was eliminated because every single one came to the floor. So that took care of that one. And there was another one who was running a horse that was not castrated and there was a female that was in heat, so I put my crop on her pussy and rubbed it on the horse's nose, so when it came time for him to jump, he could not control the horse. He was eliminated too. That's how I got back to all the bullying I got when I was eight years old. You learn to defend yourself. You can take hot peppers and rub it on their eyes, then kick them in the balls with my orthopedic shoes. – Juan-manuel Alonso

———————▽———————

Indianapolis, IN (USA)

I'd rather not remember. – Xavier Bathsheba-Negron

———————▽———————

Southern California (USA)

In elementary school I was physically bullied, shoved, pushed, and I never understood why. One day my mom asked me as a young kid if I was gay. In the area that I grew up in that was a bad word. I took offense to it, got super-defensive, shut down. In high school after coming out it was more verbal. I was constantly being put down for being gay, because I was one of three gay people at my school. There wasn't a very big GSA [Gay Straight Alliance]. Stuff like that wasn't at my school. The bullying was pretty bad throughout high school and I became a very, very, angry person. But you grow from it. – Hayley

———————▽———————

Mississippi (USA)

Mainly name-calling. I came from an abusive home in the beginning when my mom and biological father were married. He was very physically and sexually abusive toward me. I guess I wore that, it showed up. Kids picked up on it and I got picked on mercilessly. It started early, kindergarten early. I can remember feeling like a piece of shit back then. Just felt like a total misfit. Didn't belong anywhere in the world. I also started anorexia at the age of nine. I was trying to gain control of my life. Of course, I didn't know that's what I was doing by starving myself. Kids don't have the concepts. They do nowadays but we didn't have phones, we didn't have internet, we didn't have knowledge presented to us in that way, so I didn't know that what I was doing was an illness. I was really, really, rail thin, and I was picked on for that. – Jade

———————▽———————

Southern California (USA)

Severely, I tried to kill myself multiple times. Some people threw things at me. I remember in second grade one girl picked me up by my neck and pushed me up against a wall and spit on me. There were other girls who forced me down on the floor and stuck their chest in my mouth. There were other girls who undressed me and put things in my ass. I got choked a lot for sitting somewhere where someone else wanted to sit. I got called fat, ugly, tranny, faggot, dyke, all those things. Anything you can think of I've been called. Because I was not raised Christian, I was made fun of for not being Christian. I was made fun of for being fat, for having acne, and because I was queer. Or because I wasn't preppy, I dressed more in a counter subculture way. People found reasons to make fun of me. People called me a brainy bitch because I got straight A's. People always bullied me, always, always, always. – Bambi

———————▽———————

Victorville, CA (USA)
Hesperia, CA (USA)

I was. I was very petite. I was always a little bit different because I chose to have short shorts. I chose to do cheerleading, the feminine things like dancing. I got bullied a lot for it just because it wasn't a boy thing to do or a man thing to do. It was very hard. I also had long hair. I liked to grow my hair. It sometimes got to the point where I cut my hair trying to stop the bullying. I kept a lot of that to myself because I didn't want to stress out my parents. I dealt with it on my own. – Chloe DeCamp

———————▽———————

Were You Bullied in School and if so, What Form Did it Take?

Bensenville, IL (USA)

I've been wearing glasses since I was two. I can remember it as if it was happening now. We were at a bus stop and all the kids were calling me Clarence the Cross-Eyed Lion, because I did have a cross-eye. I was the only kid in the neighborhood who wore glasses. I can remember hating the way that I felt, so when I was getting off the bus to go to school, I took my glasses off, threw my glasses onto the sidewalk and stepped on them. I thought, "I will never feel like this ever again." But that was not the only time. I can remember in high school a girl bullied me – and again it's so raw right now – I can remember this girl punching me. Everybody just stood there and watched her punch me. I fell to the ground and then I got up and I looked at her and said, "Do you feel better?" And she looked at me enraged. I said, "If you would feel better, I'm happy to turn the other cheek and let you hit me again." She just looked at me and walked away. Then I went to the nurse's office. It happened a lot. – Cathy Melton

————▽————

Weymouth, MA (USA)

My name is Leslie Tisdale and the boys primarily changed it to Lezzy Titsdale and that was bullying. I would tell you that I won every scrap – I did scrap when I was a youngster against boys. The only one I lost was my only fight with a girl because I was chivalrous and let her throw the first punch. She downed me and that was the end of that. The good news about that is that I was told some tens of years later that she showed up at her 40th high school reunion in black leather with her girlfriend on the back of her Harley. So I don't feel so bad about it. But I would tell you also that I was bullied because of my weight. I had a weight problem as a child. But I will tell you also that there was a girl that was heavier than me and I bullied her. – Leslie Tisdale

————▽————

Melbourne, Victoria (Australia)

It's 1996. There was a set of rings to swing across the play equipment. I was hanging upside down. This was not unusual for me. A boy swung a single ring towards me and I fell. My eyebrow split open and I needed stitches.

1996 – 1997 The boys are consistently bullying me verbally. Things like, "Everybody knows Anita picks her nose," they also make much of me having germs.

It's 1998. I've moved to a girls' school. I'm excluded from two different social groups. I still don't know why.

It's 1999. I'm in the toilets near the canteen. The two entrances of the toilet are around the corner from each other. I'm trapped in the toilets by one girl, while the other pretends to film.

It's 2003. I've been hanging around the Chinese friends of my Chinese best friend. They've been excluding me. It's been more subtle than before. I ask why. I'm told because "I don't think like them." – Anita Morris

———————V———————

White Deer, Texas Panhandle (USA)

No, but I think I could have been. I have a twin, so it's not so much that we covered for each other or that we looked out for each other, but there was always more than one to bully. They had two to deal with if anything happened. It was just the presence of the two of us as a team. – Don Rockwell Coffee

———————V———————

Albuquerque, NM (USA)

Oh hell yes. Nearly all of it from male students, but a little bit from "teachers" too. Name calling, messing with my stuff, physical violence, a whole lot of mockery, e.g., repeating things I'd said in a high nasal whiny tone, singing songs, nonstop contempt and amusement as if I were fundamentally ridiculous and disgusting at the same time. Nearly all of it homophobic and/or sissyphobic in nature (and of course THEY didn't distinguish between gay and sissy). The teachers who participated actively would be sarcastic or dismissive and would say far more subtle things that implied the same thing, and which expressed that I was bringing everything on myself and deserved no sympathy or protection. – Allan Hunter

———————V———————

(USA)

Slightly. And yes, a bit of homophobia. It was mostly 'cause that's what nerds and geeks and people who were studious were tagged as. Not so much that they were seen as "faggots" but more, anyone who wasn't a jock or in a certain clique, were deemed this. It was a derogatory word that was wielded easily and without repercussions. Side Note: I avoided this quickly by being friends with everyone BUT the jocks, and had some heavy duty mean looking Greaser friends who stood by me. – James S

—————▽—————

Canton Township, OH (USA)

I was bullied but I have never been fey, so just typical skinny quiet nerdy kid name calling. I overcame it by developing a sense of humor and that I was always smarter than my bullies. – Mike Gifford

—————▽—————

London (UK)

I went to what in America is called a private school but in England was called a public school. Just to confuse everyone. I would have been insulted if I hadn't been bullied at some point. In my first year, I was 11 or 12, I was a fairy fat kid with glasses, little horned rim glasses. I could easily have been cast in *Lord of the Flies* as Piggy. In fact, I think I model myself after Piggy. I would frequently end up being thrown into trashcans or just otherwise set upon by the older boys. – Tess Tickles

—————▽—————

(USA)

A male cousin threw rocks at me all the time. – David

—————▽—————

(Chile)

Oh, fuck yeah. The basic ones were, I used to have a very thin voice when I was a kid, and it was slightly feminine. I got bullied for that. Every time there was a character of a woman in a novella, I got called those names. I was also bullied by the teachers, that was a super fuck-off. Everyone thought they had the right to call you names. I knew that I was different and that something was going on with myself. I didn't know which was the right path, because I was being told how to behave. My mother was obsessed with the fact that I was a little bit feminine and it turned out the teachers also noticed. I remember one of the teachers called to my mom and said, "Hey, your son is feminine," and my mom was super-pissed off with me. "You have to behave like a man" … and all that shit. I had to put up with that for years. And my grades were flawless, impeccable. I can't believe that my mom thought a t-shirt was feminine. Also, my father and his co-workers, when I was walking by on my way to school. My mom didn't like the school uniform, everyone was wearing ties and I was wearing a romper and a little bag with rainbows and a little whale. So, I was walking by and all the other kids were wearing the uniform and I was wearing shorts and this little romper and my bag. I was cute, but hey … in the middle of the fucking countryside? So, when I walked by, guys, adult guys, they would whistle at me. Construction workers, screaming at me … I was only seven years old. Now, I know, that it was because I was fabulous. I had to put up with all that shit for a long time. I had to change schools and that's where I reinvented myself. – Ives

———————▽———————

Rugby (UK)

I was never really badly bullied, as my physical stature discouraged this. Also, I wasn't effeminate or camp. I was quiet, thoughtful and sensitive, and after a few weeks in the rugby team I made my excuses and dodged team sports wherever possible (although I was quite a good hockey player). Nonetheless, it was the 1970s and what we would now call homophobic slurs and insults were rife. Most of my experiences were the ubiquitous name-calling, the occasional thump, but mainly ostracism and the need to constantly self-censor. Once you have been labelled "gay" others fear being tainted by association, so team sports become pointless (no one passes the ball to you) and the locker room banter can be purposely vicious and humiliating. I was once threatened with a knife in the long-jump sandpit when two boys sat on me, but I didn't find that particularly frightening or upsetting. You just put up with it and place your faith in things getting better. I have since learned that a few teachers and several boys I knew at school were also gay, but there was no support of any kind, from any quarter. It makes you resilient, I suppose, but only the strong survive. – Diesel Balaam

———————▽———————

(USA)

It was mostly verbal, and not about being gay but about being weird, a "spaz," uncoordinated, etc. Often the environment was one big passive bully. – David Pratt

———————▽———————

Were You Bullied in School and if so, What Form Did it Take?

Northlake, IL (USA)

Oh yes, I was bullied, but I guess because I had a best friend who was also "different" and the fact that I have always had thick skin and believed that what others said or thought about me was none of my business, it didn't really bother me that much. I was called "fag" and "homo" etc. and once I was jumped by a couple of bullies but as I was always athletic and strong, even if fey, I bested them both and that was that! The physical and verbal bullying I suffered from my own father was a bit more of a problem for me, but as we both aged and dealt with our issues, things got better. I was determined to have a relationship with him based on respect coupled with forgiveness and I am grateful that it worked out. I was a caregiver to him in his final years and count that as one of the great blessings of my life. – Paul Mikos

————▽————

Milwaukee, WI (USA)

Yes, and I'm embarrassed to say that it became a sort of food chain and I made fun of kids who were below me on the pecking order in school, though there weren't too many kids who ranked lower. I was always trying to be what other people wanted me to be and hated myself for being what many of the kids accused me of being. I tried to disappear and be as unnoticeable as possible. – Anonymous

————▽————

Niles, IL (USA)

Yes, name calling. I built a mental wall against everyone, hated all the kids, got into fights. I HATED grammar school, high school was better, but constant name calling – everyone knew I was gay. – David Plambeck

————▽————

(Venezuela)

I was always educated, but my manners were gay, I believe. People would tell me, "Oh you faggot." I had an encounter with one guy because I was always with the girls and that guy liked one who was my friend. I never liked girls in that way, since I remembered, but I had to because – Venezuela, you know.

But he just punched me in the face because I was taking his girl away from him. But it was not true. Yes, I was bullied all the time. Even when I was in high school. My family also bullied me, some of my cousins. Now I don't give a shit. I remember those days, they were not nice. – Carlos

———————▽———————

Los Angeles, CA (USA)

For some reason he always had an issue with me. The first time we met he pushed me and I fell back. All the other kids gathered behind us. I had never been in a fight. I thought, "What the hell does he want?" So I pushed him back. We became best friends – isn't that weird – we became best friends. Everything he did I wanted to copy, and we hung out together at school. As he walked to school he passed by my house. He wasn't picking me up, but in my dreams, he was picking me up. Honestly, I felt like his girlfriend. He picks me up, he drops me off. To me, I felt, "Wow! This guy is special." He made me feel special. I didn't think about it then, but I was infatuated by him. – Felix

———————▽———————

Chicago, IL (USA)

For most of my grammar and high school years, I was fat and very conscious about my weight. I remember in grammar school labeling myself Fatman as a way to lessen the pain and sting of the word. And in gym class, I could never climb the steel poles, do pull-ups on the pull-up bars or use the rings. In high school, I was usually chosen last for teams in Phys. Ed class and that was pretty humiliating especially since I loved and played sports in my neighborhood. Eventually I stopped dressing for gym. – Robert Castillo

———————▽———————

Wauconda, IL (USA)

Of course I was bullied in school, and the form it took was in verbal abuse, some shoving in the halls and such, and call outs for my lack of physical abilities and non-participation in sports. They called me sissy and were not interested in being friends with me in general. Now that I look back on it, I see how hurtful it was, but as I recall I was able to pretty much write it off at the time, unless they came at me physically which was rare. – Dean Ogren

Were You Bullied in School and if so, What Form Did it Take?

————————∇————————

Elyria, OH (USA)

I only recall a single incident. It was in junior high school and two of the rougher boys in my class pinned me against a wall. But I talked myself out of violence. – Alex Gildzen

————————∇————————

Seattle, WA (USA)

Yes, but not with any words that indicated I was gay. It was probably because I was of small stature, was very skinny, and I was not very athletic. I don't really remember being bullied but I just felt like I wasn't one of the jocks and the beautiful people. By the time I became a senior in high school I was very popular and held a student body office. I was also very active in the theater department. – OT

————————∇————————

WHAT IS THE TOP QUALITY YOU SEEK IN A PARTNER AND WHY?

Chicago, IL (USA)

Kindness. I've been fortunate (or unfortunate) to have been involved with guys with very diverse qualities but none with true kindness. – Jim

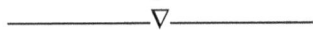

———————∇———————

Seattle, WA (USA)

I like someone that knows who they are in life. On our second date, after I went off at the mouth about some subject, my future-husband looked at me and nicely said, "You know you're full of shit, right?" Right there I knew everything I needed to know about him. He was an individual. He wasn't afraid of voicing a contradictory opinion, and most of all, he could stand up for himself. It was the first time I realized our potential long-term compatibility. – Eric Andrews-Katz

———————∇———————

Chicago, IL (USA)

I've been with my boyfriend in Chicago for seven years. I joke that he likes it so much, he broke another mirror.

After a lifetime of broken hearts, I realize I want to know what top quality I seek in myself … and why. – Thomas Bottoms

———————∇———————

What is the Top Quality You Seek in a Partner and Why?

Oakbrook Terrace, IL (USA)

Honesty and faithfulness were burned in the past by men who were neither. – Robert Hansen

—————∇—————

Nevada City, CA (USA)

Equality. I do like a man who is handsome, smart, and kind, but over the years, kindness has become the more important quality. – Louis Flint Ceci

—————∇—————

Chicago, IL (USA)

At age 62, someone who can talk, cook, spend time alone and not feel ignored, go to sleep and not want sex, who prefers sleep. – Vincent Rideout

—————∇—————

Greenwich, CT (USA)

Maturity. I have always been attracted to older men because I believe they are more emotionally stable. – Thomas Autumn

—————∇—————

Rancho Mirage, CA (USA)

Above all, HONESTY. I think because my first and only partner I ever had from 1983 – 1985 played around when I was gone during each week attending college. Since then I've never been in another relationship, but I don't feel it's because I can't trust guys and I don't think I act in any way that scares them away (although, my Vimeo video creations can be a bit "out there," but that's just creativity, folks!). I figure I still have time to find someone special because I have friends who met their partners in their 60s. Honesty is something I cherish, and I am always honest with others. – Todd Jaeger

What is the Top Quality You Seek in a Partner and Why?

———————∇———————

Cathedral City, CA (USA)

One of the most important things is somebody who's there to support me but still gives me freedom. I don't have to be joined to them at the hip. I can go do things on my own. They can go do things on their own. They don't expect me to always do what they want to do. – Art Healey

———————∇———————

Chicago, IL (USA)

Honesty!!! – Don Strzepek

———————∇———————

Cathedral City, CA (USA)

Awareness and openness and equality. I want all those things, I think they're really important. I'm not sure you can get all of those things from one person. I doubt that very much. My experiences in life have said to me that some of the best relationships I've had were in multiple relationships and open relationships, where I had great sex with one, good sex with the other, emotional stability with one, comfort and joy with another. So you can't always have that with one person. I've not had that with one person. We live a life that's so foolish, if having one person in your life works for you, then God bless you, I'm happy for you. But if it doesn't and you're living a lie, you're full of shit and you're just lying to everybody. And the bottom line is, that first person you're lying to is yourself. That's the fallacy of relationships, that nobody can be everything for you and you can't be everything for anyone. Until you love yourself, no-one can love you. – Joseph S

———————∇———————

Palm Springs, CA (USA)

Honesty. – Dan Brazill

———————∇———————

What is the Top Quality You Seek in a Partner and Why?

Chicago, IL (USA)

Self-possession. I seek lovers who know who they are, don't need constant reassurance, are who they are. I like dominant personality types best, but if a sub' is totally a sub,' confident in their submission, fearless, then that's okay, too. The problem with most bottoms is that they are just a bundle of insecurities. – R.M. Schultz

—————▽—————

Chicago, IL (USA)

Compatibility is the only real quality that I seek. I have no real preconceived notions of who would make a good lover, but I am naturally drawn to someone intelligent and with an inborn sense of elegance. The people who draw me the most are those with a certain quality of childish wonder with the world. I'm drawn to someone able to enjoy silence. In a boring way, I suppose I go for what *anyone* ultimately would: someone with an earnest desire to make a relationship work as well as an ability to adjust to whatever may help the relationship to flourish. Oh, and yeah … someone comfortable with living in his own flesh should move to the front of the love-line. – Chip H

—————▽—————

Chicago, IL (USA)

Loyalty … How can you love someone without trust and respect? – Gary Chichester

—————▽—————

(USA)

Honesty. Because without it a relationship cannot work. (really, it's having a nice ass, LOL) – Driveshaft

—————▽—————

(USA)

They need to be okay with the fact I put my animals first. I have a rescue cat now and expect to have more animals in the future. I've been a crone to a number of elder and special needs creatures, and they are my priority. Human needs are secondary. As I get older sex doesn't interest me as much, so I could go a long while before I put out for a lover. They're just going to have to deal with it. – Daniel Fisher aka Raid

———▽———

San Diego, CA (USA)

Gentleness. See this is interesting because though I think I'm part of the kink world, I am not turned on by heavy macho aggressiveness. It's not a turn on for me, but it's a super turn on for these guys to have this hard, aggressive, stance … dom, sub, and all that. That doesn't do it for me. I'm super turned on by gentleness and high intellect. Someone who really thinks about things and talks about things. – Bill

———▽———

Chicago IL (USA)

Honesty and integrity are important, couples should be able to speak about every aspect even when it may seem fleeting or uncomfortable. Being on the same page helps to strengthen the relationship bond. – Dale

———▽———

Cathedral City, CA (USA)

Honesty, integrity. I don't like games and I don't like mean people and I don't like people who are only going to be obsessed with themselves and not me. – Ron

———▽———

Chicago, IL (USA)

Passion for social causes, like the environment, animals, art and design. It

shows we have similar souls. I have zero interest in anyone who follows money, power or politics. – Martin Mulcahy.

—————∇—————

(USA)

Compassionate, romantic, honest, a friend, integrity, communication, unconditional love. All those things brought together is the essence of a great relationship. I eventually want to marry my best friend and husband. – Greg R. Baird

—————∇—————

Cathedral City, CA (USA)

I think what I look for is just being able to sit down and enjoy each other in a nice easy rhythm, no pretense, no bullshit, no extra camp or anything. Just have a conversation. – Bob Brown

—————∇—————

Cathedral City, CA

Integrity. – Hal

—————∇—————

Chicago, IL (USA)

Chemistry, honesty, trust, smart, successful. – Laurie Cowall

—————∇—————

Palm Springs, CA (USA)

Loyalty above all else – Keith Kollinicos aka Missa Distic

—————∇—————

What is the Top Quality You Seek in a Partner and Why?

Palm Springs, CA (USA)

For me it's realness. – David Vega aka Lucifers Axe

———————▽———————

Cathedral City, CA (USA)

Intuitiveness. It covers a really broad aspect, be sensitive to what's around you. – Simeon Den

———————▽———————

Sydney (Australia)

Trust and honesty are the most important qualities for me, because I grew up in a broken family where I felt very alone. Even my relationship with my siblings was very distant as we were often not living together, and my situation changed regularly. This kind of upbringing taught me to be untrusting of people in general and to put up emotional walls to keep others away.

When I found the gay scene these feelings were made worse because I was looking for love and connection with people, but all I was finding was meaningless sex with men that were only interested in my innocence and youth. Thankfully this all changed when I met my partner and realized that there was someone looking for the same thing. – Ian Davies

———————▽———————

Palm Springs, CA (USA)

Basically, having their act together. I like someone who can kiss well, who can cuddle. In fact, last night I went to the Toolshed and I was just sitting there minding my own business. This handsome older guy comes up to me and says, "I've been wanting to kiss you since I first saw you." And he was a good kisser. – Marc

———————▽———————

What is the Top Quality You Seek in a Partner and Why?

North Carolina (USA)

Chemistry. Mutual chemistry. Call it energy, if you'd like. Such is way more important than looks or even intellect. If it feels right, it usually is. – Gavin Geoffrey Dillard

—————▽—————

Santa Barbara, CA (USA)

Trust that he'll protect my feelings no matter what happens, that he'll always have my back, that he'll love me even when I screw up. Feeling this trust, I can relax and fully be myself, and share myself with him. – Daniel M. Jaffe

—————▽—————

Palm Springs, CA (USA)

Absolute openness, honesty, and humor. – Helen Macfarlane

—————▽—————

Chicago, IL (USA)

Kindness. To put up with me, he'd need a lot of that. – Mark Zubro

—————▽—————

Palm Springs, CA (USA)

Honesty, humor, patience. No drama – Siouxzan Perry

—————▽—————

Palm Springs, CA (USA)

Honesty, integrity, and not to hold anything back, because that's the foundation to a successful relationship. Totally honest, no lying. If they lie, you've done me, you've got the cross. I'll know anyway, I'll feel it. – Gib Maudey

What is the Top Quality You Seek in a Partner and Why?

————————▽————————

Chicago, IL (USA)

A sense of humor. Anyone with a sense of humor is intelligent, a quality I also value, and those two things together make for a life of good times. Compassion and good communication skills are really important as well. – Yvonne Zipter

————————▽————————

Cathedral City, CA (USA)

Understanding, compassionate, smart. I like intelligence. – Bart

————————▽————————

Cathedral City, CA (USA)

Honesty. From my perspective there's nothing I wouldn't share with Charlie. And my expectation is the same. I'm not saying you have to merge everything, your deepest, darkest, thoughts and stuff. Just honesty. You come to an agreement for certain things, whether it's are you're going to be monogamous or not, or what you're going to do with your finances, or if you're not coming home in the evening, where are you going? … just things like that. Honesty. – Cody

————————▽————————

Cathedral City, CA (USA)

Compassion because if that person isn't compassionate toward other people there's something missing in that person. – Michael Wayne

————————▽————————

Chicago, IL (USA)

It would be more than one quality. A sense of humor is a must. I can't relate

to someone who doesn't know how to laugh. Besides that, he would have to have compassion, intelligence, a sense of responsibility, and enough self-confidence to make it all worthwhile. In other words, he'd have to be perfect. This is why I'm alone. – Xavier Bathsheba-Negron

————▽————

Oxford, (UK)

I like a partner that enjoys the same things I enjoy, like opera and theatre and good food, nights out, conversation, politics that aren't my anti-politics. That doesn't have to be sexual. For me, a partner doesn't have to involve sex as such. But for a sexual partner, or slave in my parlance, it's obedience I like. To be obeyed in what I say and what I want, to the point where they would know before I say that I want it. They learn what would please me or what I want from them and they do it without asking. It's ingrained into them. – Martin

————▽————

Palm Springs, CA (USA)

Humor. Intelligence. You gotta be able to carry on a conversation with me. And I want to talk about more than just what you're wearing. I like to talk about a lot of things. I feel like I'm pretty worldly, not worldly well-traveled worldly but I read a lot. I look up a lot of stuff. – Jade

————▽————

Chicago, IL (USA)

At this point, it's empathy and intelligence, but that evolved out of experience. – Mike Gifford

————▽————

Cathedral City, CA (USA)

Emotional intelligence. I need them to know what their love languages are, I need them to be understanding of my love languages. I need them to be aware of what a healthy relationship looks like and be aware of boundaries. I want them to be emotionally intelligent. You need to be aware. You need to be awake up here, otherwise we're not going to click. – Bambi

———————∇———————

Palm Springs, CA (USA)

Honesty. I can't stand somebody who's fake. I was raised by a guy who was born in 1896. He was the son of a Methodist minister, a traveling Methodist minister in New Hampshire. He gave me some really good skills, a set of skills about the world. He adopted me when he was just retiring from his work life. It was me and him running off on vacation after vacation, taking me out of school, driving me across country, taking a trip to Morocco, this kind of stuff. I got old school values. He gave me values like honesty. He gave me a desire for education and higher education and a lifelong education. I think within that there are two things: one of them is a sense of humor, the other one is honesty. And I really like femmes. – Leslie Tisdale

———————∇———————

Palm Springs, CA (USA)

Integrity. I have to tell you that Leslie is that person. Leslie is a person of integrity. Only a handful – five maybe – that I know are like she is. If she says she's going to do something, she's going to do it. If she says she's committed to you, she's committed to you. She's a person that doesn't gossip at all. She has the most character and integrity of anybody I know. Honest to a fault. – Cathy Melton

———————∇———————

Cathedral City, CA (USA)

Being down-to-Earth. I think a lot of our community is emphasized on looks and oversexualizing people. From my experiences dating I have noticed that I am more of a sexual object to most. I want to hold a conversation with someone that isn't asking about my genitalia and stuff like that. I want to be treated as a regular person. I know that sounds like how it should be, but, unfortunately, it's not. It's something, for me, that's so rare that if I see that quality in a person, I'm automatically attracted to them. – Hayley

————▽————

Cathedral City, CA (USA)

Understanding and acceptance. For me, my girlfriend now, she didn't care that I was trans. She was very accepting, very supportive, it wasn't even a question in her mind. That to me is very attractive. It makes me bond closer with someone, it makes me open up and feel comfortable, safe enough to say something. Safety has to be my priority in life because of what happens to trans people a lot. It's something I always look for, because if they're not accepting, I can't trust it, and if I can't trust it, then I put myself in a dangerous situation. – Chloe DeCamp

————▽————

Chicago, IL (USA)

The top quality I seek in a partner is a mental connection. I want my mind to be challenged. I want to be provoked to think differently. If that connection isn't there, I lose interest very quickly. I was grateful to experience this with both of my partners. Sex is important, but in my opinion the mental connection surpasses it. – Yehuda Jacobi

————▽————

Loyalty of the heart. The rest can be negotiated. – Diesel Balaam

————▽————

New Orleans, IL (USA)

Honesty and loyalty. Both are hard to find. – Terry Gaskins

————▽————

Chicago, IL (USA)

A sense of humor. – Anonymous

————▽————

What is the Top Quality You Seek in a Partner and Why?

Chicago, IL (USA)

Kindness. Because there is not enough of it in the world. I have a T-Shirt I got from an AIDS Ride many years ago which reads "HUMANkind; Be BOTH." It says everything. – Paul Mikos

—————▽—————

Chicago, IL (USA)

I'm not really seeking a partner because I was spoiled by my late husband John and I'm okay with that, but you never know. – Robert Castillo

—————▽—————

Cathedral City, CA (USA)

Trust. It surprises me how many couples that I know have come to me individually and told me secrets about their relationship. Inevitably it leads to mistrust, whatever they're trying to hide and then when you start lying in a relationship then you may as well not have the relationship. It's like a female friend of mine came to me a few years ago and said she thought her husband was having an affair and she wondered how she could spy on his email or put some software on his laptop so she could find out what she was doing. I said to her, "What is your point, because if you don't trust him now, why even go to the expense of buying spyware. You just need to decide if this is a relationship you want to keep going or not. Then have a conversation." They split up. – Tess Tickles

—————▽—————

Chicago, IL (USA)

Loyalty. A partner must be always there for you, and when you have that you really have it all, because they will be there through the good and the bad. Through hard times, and illness, and challenges. I have seen that loyalty is probably the greatest gift one can give to another. Yes, even better than that awesome sex, and for me to say that is giving up a lot. – Dean Ogren

—————▽—————

What is the Top Quality You Seek in a Partner and Why?

Fort Lauderdale, FL (USA)

Intelligence combined with a sense of humor, because otherwise, what's the point of putting up with someone else's shit. – Rick Karlin

———————▽———————

Cathedral City, CA (USA)

A creative sense of humor. It's important, because if you can laugh, you can get through anything. – Ian H

———————▽———————

Milwaukee, WI (USA)

Probably a tie between a sense of humor and a sense of adventure. – Anonymous

———————▽———————

WHAT WAS THE MOST MEMORABLE LGBTQ EVENT YOU EVER ATTENDED?

Tampa, FL (USA)

To this day, it would have to be the visiting exhibit of the AIDS Quilt Project when it was on display in Tampa, Florida. At the time, AIDS had taken at least three friends and co-workers and I went with my best friend. When we walked into the auditorium, there were several thousand panels laid out on the floor with narrow walkways between them, almost like a city street grid. At various intersections, a box of tissues sat. I wasn't quite sure why there were all these boxes of tissues on the floor, but as I began walking through the exhibit and reading these astoundingly beautiful and sad fabric memorials, the emotions became overwhelming and I spent the rest of the time sobbing as I walked around. I was thankful for those Kleenex. – Timothy Juhl

————————∇————————

Denver, CO (USA)

It wasn't my first Pride event, but it was the second or third and it gave me hope. I would claim the Denver Pride 1994 before I started college. I hung out with close loving friends. I smiled and sang and danced. A friend had recently had an appendectomy. We put her in a red wagon and wheeled her around, taking turns so she could be featured in the parade. The parade walked down Colfax Avenue to Civic Center Park, across from the state Capital. The Civic Center put on a great drag show, one performer arguably being a better performer than Whitney herself. – Thomas Bottoms

What Was the Most Memorable LGBTQ Event You Ever Attended?

—————▽—————

Los Angeles, CA (USA)

It would have to be when I used to go to the parades in West Hollywood. They were always pretty memorable. I would always be out there with friends. Go to the festival afterwards. I can't remember any other specific event other than going to the bars and going to the Parade once a year. – Tim Barela

—————▽—————

Chicago, IL (USA)

A function celebrating the anniversary of the "first" LGBTQ student association at a Catholic college in the world ... DePaul University ... I was one of the founders and I am now in the historical archives at DePaul. – Don Strzepek

—————▽—————

Chicago, IL (USA)

Two spring to mind both here in Chicago:
   First. Being at Sidetrack for Election night 2008 when Barack Obama was elected. It was such a joyous night, and everyone was wildly excited for both a progressive Democrat and for a hometown politician.
   Second. I went to the HRC dinner when Michael Sam spoke. I was so impressed with his courage to come out in such a macho environment like football. He struck me as strong, courageous, and principled. Additionally, I thought he was so handsome. It was a great evening. – Jim

—————▽—————

Washington, DC (USA)

(Aside from my five weddings to the same husband) ... The 1993 March on Washington DC. I'd never seen that many LGBTQ people in one spot. The voice we used as a united group made me realize the power we have when a group is united. –Eric Andrews-Katz

—————▽—————

What Was the Most Memorable LGBTQ Event You Ever Attended?

Washington, DC (USA)

A fund raiser/silent auction for an AIDS support group in Washington DC hosted by Nathan Lane. I donated a piece of my own and attended with my lover. – Vincent Rideout

———————▽———————

Chicago, IL (USA)

That would have to be Chicago's pride parade after the Supreme Court ruling. The Gay Games at Soldier Field in Chicago was pretty amazing too. – Robert Hansen

———————▽———————

St Louis, MO (USA)

While it would not have technically been considered an LGBTQ event, because HIV/AIDS was hitting hard in the gay community mid to late 1980s a memorial event in downtown St. Louis in a big open area across from the courthouse was basically related. A very large group of people attended, and we were all given candles. A mic was handed around for each person to say the name of a loved one who had died from complications of AIDS. I mentioned Ron, who I had had been in a three-year relationship with. It's an event that I remember vividly and has stayed with me all these years later. – Todd Jaeger

———————▽———————

Seattle, WA (USA)

The 1989 GALA Chorus Festival in Seattle, Washington. I was a member of the San Francisco Gay Men's Chorus at the time. It tore my heart open: I wept, I shouted for joy, I laughed until it hurt, I had my mind blown by the beauty and daring of the singing. I went on to attend GALA festivals with the Lesbian/Gay Chorus of San Francisco and the Silicon Valley Gay Men's Chorus. – Louis Flint Ceci

———————▽———————

San Francisco, CA (USA)

In 2007 being at Gay Pride in San Francisco in the marriage window. Having

over 500 couples that had gotten married during Gay Pride at the Gay Pride celebrations in San Francisco and being one of those couples. I was married in 2004 when Gavin Newsom did the weddings on Valentine's weekend in San Francisco, that they had thrown out. Joe and I were part of the 18,000 couples who were in the lawsuit that caused the window to happen and then probably to end up on the ballot. We were legally married so they couldn't do anything about it, but nobody else could get married. – Art Healey

————————▽————————

Palm Springs, CA (USA)

The most recent one would be the Steve Chase Awards in Palm Springs at the Convention Center last year. Steve Chase was a philanthropist who was very wealthy, designed furniture, interior design, very fancy. Very pricey. The awards go to people in the community who are uplifting and philanthropic to the LGBTQ community. So it's a very self-serving organization but I got to work the red carpet and it was amazing. The amount of money in this area and from LA is just unbelievable. There's hundreds and thousands of dollars being donated on a regular basis. Way more than Florida, way more than New York. That was the most recent event. – Joseph S

————————▽————————

Chicago, IL (USA)

"Art AIDS America" was a show at Alphawood Gallery in early 2017 showcasing artwork created in response to the AIDS crisis. I went on my day off and only saw about a third of the show before I was overcome with sadness and had to leave. Some of the artworks were about people I knew, places I had been, events I had attended, and it was simply too much. A week later, I went back and tried again; still couldn't finish. Got through the whole thing on the third try. On the way out, one of the curators stopped me and said, "This is your third visit; you must really like it!" I just busted out crying. – R.M. Schultz

————————▽————————

Short Mountain, TN (USA)

My first Beltane Gathering at Short Mountain Sanctuary, in Tennessee. It was an eye-opening mind-expanding experience. It shaped a chunk of my life for good, bad and odd ways. Driving down in an old hearse, with a mess of freaks spending 10 days in the middle of nowhere surrounded by queer people, easy sex, drugs, awesome and terrible music as well as metric tons of drag will change a person. I didn't even say anything about the goats or chickens, an Appalachian paradise. – Daniel Fisher AKA Raid

—————∇—————

San Francisco, CA (USA)

The San Francisco Pride Celebration. Seeing Jennifer Holliday on the main stage in 2003 singing *And I Am Telling You.* She made tears run down my face. – Driveshaft

—————∇—————

Sydney (Australia)

The White Party. You know the Fox movie people, well they have a huge installation in Sydney? Sound stages go on forever. For this weekend the gay organizations there just take over the whole thing. Bands, DJs … my God, there must have been eight DJs at any one time in different theaters. – Dan Brazill

—————∇—————

Washington DC (USA)

There have been so many wonderful events that I have been fortunate to attend. The one that stands out was being a volunteer at the first national display of the Quilt. – Gary Chichester

—————∇—————

New York, IL (USA)
Chicago, IL (USA)
Cleveland, OH (USA)
Paris (France)

I have attended so many gay events that it's difficult to pinpoint just one. Stonewall 25 was definitely memorable. Chicago Gay Games in 2006 is also one for the books. Taking silver in bowling was way better than expected. Hanging out with old and new friends. I have gone on to take a bronze in Cleveland 2014 and Gold in Paris, Fr. in 2018. – Tripp

What Was the Most Memorable LGBTQ Event You Ever Attended?

———————▽———————

San Francisco, CA (USA)

Folsom Street Fair. My first time was two years ago. I'd never been to Folsom and I was curious. I'm not saying it was the best or most fun time I've had, too many people. It was certainly the most memorable. There was a certain amount of freedom, you could walk around naked, which I did, and other guys did. To see everyone having a blast was … wow, what an event. And to think that it's a world-renowned event, a big deal. I felt, "Oh wow, it was really neat to see this. I don't want to go back, thank you. The crowds and all that." – Bill

———————▽———————

Chicago, IL (USA)

The premiere of my first film at the Chicago REELING gay film fest. – Martin Mulcahy

———————▽———————

New York, NY (USA)

My first Gay Pride Parade in NYC. As a young Caribbean boy seeing all these people who were just like me made my jaw drop, people were dancing and kissing, holding hands and having an amazing time. It was the first time I felt I could let my hair down and just be, it was refreshing and invigorating. – Dale

———————▽———————

New York, NY (USA)

My first New York City Gay Pride about 1977. It was overwhelming in every way. You looked around and everybody was friendly, happy, having a good time. It was exhilarating. I went with Sal and his apartment was right on 5th Avenue, but it was 9th street, which is also Christopher Street. We were right there. It wasn't as big as it is today, but it seemed like a mass of people. – Ron

What Was the Most Memorable LGBTQ Event You Ever Attended?

——————▽——————

Los Angeles, CA (USA)

One of our friends who was a dancer, he was in the original *West Side Story*, did the movie as well, had a cancer of the throat and had a vast amount of medical bills to pay. Somebody organized a get-together in the gay movement to donate money. I went to it and it was just amazing how many people showed up. People like Russ Tamblyn who danced in *West Side Story* and in various MGM musicals. It was at the Bob Hope Center – unusual because Bob Hope was a little bit homophobic. But the money that came in that night was amazing. It was the first time I had gone to a fundraiser which was attended by gay people. It's incredible how they all came out and put the money in the hat. – Bob Brown

——————▽——————

Washington DC (USA)

When I went to the last full showing of the Names Project AIDS Memorial Quilt in Washington DC in October of 1996. I was with my former boyfriend James. We came on two separate bus trips and met there. His health was declining and as we walked through the moving and emotional quilt panels he said, "I feel like I am walking through my own graveyard." We then joined others on the March on Washington and it was incredibly empowering. – Greg R. Baird

——————▽——————

San Francisco, CA (USA)

San Francisco Gay Pride 1989 with my then companion who had lived in San Francisco for several years, before moving to San Diego where I met him. That year the parade started at the Castro and went all the way down Market, that's a long parade. But it was amazing. We were at Church and Market, there's a Muni stop there. We sat on the railing by the car stop, so we didn't even have to stand. Cute little things happened. One was the cops had to stop the parade periodically to let the Muni streetcars and trolley buses cross Market. The cop stopped the traffic and here comes one of the gay guys in the parade and hands him a rose. Only in San Francisco. Then across, there were two guys standing on the ledge of these tall windows. One of them was not amused that I was cruising his boyfriend. The boyfriend was smiling but the other one "Grrrrr!" – Hal

What Was the Most Memorable LGBTQ Event You Ever Attended?

—————▽—————

Sydney (Australia)

The first time I went to the Sydney Gay and Lesbian Mardi Gras in 1980, it was unbelievable to see so many people like myself, after thinking for so long that I was the only one that felt like this. I had never felt so included and excited, however, at that time Mardi Gras was still in its early years and was despised by the general public.

Even though there were a few times when we were being abused and having rubbish thrown at us, there was such a sense of solidarity that we were not going to accept this behavior any more. This was my first feeling of pride and empowerment. – Ian Davies

—————▽—————

St. Petersburg, FL (USA)

It was about three years ago. It seemed like days after the Pulse shooting. I knew two people who were in Pulse. One girl stands out, I still see her face. That Pride year was so difficult. I had talked to my partner about whether we were going to go or not because of the safety issue. Then we talked about … we can't hide, it's more important now to be visible. We usually go in a flamboyant way, dressed like pink fairies, it's always with a kink, leather, fetish, but we knew because of what happened it had to be different. So we did it tastefully as fairies but more on a conservative level. That year it was so hard to talk to people, so difficult without breaking down in tears. There was so much love from everybody that was there. It was packed. They brought in the Guardian Angels that year and one of them I remember from New York when I was very young. It was such an outpouring of love from everybody. Out of all of them, and I've been to so many, that was the most memorable one. – Keith Kollinicos aka Missa Distic

—————▽—————

New York, NY (USA)

The first Pride I went to with my brother Danny. I remember because it was quite an interesting weekend. The day before Pride I was in the city and I knew my brother was in town. Shortly before, I came-out to him. We decided to go to Pride together. So I went out that Friday before and needless to say I didn't make it home, because I frequented a few of my little hot spots. At the time, I was living in Jersey, but working in the city. So I'd been up the entire night, I was a complete mess. I hadn't showered, my hair was wild – I used to have long hair back then. I thought, "I don't have time to go home to change and come back for Pride." So, I thought, "Fuck it, I'm just going to stay in the city." Now I'm in my nighttime going-out clothes during daytime. I was a mess, but I was happy to see my brother because a friend of his who he knew – his name was Gary – he helped organize the giant balloon arches and since Danny was there visiting, he wanted Danny to hold one of the arches. Now this was a big deal for Danny because he's not out to anybody. Nobody knows he's gay. In the closet, yet here he is carrying a rainbow arch in Gay Pride in New York City. I went to the beginning of the parade and followed him all the way to the end and when I got to the end they put me in as one of the volunteers to help out and manage the crowd. They gave me a t-shirt and I thought, "This is kind of cool, this is my first Pride with my brother and we're both in the parade together. That was the first time I experienced Pride in that way. I got to see all the floats, I didn't have to worry about the crowds because I was in the parade. That was the most memorable and I took a lot of pictures that day and just being with my brother was just different. – David Vega aka Lucifers Axe

———————∇———————

New York City (USA)

In the summer of 1979, I attended a Pride Parade for the first time, New York's. The march up Fifth Avenue just kept coming and coming and coming. I couldn't believe the throngs. One marcher, in particular, stands out in memory: sitting on a vehicle of some sort, a Jewish-looking man in dangling earrings and a pink boa waved at the many Jewish seniors standing on the sidewalk with mouths agape, then he called out, "Hello, *landsmen!*", using the Yiddish word that Jewish immigrants used for "countrymen" or "people from the same village." I jumped up and down and waved back at him, my *landsman*. – Daniel M. Jaffe

———————∇———————

Seattle, WA (USA)

Nights at the disco on psychedelics, feeling 100% free and in-charge. Especially my first disco, Shelly's Leg in Seattle, walking dark streets at night in a strange big city wearing nothing but my black Capezio dance skirt and black-painted nails. The first tastes of freedom are the most profound. – Gavin Geoffrey Dillard

What Was the Most Memorable LGBTQ Event You Ever Attended?

──────▽──────

New York City, NY (USA)

Being outside the Stonewall Inn in New York City the moment they announced the Supreme Court decision on marriage. – Mark Zubro

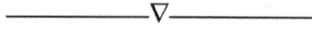

──────▽──────

Palm Springs, CA (USA)

That must be the first major Pride that I went to as an "out" lesbian 2011 and it was the day after I came here to meet Siouxzan. I lived in Austria for 25 years and I was out to my friends and family, but not in my work and in my being in Austria. I was quite active and known in Salzburg. For me it was so joyful and exhilarating, standing there holding my new girlfriend who I married two years later. That energy it was lovely – Helen Macfarlane

──────▽──────

Palm Springs, CA (USA)

We had just gotten married and they asked us to ride in the Pride Parade. It was really a big deal for us, because Helen had just gotten here and it was right near the legal marriage thing and we were all a flutter and it was really cool. They did an article on us in the paper and it was really a nice thing. Then as we were getting in the car, two drag queens got in and pushed us away. It was horrible. All our friends who were lined up on the street, were like, "What happened?" And we had to tell that story. We couldn't get them out of the car. They were horrible. They just decided they were going to do it. We had our little chihuahua with us and she was dressed in a rainbow leis. They had built up to this with the article and everything and we weren't there. That was memorable. There's been a lot, like the people in the parades. When my friend Bob was alive in San Francisco, I used to go to the one in Palm Springs, then to San Francisco, and they would come back with me to LA. Watching him and the Gay's Men's Choir when it first started and watching him singing, just the whole start of it. Being able to be one of the first people in the Hollywood one when it was 10 people. It was just watching it from the very beginning up until now, when every parade makes you cry. The way that we are becoming everyday people and before we weren't. – Siouxzan Perry

──────▽──────

Los Angeles, CA (USA)

My first Gay Pride. It was after I moved here to California. I was blown away by the amount of gay people. I grew up in a small town, up until I was 15 I really believed there were only a few gay people. I knew of them. But in our local library, all the books on sexuality and homosexuality, were written in 1950 and before. So, it wasn't helpful. We didn't have role models like we do today. There was no Ellen. – Bart

—————∇—————

Auckland (New Zealand)
Sydney (Australia)

Mr. Gay Auckland. I think it was 1989. I worked so hard for it, and I came second from 15 contestants. The guy that won had a boner, so obviously he was going to win. I just wanted to see if I could get up there in front of people and do it. You had to do a little show and I did Village people – I love the Village people. The construction guy … fuck! Hot! So I did a Village People number and we had to do swimwear, it was like a male pageant. The drag queen that hosted that was Bertha. There have been many others like the Hero parade in New Zealand. It's like Pride but they call it the Hero parade for Gay Pride Month. It's brilliant. Mardi Gras, Sydney … amazing. My first Mardi Gras in Sydney was mind-blowing. One million people on the streets. – Gib Maudey

—————∇—————

San Francisco, CA (USA)

The first Folsom Street Fair in San Francisco, about 1985 just after I moved there. My friends took me there. The next year I got a pair of chaps and had a great time. – Marc

—————∇—————

Palm Springs, CA (USA)

The first Palm Springs Pride parade I attended. I've been to the ones in LA and they're big and extravagant. But I remember feeling so good about the Palm Springs parade when I saw the high school marching bands. I thought, "Oh my God, we have to live here someday Charlie. Look at this, the whole freaking valley is participating in this." And we made a plan and it took a number of years longer than we planned but now we're living here full time. And this has been such a blessing being here. – Cody

——————▽——————

Chicago, IL (USA)
Washington DC (USA)

With so many from which to choose, selecting one is nearly impossible. As a 1999 inductee into Chicago LGBTQ Hall of Fame, the first time I rode on the organization's float in the Chicago Pride parade was unforgettable.

The first AIDS Walk in which I participated in Washington DC in 1986 began with Holly Near leading the participants in singing *We Are A Gentle, Angry People*. I can still hear it to this day.

I was fortunate enough to attend the 1987, 1993, 2000 and 2017 National Marches on Washington for Lesbian and Gay Rights. The 1993 National March on Washington for Lesbian and Gay Rights was the most memorable for many reasons, not the least of which was participating in the mass wedding with my husband Rick, led by the Reverend Troy Perry, on the steps of the Social Security Administration building.

Also, with the 50th anniversary of the Stonewall riots on people's minds as I write this, attending the Stonewall 25 celebration in New York in 1994 was especially memorable. – Gregg Shapiro

——————▽——————

New York, NY (USA)
Palm Springs, CA (USA)

The parades in New York. This past Gay Pride here in Palm Springs there was a ceremony for a three-story mural I painted for the Center. So that's something I will remember because it was an incredible experience, a celebration of gay pride. That was very meaningful for me. – Juan-manuel Alonso

——————▽——————

Chicago, IL (USA)

I had been in Chicago since July the previous year, so I was finishing up my first year at DePaul. I decided I was going to do some errands and I was walking around the neighborhood – I had an apartment on Pine Grove. I was walking and I kept hearing this noise, screaming and laughter, and I made a left and found myself on Broadway, and it was the Gay Pride Parade. I wasn't even aware it was going on. All of a sudden it opened up in front of me. I felt like Dorothy in *The Wizard of Oz* landing in Munchkin land and they're all singing and dancing around her. I was going, "Oh my God, it's the Pride Parade." – Michael Wayne

———————▽———————

San Francisco, CA (USA)

Probably the first Pride Parade I ever attended, in San Francisco. I think the year was 1978. My straight male friend brought me there. Sylvester was in the parade. And Harvey Milk. And every kind of grouping you can think of – gay dads, gay phone company workers, etc. I cried through much of the parade, as it passed by, for the sheer joy of seeing so many people so out and so happy.

That same year, I attended a No on Proposition 6 event. Proposition 6, otherwise known as the Briggs Initiative, sought to ban LGBT people from teaching in California's public schools. Harvey Milk was there, as was Jane Fonda. That was pretty memorable as well. – Yvonne Zipter

———————▽———————

St. Petersburg, FL (USA)

St. Petersburg Pride, the very first one. Now we're third in the nation. They have one of the largest, outside of New York and San Francisco. But the very first one was my favorite. It was tiny. It was back in 2000 or 2001, because Tampa had closed its doors to gay people. They had decided that they were no longer, no more, "You queers gotta go. We're not serving you anymore. You can't have your Pride here anymore. We're shutting the doors and bolting them. You can't come in." St. Petersburg decided to take it on and the very first year was amazing. Small, not a lot of people, but we had the best parade ever, with the big long flag. It was brought to St. Pete and we made national news because of it. – Jade

———————▽———————

Santa Monica, CA (USA)

It was the day I came out to my dad as trans 100 percent. I went to a 12-hour conference in Santa Monica, my senior year of high school. It covered everything from misogyny, to being trans, to the prison industrial complex. It was an expansive conference and there was a panel of trans people. I heard them talk and one of the transmen said, "I tried to kill myself and when I came out as trans and walked into the fire, it was worth it." On the drive home I said, "Dad, I'm a boy. I've figured it out now. I have to come out." That's probably the most memorable LGBTQ event for me. – Bambi

—————▽—————

Palm Springs, CA (USA)

I went to this last Harvey Milk event in Palm Springs and that was the first event that I've been to. Just seeing the support from the community, kind of gave me hope. Just seeing how people genuinely care is so refreshing because where I come from that's not a thing. So being able to move down here to Palm Springs and experience events like that, there's just so much love in that room. It was kind of overwhelming but amazing. – Hayley

—————▽—————

Los Angeles, CA (USA)

LA Pride by far is one of my favorite things because it let me be free to just enjoy myself without the fear of someone watching me, judging me, hating on me. I didn't have to worry about where I was going, where I would have to be. I was just able to be in the moment and just be with other people who were in the moment and about the moment. I could make friends with someone and not know who they were. We had something in common which was being a part of a community that's growing and caring for each other. – Chloe DeCamp

—————▽—————

Palm Springs, CA (USA)

My first L-Fund dance. It was the Gumbo Gala in Palm Springs. The L-Fund is for Lesbians in Crisis. I remember going to it and being in a room with all-women. I can remember sitting at the table and looking around and thinking, "These are all my people. We are all alike. We might be different colors, but we are all alike. We all love women and we all care about women, we want to help women." I remember what I wore, I remember who sat at the table, I remember everything. I remember looking around and thinking to myself, "Does it get better than this. The other events I'm going to go to, do they all look like this?" And they do. Now I volunteer for the L-Fund and I strive to help women in crisis. There's a lot of women in crisis. And we're all silent a lot. Every time they have an event to raise money for women, I volunteer. Now we're dividing the cause and now it's not just for women in crisis but for educating lesbians of all ages, young and old. That's probably the things I'm most passionate about today. – Cathy Melton

————————▽————————

San Francisco, CA (USA)

I would tell you that one of the NCLR (National Center for Lesbian Rights) galas. When I lived in Oakland, I was married previously. My ex-wife and I went to several, and I may have gone to one after we broke up. It was very motivating because it was obviously a fundraiser and celebration all at the same time. It was special because it was mostly women and it was for a cause I believed in and it was a chance to become a little more political than I had been previously. Plus, one time I saw Tracy Chapman and her girlfriend there and that was cool. – Leslie Tisdale

————————▽————————

Melbourne, Victoria (Australia)

Festival day, Midsumma 2006. I'm recovering from a break-up. I'm there with a group of three friends. There's an FTM and female couple, and a third female friend. Most of the stalls are selling or promoting things. We're walking so the m/f couple are in front, the female friend and I are behind. People keep assuming the other woman and I are a couple. It's still amusing. – Anita Morris

————————▽————————

London, (UK)

Some of the Gay Pride events in London back in the 1980s – just for the sheer exuberance of them, before Pride got over-commercialised and while it still had some political integrity and message. Other than that, some of the Gay West social events in Bath and Bristol, back in the late 1980s and early 1990s were very convivial – more involving and personal than the commercial scene which can be a cold and lonely place for many. – Diesel Balaam

What Was the Most Memorable LGBTQ Event You Ever Attended?

————————∇————————

Palm Springs, CA (USA)

Last year. We were sitting on Hunter's porch for Gay Pride. That one took the cake. The Chicago parade is also fabulous, but Palm Springs definitely. – Jack Farquhar Halbert

————————∇————————

Clearlake, CA (USA)

Levi/Leather Weekend was nice. It was a campsite and clothing optional. I just love being naked. I had a great time with a lot of people. It was fun. Those are the types of gatherings I've been doing. – Paul

————————∇————————

Chicago, IL (USA)
New York, NY (USA)

The first AIDS Ride in Chicago. I was on the press platform when all the riders came in. There was not a dry eye on the stage. Second was being in New York for Stonewall. My friend Chris Kellner and I stayed in front of the Stonewall that Saturday night and I met Sylvia Rivera – one of the remaining people who was in that historic event. And seeing the Quilt. – Terry Gaskins

————————∇————————

Chicago, IL (USA)

Cruising the Nile by the Lincoln Park Lagooners at the Aragon Theater in the late '70s. – Anonymous

————————∇————————

London (UK)

1988. My first Pride in London. When I was out. It was just such a joy to be in that crowd, for me it was a massive crowd, starting in Hyde Park and then walking down Oxford Street with the parade. Just such a diversity of people, men and women, all kinds of costumes, all kinds of floats. But one of the things that was the biggest charge in those earlier pride parades was politically, we weren't accepted at all. So this was as much a protest, a sticking my finger up at society and the establishment, saying, 'You know what, I'm here and I'm not going away. I'm going to be who I want to be." And because I was newly out then, of course it felt even more of that and I remember a group of lesbians leading a cheer as we walked down Oxford Street, "We're here, we're queer, and we're not going shopping." – Tess Tickles

———————▽———————

Milwaukee, WI (USA)

The Names Project AIDS Quilt unfolding ceremony. So powerful. Those panels made me see AIDS in a very different light. It humanized the numbers. I didn't know a lot of people who died so it was hard to understand. – Anonymous.

———————▽———————

Washington DC (USA)

1987 and 1993 March on Washington. 1987 because that was the first time I was in a city that had more gay than straight people. I remember thinking, "This is what Jews must feel like when they go to Israel." 1993 because I married the love of my life there. – Rick Karlin

———————▽———————

San Francisco, CA (USA)

There have been many, but the most memorable event/occasion was the time John and I flew to San Francisco in February of 2004 to get married at San Francisco's City Hall. We stood in line with hundreds of other same-sex couples for hours and while in line, flowers were being distributed to couples by local florists. The flowers were being sent from folks all over the world! People were also saving peoples' place in line so they could go get something to eat. it was one of the few and only times when I truly experienced and got to witness COMMUNITY. John and I ended up not being able to get married that day but made an appointment and were married at San Francisco's City Hall on March 5th, 2004. That was the most memorable MOMENT of my life and marrying a man was pretty gay at the time. – Robert Castillo

———————▽———————

What Was the Most Memorable LGBTQ Event You Ever Attended?

Guadalajara (Mexico)

My first gay pride was in Guadalajara. It was huge, maybe two or three hours going down the street. Everybody was so happy, because it's a big thing there. To see people being themselves and having fun with no pressure. The police were taking care of them. And, believe it or not, the party was behind the Cathedral in Guadalajara. It was awesome. At the back of the Cathedral there's a big plaza, the main party was there, so it was a riot. Everyone was taking photographs with the church in the background. – Carlos

————∇————

Washington, DC (USA)

That would have to be the last time they had the AIDS Quilt in Washington DC. We traveled there from Chicago specifically for the event. It was very sad, because I found a panel for someone I had known years earlier, but I had not known had died. It was a very sad event, but one where I felt very connected as well as very angry. – Ian H

————∇————

New York, NY (USA)

The Best of the Best benefit show for AIDS research at Metropolitan Opera (1985). – Alex Gildzen

————∇————

New York City, NY (USA)

Again, the late '90s. I attended a candlelight march for Matthew Shepard. Several hundred, if not thousands, assembled in front of the Plaza Hotel and marched south down 5th Avenue. Apparently, the organizers only had a permit to use the sidewalks, but so many people turned out that it was impossible to contain them on just the walkways. The police were attempting to keep everyone contained, but it was not possible. They began to arrest the organizers and many others who were just marching in support. I narrowly escaped being arrested. Incidentally, when we were lighting each other's candles before the march, I turned to light the candle held by the man next to me and came face to face with Harvey Fierstein! I had met and partied with him and some friends at a stripper bar in Montreal a year earlier. As I turned toward him, he croaked in that unmistakable voice, "You again!" – Paul Mikos

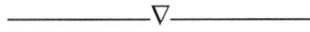

———▽———

Washington, DC (USA)
Chicago, IL (USA)

Every time I attend a presentation of the AIDS Memorial Quilt, I am moved like no other event. As a visitor, and then as a member of the many committees that have presented it in Chicago and all around the country over the years. The memory of all that have been lost over the years is both overwhelming and breathtaking, to see how their loved ones have shared their lives and a lasting memory of their loved ones. Two displays stand out for me. The last full display on the Mall in Washington DC where we had reading of names going on all up and down the display. Reading my list while looking out on the quilt spread as far as you could see, was a very memorable and moving moment for me. I would have to say that it was equally memorable when we presented the 12X12 sections at the opening of the Gay Games in Chicago at Soldier Field. All it represents were all there with us that sizzling summer night. – Dean Ogren

———▽———

WHAT'S THE BEST DRAG SHOW YOU EVER SAW?

Kansas City, MO (USA)

Well, I didn't see it, but I was a contestant in the Miss Spring Thing pageant in Kansas City, MO in March 1997. I hadn't really done drag, and since I was in a new city, I decided to complete. I was obsessed with Pam Grier and decided to go as Miss Moonshine Jones. Clad in a blonde afro, velvet dress that showed off my legs in thigh high stockings, and way too much blue eye shadow, I humped the floor to *You Suck* by the Yeastie Girls. I won Miss Congeniality. The judges called me raunchy and questioned why I did a rap song, something so underground. I hoped my eye roll wasn't blatant. – Thomas Bottoms

————————▽————————

London (UK)

Lily Savage, Two Brewers, London probably around 1990. – Matt D

————————▽————————

Chicago, IL (USA)

Still the one and only Chili Pepper and the group from THE BATON!! – Don Strzepek

————————▽————————

What's the Best Drag Show You Ever Saw?

San Francisco, CA (USA)

Lypsinka doing "Lypsinka! A Day in the Life" – although John Epperson does not call his performances "drag shows." – Louis Flint Ceci

─────────▽─────────

Wilton Manors, FL (USA)
Chicago, IL (USA)

Without a doubt Nicole Halliwell and the "Drink n Drag" girls that perform at The Pub in Wilton Manors FL. Though will always love the Baton Show Lounge girls, Ginger Grant was always a favorite of mine. – Robert Hansen

─────────▽─────────

Miami Beach, FL (USA)

In the early seventies, a friend took me to a huge club (I don't remember the name). The area, now South Beach, was very gay at the time. The production and the talent was amazing. – Gary Chichester

─────────▽─────────

San Francisco, CA (USA)

What's that thing in San Francisco, just closed down? It went on for years … Beach Blanket Babylon Goes Bananas. It was unbelievable. All these guys in drag, they weren't like your normal gay drag where everything is so exaggerated … except for the crazy hats. That was about as exaggerated as it got. They would talk about San Francisco in a particular year, a little vignette. It was just hilarious what they were doing. – Dan Brazill

─────────▽─────────

Asbury Park, NJ (USA)

The old M&K in Asbury Park had some of the greatest drag shows I will ever see in my entire life. It was the most incredible bar in its day. Again, this is probably the '80s, everyone had big hair, and I was the king of big hair, that was my thing. There was a very famous drag queen called Wayne Mills and this was in the time of Donna Summer, so he was the drag queen that did her. Every show, the hair, the wigs, the costumes, the music. It was current, it was fabulous, it was fun. He was one of the most incredible people I ever met. I had never had a drag queen as a friend before. Noting more than just friendship with him, but I loved him as a person. His shows were freakin' unbelievable. It was the '80s, big production numbers, big hair, big clothes, loud sound systems, people dancing on boxes and carrying on like crazy. It was fun as hell. – Joseph S

———————∇———————

Savannah, GA (USA)

The Lady Chablis (RIP) – Driveshaft

———————∇———————

Chicago, IL (USA)

The best drag show I ever saw was at Finkle Steele in Chicago, IL during the Hearts on Fire Party in '04, starring the one and only Circuit Mom. When that bitch traveled across the top of the dance floor in that hot oar bucket, I completely fell in love. The Best! – Tripp

———————∇———————

Philadelphia, PA (USA)

Joey Arias performing at the Trocadero in Philadelphia circa. '95-'96 ish? I made the props for her show. A giant paper-mache volcano with smoke rising out of it. I thought it was brilliant. Cheri Vine and someone else were there. Honestly it was all about the spectacle for me, their performances were good, but my sets were fantastic. Even if the promoter was a D-Bag who ripped me and the stage hands off, I was proud of the work I'd done. – Daniel Fisher aka Raid

———————∇———————

Cathedral City, CA (USA)

Les Dames du Soleil at the C. C. Construction Co. They put on a show there for some charitable AIDS thing. It was the original group and they were really, really good. – Rory

What's the Best Drag Show You Ever Saw?

—————▽—————

Chicago, IL (USA)

Baton nightclub in mid '80s. It felt so much more real than today's over-stylized kitsch shows. It was gritty, amateur but genuine. – Martin Mulcahy

—————▽—————

Fayetteville, AR (USA)

I rode my motorcycle to see a friend in Fayetteville, Arkansas. There were two gay bars there and one of them was having a drag show. He took me. I've had friends that were female impersonators, but I never really saw a drag show before that. That was only 17 or 18 years ago. There was a whole big audience and the drag queens were running around, up and down. It was a contest. – Ron

—————▽—————

Orlando, FL (USA)

Miss. P at the Parliament House in Orlando, FL. I went with my brother, who is also gay, and his two friends. The drag queen was boozy, filthy and hysterical … I loved it. – Greg R. Baird

—————▽—————

Miami, FL (USA)

I've seen a lot of drag shows. The best show was Lou Paciocco's La Cage. He had a Dolly Parton look-alike, a Cher look-alike, Joan Rivers, that was the best, it was in Miami. Those girls were fantastic. They looked like dead-ringers for their characters. – Keith Kollinicos aka Missa Distic

—————▽—————

London (UK)

It would be Danny La Rue at a nightclub called the Pigalle in London. That was, '54, '56, around that time. I loved him. Later on, I worked at Wig Creations and we used to do his wigs for him, but this was before I ever

235

thought about wigs. I loved him because he came out so beautifully dressed and then would suddenly go into a deep man's voice, "Well what kind of thing do you think I'm gonna do?" – Bob Brown

————————▽————————

Chicago, IL (USA)

Chili Pepper at the Baton. Chili was like a drag queen but like a real person. She had pixie hair, fabulous legs. I have friends who are friends of hers, so I saw her a few times socially. – Laurie Cowall

————————▽————————

Chicago, IL (USA)

The Baton Show Lounge. I had never experienced such beautiful women in a perfectly choreographed production. – Dale

————————▽————————

Sydney (Australia)

I've seen hundreds of drag shows over the years, but the first show I ever saw had the biggest impact. It was at Patch's nightclub in Oxford Street Darlinghurst in Sydney in 1979. I still remember the names of the cast, there was, Trixie Lamont, Pola Negre, Flange Desire and Cindy Pastel.

I came from such a straight and boring town (Maitland, NSW), which was basically, Christians, cows, coal miners and rednecks. No one even spoke about stuff like that, so it was the most exciting, glamorous show I had ever seen. It was not only the first drag show I saw, but it was also the first time I went to a gay nightclub. Before this night, the only reference I had seen about cross-dressing was on comedy TV programs like Dame Edna Everage and *The Dick Emery* show from the UK. – Ian Davies

————————▽————————

Dallas, TX (USA)

When I was coming-out, when I was younger, I never had a lot of experience with the drag world. I'd seen a couple of drag shows in the city and it's interesting that I knew about drag history because I watched a lot of PBS. I knew it was out there but to see it live in front of me, there weren't a lot of good drag shows I saw. It's not because my partner is into drag, but quite frankly some of the best shows that I've seen are the shows that he's performed in. But that's also because I've seen the background of the drag world, not just as an audience member. I've seen the preparation, the time it takes, what he's going through, how dedicated he is. Being in that dressing room seeing the other drag performers and see how dedicated they are. One of the best shows that I've seen was the USO Show in Texas, when Missa Distic did Amy Winehouse. The other people who did their characters were just as good, doing their style of drag. Not a lot of people do Amy Winehouse. He did it in the comedy fashion. It wasn't serious. It was at the Dallas Eagle. – David Vega aka Lucifers Axe

———————▽———————

Chicago, IL (USA)

Well, I have a story about the most memorable drag show I ever saw. When I was in college (and sneaking into the boy bars, as I was slightly underage), there was a heavyset drag queen who was all rage. She seemed to host all the events and Julie Brown's *Homecoming Queen Has Got a Gun* was one of her favorite numbers to lip sync/act out. I was at Bistro II in Chicago almost every weekend and they had a little wooden runway they would attach to the main stage and this particular performer would charge down it, with energy and commitment, frantically acting out the chaos as everyone was fleeing from the deranged heroine in the song. The runway would, literally, shudder and almost collapse as she pounded, enthusiastically, upon it. One night, Chuck Renslow, who was a legendary figure in the gay world and the owner of the club, watched her as she did the number and he turned white as a ghost when that stage started vibrating under her impact – visions of broken bones and law suits dancing, I'm sure, in his head. When she was through, he grabbed one of the nearby bartenders and still shaking his head in dazed wonderment, he gasped out, "I love her. I really do. But someone just has to tell her ... she's too big a girl to do the number that way!" Every other time I saw Renslow, he was cool as a cucumber, totally in control. That was the only time that I ever saw him waver in the slightest. – Brian Kirst

———————▽———————

San Francisco, CA (USA)

I most remember Finocchio's in San Francisco, in part because it was my first, in part because it was so deliciously horrible. The gurls did three shows a night, so they pretty much chewed gum throughout their routines. It was exotic and hysterical. On the other hand, my suite-mate at the time was Paul Rubens, who attended class most every day in full Carmen Miranda attire, along with a few other classmates who all ended up part of *Pee-Wee's Playhouse* – so, basically, every day was a drag show. – Gavin Geoffrey Dillard

———————▽———————

San Francisco, CA (USA)

It has to be Peaches Christ. One of my very dear friends and when I was working with all the Russ Meyer people, we took Tura Satana to one of his shows and that's when we got to be backstage and watch everything. I knew Josh as Peaches. When he came to the airport, he was Josh, a little farm boy. I said, "Where's Peaches?" ... "Peaches is in here." ... Then watching the whole thing happen and then everybody I knew out of drag, and watching the whole performance, and being involved in this whole thing was extraordinary. – Siouxzan Perry

———————▽———————

Sydney (Australia)

When I was visiting a friend of mine in Sydney, the Imperial Hotel. Those Aussie drag queens know how to do drag. They were absolutely fabulous. They were not just comic versions of women ... some of them could actually sing. – Marc

———————▽———————

Sydney (Australia)

Priscilla Queen of the Desert at the New Town Hotel back in 2000. It was like the movie, the whole cast. It was out of this world. It was a live drag show, in a neighborhood of Sydney called New Town which is very gay now. It moved me totally, and I'm not really into drag shows myself. – Gib Maudey

———————▽———————

Cathedral City, CA (USA)

Back in the early '90s there was a club out here in the desert – Charlie and I would come out here to vacation – it was called Rocks. There was a trio of drag queens called the Pigeon Sisters. They would do this wonderful USO-type show. It was comedy drag, they would have big red beehive hairdos and have their USO outfits on. The crowd just loved them. We just really enjoyed seeing them and any time we came, we would make sure the Pigeon Sisters were here. – Cody

———————▽———————

New York, NY (USA)

It wasn't really a drag show but I saw Jinx Monsoon do her Off Broadway cabaret show about four years ago. I'd seen her on Ru Paul's Drag Race and she's a theater nerd. When I was planning my trip to New York, I found out she was going to be performing. I thought it was absolutely wonderful. So funny and so talented. – Michael Wayne

———————▽———————

Ko Samui (Thailand)

It's quite a big resort town. We went to a Swiss Alpine restaurant and had Thai food, and there was a drag show. I was with my brother, his wife, and my parents. The bus had broken down for half of the troop of drag queens. They had to get out and push the bus. They were a bit grubby around the edges. They got there but they were going to meet half the troop at the venue but they got lost, so they managed to rope in some friends who didn't know the routine. So, you had half the troop covered in engine oil on their frocks and the other half didn't quite know what to do. It was hilarious. It was fabulous. Luckily, we filmed it. I have a film of this event. – Martin

———————▽———————

South Beach, FL (USA)

It was at a club I worked at in South Beach. It was at 1235 Washington Avenue. I used to be in charge of doing their stage set and decoration. I had never seen a drag show before. I was never into it. But by working with all the drag queens I started to appreciate it. Even before that I was a maître d' at a restaurant in South Beach modeled after *The Birdcage*. I was the maître d' so my drag was in leather, and the waiters were drag queens and they did the shows. It was called Lucky Chance. They first opened on Ocean Drive but they weren't having too much business, it was out-of-the-way, so they moved to Lincoln Road. There it became a scene. There were three or four rows of people outside trying to look at the shows through the glass. That was quite an experience because every performer was a professional. They took two hours to get themselves together, but when they came out very few people would have known they were guys. – Juan-manuel Alonso

—————————▽—————————

New York, NY (USA)
Banning, CA (USA)

I didn't get to see it live, unfortunately, but someone I was seeing at the time was performing in New York. They did a really, really, cool total gender-fuckery of their own little character called Bear Lee Legal. They did this whole performance to *Coin Operated Boy* and it was super-colorful. The Dresden Dolls were black and white and mime type of thing, but they did a bright and colorful version of that. Seeing a trans person perform was exhilarating and they did an amazing job, it was very well done. They have amazing star power and I'd never really seen a trans masculine-ish person perform before. So that was really cool to see as well. I didn't know that there were a lot of trans guys that did drag. – Bambi

—————————▽—————————

Long Beach, CA (USA)

I went to Hamburger Mary's and I was completely blown away as the stage itself was visually impressive compared to what I'd seen. I saw my first female drag queen. She had a song on iTunes that she sang. Very raunchy, it was hilarious. That was the most memorable drag show I'd ever seen. It was quite interesting. – Hayley

—————————▽—————————

Riverside, CA (USA)
Victorville, CA (USA)

That's a tough one. VIP used to put on a really good drag show. Compared to being up in Victorville, the only place out there is Ricky's – they weren't really doing a lot of drag shows at the time when I was going there. When I went to VIP they had this really outrageous couple of performers who were all over the place. They were vulgar, they were funny, you could tell they were very confident. They wanted everyone else to engage and have a good time with them. It was just a whole lot of fun. The whole place was packed. It was great. – Chloe DeCamp

What's the Best Drag Show You Ever Saw?

——————▽——————

Lumberton, MS (USA)
St. Petersburg, FL (USA)

I was with my first girlfriend and this was prior to us moving to Florida, we lived in Lumberton, Mississippi. We flew down to Florida to visit her brother. We decided to stay at the very first gay resort in that town. It was Suncoast Resort in St. Petersburg, Florida. We got there a week after their grand opening. They had a couple of bars, one was the Tropicale, and they had a drag show. It was an Asian drag queen. I don't know what the show was about, all I remember was this – I was a little Southern girl; country come-to-town girl – watching this Asian drag queen up on stage. She had on one of those one-piece leotard outfits with tight stockings. Looking at the front, there was no bulge, no package. My mind is going, "Where the fuck did she put it? OK, where did she put it?" She's sitting on a stool talking and she stands up to do another routine and as she turns around and there was a line of feathers that went from her ass crack all the way up to the top of her neck. So, I can only imagine … the girl I was with told me that she took her penis and wrapped it up between her butt cheeks and that's why she had the feathers. Of course, I couldn't get the image out of my mind. It was just mind-blowing for a little country come-to-town lesbian. I've seen some drag shows, and I've seen some good ones, but that one was by far my favorite. – Jade

——————▽——————

Albuquerque, NM (USA)

It's not an art form I have much affinity for. For complicated personal reasons I have always felt mocked and made fun of by male folks in drag rather than somehow included and celebrated. – Allan Hunter

——————▽——————

Palm Springs, CA (USA)

I'm comfortable with Bella Da Ball. I think she's wonderful and such a good representative for our city. She does a lot of good and seems to always show up. Anything she's involved in, I approve of. I support drag and I've been involved with some of the queens but I don't know how to react. I appreciate the shows they do and the good they do for the city, but I don't have a one to one relationship with any of them. Bella recognizes me and she may be the only one. – Don Rockwell Coffee

—————∇—————

Palm Springs, CA (USA)

I'd say Varla Jean for comic. She's pretty funny. I see him at the gym, he's a big hunky man. What's that one at Toucan's? Whatever her name is. – Jack Farquhar Halbert

—————∇—————

Columbus, OH (USA)

I've never been to a drag show I didn't like but I don't think I have a favorite. I do recall the first drag show I attended when I was about 19 years old at a nightclub called Axis. There were both male go-go dancers and drag queens. One especially muscular stripper grabbed me because I was extraordinarily thin and flipped me about like a rag doll. Not my favorite drag show but quite memorable for me. – Mike Gifford

—————∇—————

San Francisco, CA (USA)

I saw Charles Pierce, he did Betty Davis. I don't think I saw anything in Boston when I lived there. You know, the best drag shows are down here. Most of these guys are actors anyway. The ones up north are not as good. There was one fellow who was very good up in San Francisco. He was a San Francisco Gay Men's Chorus member. I remember when he started out, he was trying it out in one of our skits for a camping weekend we did. A choral weekend. He tried it out and ever since then he's been a major drag queen in San Francisco. I can't remember his name. – Paul

—————∇—————

London (UK)

Madame Jo Jo's in London. That was an actual drag revue bar. All the wait staff, the bar staff, everybody was a drag star and they could sing and dance, tell jokes. It was just an amazing bar. – Tess Tickles

What's the Best Drag Show You Ever Saw?

———————▽———————

New York City, NY (USA)

2016. I think Taylor Mac's 240-year history of American song counts. He was in some kind of drag (costumes by Machine Dazzle) the whole 24 hours of it. – David Pratt

———————▽———————

Santiago (Chile)

We have this club called Bunker. They have, of course, the pretty boys. It was super expensive for us but they have a two-for-one at the entrance if you get there before midnight. So people in line try to pair off and pay half. So suddenly you're in there in a corner with one drink. It was so campy. So this guy has a show that happens at 2 a.m. that lasts for an hour. The place was an old theater, so they have all the whole infrastructure around. The drag show was just marvelous and gorgeous and funny, people flying from the roof. It was literally Cirque du Soleil drag. Every single week it was a different show for years. – Ives

———————▽———————

Boston, MA (USA)

Certainly, it was the most creative drag show I ever saw, a Gay cabaret put on by the gay student's group at college. One of the theatre majors came out singing and dancing as, so politically incorrect now, Aunt Jemima. He then did a strip number and transformed himself into Diana Ross. – Ian H

———————▽———————

Nashville, TN (USA)

At Play in the Broadway district of Nashville. It's a bar with a drag show. I was totally amazed. Those guys were the hottest chicks ever. There was not a hint of maleness to them. It was brilliantly done, a brilliant show. Shocked the heck out of me. Shocked the hell out of the relatives I encouraged to go with us. One of the men turned to me and said, "Those can't be men. Those have to be women." His wife got very upset, because he was ogling them constantly. – OT

What's the Best Drag Show You Ever Saw?

——————▽——————

Chicago, IL (USA)

Remembering that La Cage on Oak was a fun place. – David Plambeck

——————▽——————

(UK)

Probably Lily Savage – unlike most drag, which is pretty lame in my opinion, this act was well-constructed, properly witty, socially and politically aware, incisive. The things she said about the Liverpudlian singer, Cilla Black – in the days before Paul O'Grady became her hag-fag – were outrageous! – Diesel Balaam

——————▽——————

Pomona, CA (USA)

It was at the Alibi. There was another bar close to it where they had other drag shows and that was called Robbie's. They were sister bars, so everybody would go from one bar to the other. Once they finished with the show at Alibi, they would go see the show at Robbie's. They were amazing. I couldn't believe they were women … I mean, men. – Felix

——————▽——————

West Hollywood, CA (USA)

The revue at La Cage Aux Folles emceed by James "Gypsy" Haake. – Alex Gildzen

——————▽——————

Chicago, IL (USA)

The best drag queen I ever saw would have to be RuPaul. Saw her at a screening in Chicago and loved her look and whole persona. I have a wonderful photo from that screening of her and I. The best drag show/performance I've seen was here in Chicago. It was at the Latinx Pride Picnic in Humboldt Park and while it wasn't a drag show per se, the entertainment at the Picnic included performances by both Andres De Los Santos and Dimples. They are drag kings and were absolutely amazing!!! – Robert Castillo

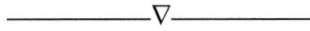

—————∇—————

TELL US ABOUT THE FIRST TIME YOU FELL IN LOVE?

Iowa City, IA (USA)

This is a continuation of the first gay bar I went to, That Bar in Iowa City. Once I'd had a few beers in me and gotten the courage to dance a few times, I began to enjoy myself (more likely, I felt like I was where I should be). I was standing at the bar when I felt a tap on my shoulder and I turned around and, in that instant, I fell in love. I know this sounds cliché, but both Michael (my first love) and I still confess to both of us falling in love at first sight. We were together for nine months (we remain close friends 40 years later). I feel incredibly fortunate to have experienced something as wild and fiery as love at first sight, but there is the problem; love that ignites that suddenly and passionately is doomed to burn fast and burn furious and as two boys 18 and 19 years old, we had no experience in dealing with such explosive emotions and as quickly as it began, as hot and wild as it was, it ended with the same ferocity. It took us many years to find a comfortable ground on which to have a friendship. – Timothy Juhl

———————▽———————

Long Beach, CA (USA)

I don't know, there were infatuations. There was this guy called Chip. I lost touch with him a long time ago. I was really in love with Chip. Some other guys, and myself, started this gay Harley owners loose group of gay Harley Davidson motorcycle owners. There was this guy Chip who was moving out to California from New Jersey. He was a computer person and was one of those people who would go from job to job. He would be transferred here, transferred there, this city, that city. He was living in New Jersey and they were transferring him to offices in Orange County and he was coming out to look for a place to live. We met at another favorite bar of mine in north Long Beach, it was called Mike's Corral, it's still there, it's called something else now. I really can't remember what it's called because I really haven't been there since it changed names. Anyway, I met Chip there and we became very good friends and I fell in love with him. I know he had feelings for me, but the thing is that he had a partner in New Jersey who wasn't going to join him until months later. He was out here by himself, not knowing anybody, except me, for a long time until his partner Peter came to join him. Chip always said, "You and Peter are going to get along really good. Peter's going to like you." Peter did not like me. I never could figure it out, until one time I was talking to his landlady. She was one of those gossipy little landladies who's into everybody's business in that building. She was telling me, "So don't you realize, he feels threatened by you." I was taken aback but Chip was between me and the guy that he lived with. It was a mess. But I still have feelings for Chip. I think that he eventually got out of that relationship and into another. He ended up living in Fort Lauderdale, Florida, last time I talked to him. I still miss him. – Tim Barela

—————∇—————

Denver, CO (USA)

Sadly, it took me a long time to realize I had fallen in love with my college boyfriend. I met him at a New Years Eve party, literally falling on him as he laid on the couch. We just cuddled as the gang watched *Pink Flamingos*. We dated most of my second semester of college, spending the night, exploring each other. His birthday would probably qualify as one of the best 24 hours of my life. Oh, to be young, in love, and not caring if you're stupid. He was the first guy I ever had sex with without a condom, after many months of dating and discussion. The first guy I let "come inside," I guess.

We broke up after my older brother died. Two dead brothers in five years at such a young age damages you. An abusive family and severe bullying makes one even worse. Decades later I can only begin to fathom how much of a mess I was.

He bounced around in my life off and on for seven years. We would try to get back together, but it never worked out. My leaving Colorado probably didn't help.

He passed away in February 2004. At the time I didn't know, and although we had not spoken in some time, I kept trying to call him. I only gave up after my calls weren't returned and the answering outgoing message had changed. It took almost a decade before I learned he had passed. No one I know has a clue how he passed. – Thomas Bottoms

—————————∇—————————

Chicago, IL (USA)

It was with a man I went on a date with who was a friend of a friend in college. I thought he was the most magnificent man I ever met as I was dumbstruck and starry eyed like a teenager. Broke my heart but made me smarter about love, romance and sex. – Jim

—————————∇—————————

Montivideo (Uruguay)

I remember the day, August 1, 1980. I met a soldier and he was 30 years old. We went to a hotel in the old city section in Montevideo and I liked him so much, he treats me like a lady and the best fuck. But the story ended badly. He looked for a richer person to live with. So I learned a lot about feeling and reality. – Dr. Eduardo Levaggi Mendoza

—————————∇—————————

Elmhurst, IL (USA)

It was in 1990 and though I'd had other boyfriends, the first time I truly fell in love was with the boy next door, Steve, he was 28 I was 30, I was living with my sister in her house in Elmhurst IL, and he was living with his father right next door. They had an above ground pool in their backyard, and though we didn't I still liked to sunbathe in my speedo in ours, and it seemed like he was always up on the deck of his pool skimming it while I was in my yard. I'd always think to myself, "Is that cute guy ever going to invite me to his pool?" Some weeks later he ran into a former classmate who also knew me and told him he knew of another gay man that lived on his three block long street, and that he was a mailman. He responded ... the only mailman I know of on my street is straight and lives with his wife next door to me. (He thought my sister was my wife). To clear things up our mutual friend set up a meeting at the Nutbush bar in Forest Park IL for the three of us to determine if I indeed was the gay mailman next door, and lo and behold I was! We hit it off instantly and come next April we'll have been together 30 years (six years married). – Robert Hansen

Tell Us About the First Time You Fell in Love?

————————▽————————

Milwaukee, WI (USA)
San Francisco, CA (USA)

I first fell in love with Linda Ackerman, a beautiful girl in my first grade class in Milwaukee. Though we lived more than a mile apart, I walked to her house for a "date" twice. She introduced me to hamburgers and chocolate malts, since she lived next door to a drive-in. I still like hamburgers and chocolate malts.

In San Francisco, I fell in love with a man for the first time. Bob was tall, thin, bearded, and a PhD student in pharmacology at UCSF. He was also dating my best friend at the time. I told my friend about my attraction to Bob and he said, "If you steal him, I'll scratch your eyes out." But I did anyway. – Louis Flint Ceci

————————▽————————

San Jose, CA (USA)

I was 19 and I was separated from my wife. I was going to school in San Jose, taking a special summer class. I fell head over heels for my instructor at the university. He was just out of a relationship and we had a fabulous summer. Unfortunately, when summer was over, I had to go back home. I came home and got divorced. We saw each other off and on for about two years. Time, circumstances and being a college student, I couldn't go where he was, and he wasn't willing to come where I was. I haven't seen him in forty years. – Art Healey

————————▽————————

Gainesville, FL (USA)

The first person I felt "love" for was named Karl. I was 16 and he was 23 (looking 17). He had a boyfriend (I didn't mind, he said he loved me). He had a (lesbian) wife for public appearances (I didn't mind, he said he loved me), and was a kept man by another gentleman (I didn't mind, he said he loved me). When his boyfriend found out, Karl moved five hours away saying that he and I would stay a couple. (I didn't mind, he said he loved me). When I went to visit him, I returned home with crabs and an STD (curable, thankfully). I minded. I began to doubt his love for me. – Eric Andrews-Katz

————————▽————————

249

Tell Us About the First Time You Fell in Love?

St Louis, MO (USA)

In 1982 I went to a bar and within the first five minutes there, a guy named Ron walked up to me and was very direct when he said "Hi, I'm Ron. Wanna go back to my place?" He liked my lanky body and my beard, and he was definitely my type with his facial hair (a Glenn Hughes-style moustache) and decent amount of body hair (NO manscaping thankfully). I was in college at the time, and during the week I was about 35 miles away and lived on campus. I came into St. Louis on weekends to have fun. He asked to see me the next weekend, and it became a regular thing. We were soon in a relationship and I was in love. It felt so great. Unfortunately, during the week, he sometimes still went out looking for tricks and going to the baths. I found out a bit later and even stayed in the relationship when he promised (oh, how naive I was) that he wouldn't do that again. In late 1985 I decided I didn't want to deal with that drama and as I was finishing college, I got my own apartment. Soon after he started becoming ill from HIV, as back then there were no meds yet that could help. I still cared and helped him get an apartment in my building. I checked in on him and could see his bedroom window from my apartment. He died in December 16, 1987 and I had visited him every night after I got off work. To this day, my relationship with him was the only one I had ever been in, I felt at first, I was truly in love. I'd like to think it WAS love. Some would say I just didn't want to be alone. In any case, no regrets. – Todd Jaeger

––––––––––∇––––––––––

New Jersey (USA)

That's a hard question. I've been in love many times in my life. The first time I was in love was with my wife, no question. I was 15 years-old, she was 17, blond hair, beautiful woman, tall, slender. I was tripping on acid. She was straight as an arrow. We were on a group trip on a hayride in western New Jersey. I decided on the bus going there, I was going to drop a tab of acid and have a party. I was 15. I tripping out off my ass on this thing and I ended up sitting next to her on the wagon. We were talking, and I don't even remember if I knew what she looked like that night because I couldn't see. I'm not sure I was seeing anything other than colors and blurs. We had a marvelous time and I ended up sitting next to her on the bus coming back to the city after this hayride. I remember laying my head on her shoulder and still being as high as a kite, but being able to focus and saying to her, "You know, I think you're the most beautiful person I've ever met. Can I kiss you?" She said to me, "Oh please do." That was it. We were an item from that moment. I explained to her afterward what I'd been doing, and she said, "I knew you were high, I was waiting to see what was going to happen, if you were going to be OK. If you were going to throw yourself off the wagon. I didn't know what you were going to do. You were all over the place but I thought you were the most handsome person on the whole trip that I met." She was the Virgo and I was the Pisces. I'm telling you, there was an alignment of stars. It was a volatile relationship from the beginning, but she was the first person I fell in love with. That was the first time I felt desire or want for anybody. – Joseph S

——————▽——————

Detroit, MI (USA)

I met this guy called Tommy ———, he was an artist. Tall, thin guy, just stunning. It never got to the point where we were going to live together, but we would often have sex. Over the course of a year or so, I wanted to start talking about living together. Then Tommy's lover got out of the military and he and Tommy were an item. – Dan Brazill

——————▽——————

Chicago, IL (USA)

I was in between 8th grade and freshman year and I met another boy who I spent all my time with. That is, until our parents found out. Catholic Charities after that. – Kbro

——————▽——————

Chicago, IL (USA)

I don't think I have truly been in love ... yet! – Don Strzepek

——————▽——————

Chicago, IL (USA)

When I was fourteen, my friend Wally and I had a crush on the same girl and pretty much obsessed about her. When it became obvious that the girl was totally out of our league, we began experimenting with each other just for a sex thrill. Blow-jobs at first, but then the whole shot; anal, fisting, rimming, anything we could think of. It was just magic discovering sex with Wally and, without realizing it, we became very devoted to each other. We kept company

251

all through high school and dated around too. We had sex with other boys, and always had girlfriends that we usually had sex with, because we thought of ourselves as "straight guys who like sex with boys." After we graduated high school we went to different schools, and his parents moved out of town, so we were never intimate again. It was only then that I realized how much I loved him, how truly intimate we had been. Of course, we never kissed or held hands, because that would have been "faggot stuff." Even in high school Wally seemed to favor boys more than girls, so it didn't surprise me when I found out that he had died of AIDS in 1986; by then I was married with a kid on the way. – R.M. Schultz

———▽———

Chicago, IL (USA)

When I first met up partner, Richard. I am still in love almost 50 years later. He was so good for my head (as they said back in the day). There have been others, but Richard was the first. – Gary Chichester

———▽———

Chicago, IL (USA)

The first time I fell in love, true love, was/is with my husband of now 26 yrs. I believe all my past boyfriends were preparing me for the road I'm on now. Even though infatuation made me do some pretty stupid shit. LOL. – Tripp

———▽———

Santa Barbara, CA (USA)

I'll cry. I can think of both requited and unrequited love. I was at college. I went to UC Santa Barbara and I fell in love with a little Filipino surfer boy. He was gay, he was out. He was so cute, he was gorgeous and shy and slightly androgynous looking. I was a junior and he was a freshman, so he was discovering who he was, so he liked my attention and our intimacy. I don't think he really knew what he wanted yet, though. It didn't go very far. Later on, a year or two later, I met up with him and he had a girlfriend and thought that he was bisexual. So even several years later he was still finding out where he was. – Bill

———▽———

Tell Us About the First Time You Fell in Love?

Guerneville, CA (USA)

It was with my first partner. I was at a local bar, I stopped in and I DJ'd there so I went into the bar and I was sitting there. I looked across the bar and I saw this really good-looking man and we both smiled at each other. Next thing you know, it was a month later, I was moving in with him. He was a great guy. We were together nine years until he passed away with HIV. – Rory

———————▽———————

Nashville, TN (USA)

The first time I fell in love I was 14 and it was with my best friend. He didn't feel the same so, I guess, that was by first heartbreak also. – Driveshaft

———————▽———————

(USA)

I have never been in romantic love with a person. I have loved many people, however not as a partner. Never saw the point of it. Now that I'm older and hopefully wiser, that will all change one day. – Daniel Fisher (Raid)

———————▽———————

Chicago, IL (USA)

At 53, after decades of cruising, addictions, self-loathing, and fear, I feel I am in reciprocated love for the first time with a man I've been dating for one year. I'd seen this handsome, stylish geeky guy on the bus for months, and finally got up the nerve to write him a note with my number on a piece of paper. He texted that night. – Martin Mulcahy

———————▽———————

Los Angeles, CA (USA)

That was tragic. All the individuals that went to my junior high school then went to my high school. At the junior prom, and I think his senior prom. I had gone by myself and he was supposed to have had a date and didn't. He was six foot something or other and just gorgeous. However, it happened, he picks me up and we went to the prom. We were coming back in his little

Volkswagen and I guess he had a big fantasy built up in his head, that he was going to get some. Since I was there, it was better than nothing ... I don't know. We started making out and one thing lead to another and then he used that magic word, "I love you." All of a sudden, I saw the picket fence, the house, and my legs spread like the gates ... That was a few minutes of bliss ... for him! He was ready to go and then suddenly he was back to who he was. I was devastated. Two or three days later I had a little bit of bleeding, so that freaked me out. Later, as it turned out, he must have discovered that he was gay, so every now and then at a bar I would see him. If there was a situation where he could cut me from the herd, out would come all these promises again. Later, when I started going to the bathhouses, he was there. – Kalvin

—————▽—————

New York, NY (USA)

Probably with Sal, he was a New York State Attorney. We met at the Ramrod in New York. We went to his place, had sex. He was living in Manhattan, and I was living out on Long Island. I went home and he called me and said, "You forgot your shirt here." I went back and we dated again, and I fell in love with him. It didn't end well. – Ron

—————▽—————

Flint, MI (USA)

It was with my first boyfriend in college, James. On a Friday weekend outing a group of us from Central Michigan University went to Flint, MI to go to the Copa. My friend, Ted, and I were looking over the balcony to the dance floor below and to my right I notice James, sitting back from the balcony. We both smiled at each other. This went on several minutes. My friend, Ted, encouraged me to go and say hello and ask him to dance. I walked over, thinking he was going to say no, but he said yes. At that very moment the tempo of the music changed to the DJ playing, *The Lady in Red* by Chris De Burgh. It was pure magic dancing with James, and we clicked. A week later, we had our first date at the Copa and I brought a copy of *The Lady in Red* on a cassette single as a gift. Within weeks we were in love. We had met in April and the following summer we worked together in Connecticut at a summer camp. When I started back at school again, James moved in with me. By December of that year he was missing being home and unselfishly I said, "James, if you are going to be happier at home, then move home." And he did. I was heartbroken.

I did not see him till the following year in October when I learned he had contacted HIV from a hook up with the owner of the Copa, which James often referred to him as the dick of death. I told James that although we were not together, that when I said, "I love you," it was forever.

I did not see him till five years later when I reached out to him and he had full blown AIDS. I would drive four hours every other weekend and drive back to Northern Michigan to give him a break and take care of him. He eventually moved in with his mother, whom I am still close with. James passed from complications due to AIDS in January of 1998. I learned the best lesson of unconditional love and friendship through him. I made a quilt panel after his death for the Names Project AIDS Memorial Quilt. I still think of him to this day. My life is better having known him. – Greg R. Baird

—————▽—————

Amersham (UK)

Tony M_____ . I was 13 years-of-age and we were all in gym class. Gordon —— the gym master, we were told the only thing we could wear in the gym was shorts. No vests, no underpants, no socks, just plimsolls and shorts. We were all in the gym doing our exercises and the gym master said, "There are two people wearing underpants in this class. Step out!" Nobody moved. He said, "Tony M_____ , Pete J_____ , in the middle of the room." They had underpants on under their shorts. Tony pulled his shorts off, then took his underwear off, and I saw him naked and I just fell in love with him. We were friends, sexually, up until we were 17 years of age. – Bob Brown

—————▽—————

Washington DC (USA)
Arlington, VA (USA)
Virginia Beach, VA (USA)

I can't say I was in love with the woman I married. I liked her beauty and her talent. She had a beautiful voice like Beverly Sills, but she was too lazy to do anything about it. The first person I fell in love with, other than my cousin when we were teens, was when I was stationed at the Pentagon. I was going for an assignation with a fellow I was seeing periodically. I was at a stop light in Arlington, Virginia, and this car pulled up next to me and a fellow waved and I said, "I don't have time right now." He said, "Pull up in the parking lot." So I pulled up in the parking lot. We introduced ourselves to each other and arranged to meet sometime later. He was a civilian working in one of the extensions of the Pentagon. We later got together – his name was Greg.

Fantastic. Here I was in my late 40s and he might have been 30. He came out to his parents on New Year's Eve when he was 16. He was comfortable to be with and we really did fall for each other, but we both had a problem. I lived in a marital household with two grown sons and a suspicious wife. He was still living in his parents' home in Maryland. Finally, one day he said, "I can't handle it, our time together is so amazing, I'm so in love with you, but I go home to my room in my parents' house and you go home to at least the warmth of your children." We parted ways, reluctantly. There's a sequel to that. I'd gone to Virginia Beach for a weekend. I went for a walk on the boardwalk and I got about two blocks distance from the hotel and I heard this deep voice behind me say, "Aren't you Hal?" Without turning around, I said, "Greg?" It was him and he was with someone who was probably jealous. Greg said, "You know what the biggest mistake I ever made was. It was parting ways with you, way back all those years." I went to dinner with him and his lover, who was not very pleasant. Greg was embarrassed as hell. Nothing terribly overt, it was just weird. So ships passing in the night. – Hal

—————▽—————

Chicago, IL (USA)

Still painful. My best friend in high school. We played and I was in love with him, but he got married. He's still married to the same girl. Later on, they asked me to do some design work for them – I don't think she ever knew we played around – and I never got around to doing it. I just couldn't do it. It had to be some kind of mental block. – Laurie Cowall

—————▽—————

New York, NY (USA)

I was going to beauty school at night. It was the Brittany Beauty Center. I'd been working as a hairdresser. But I got caught without a license. So I had to go to school. Nighttime because I worked in a salon during the day. I went to school with a man named Peter and he kept telling me, "I have somebody for you. You have to meet them." My head was in a different space than meeting somebody. But Peter said, "We're going out for a drink one night after work. We're going to go to Millennium's." It was on Long Island on Route 110 and Huntington. Peter and I were having drinks inside, and I remember I was drinking a melon ball that night. Peter says, "I have to go to the bathroom, I'll be back." I didn't think anything of it. He comes back and he says to me, "Come with me, I have someone you have to meet, they're outside. They don't want to come in." I was like, "OK." So we go outside and he introduces me to Joseph DeBono and I melted. He had long hair, he had the Jesus Christ beard. It was the first time when I met somebody that I just … it was a different feeling. This was different. Peter went back in and we wound up talking. Then Peter came back out and said goodnight. It was already last call and we were still talking outside. We left there that night – I left my car in the parking lot – and we drove around and went to a parking lot on Long Island. We were in that parking lot until the sun came up the following morning. I went with him for a long time. I was crazy about him. – Keith Kollinicos aka Missa Distic

─────────▽─────────

New York, NY (USA)

It's hard to say for me, and I say that because I sometimes think I have a soft heart, especially when I was younger. I always felt that I was in love. For me it would have to be between two different people. Old friends or someone I met years later. I'll tell you about the first one. I'm not going to use names. As friends growing up it was the first person who accepted me for me. Completely 100%. When that moment happens, I really had feelings for the guy, it was a sexual tension for me. But I thought, "This is my friend, I can't take it there." Once I realized he accepted me in that fashion, is when I realized this is the person I'm in love with. I felt those feelings of – I don't even know how to describe the feelings, because it was emotional, the body feelings, and mental feelings combined. Whether we were together or separated we had a bond connection. But then over the years my love that I had in my head for him changed, because it wasn't reciprocated in the same way. I realize he loves me. He told me he loves me, but it's a different kind of love. I look at it differently. Once I realized there were different kinds of love out there that's when I knew that I can't keep falling in love with people because they're not falling in love with me. – David Vega aka Lucifers Axe

─────────▽─────────

Honolulu, Hawaii (USA)
Waikiki, Hawaii (USA)

When I left college, I was in a disco in Honolulu dancing and somebody saw me dancing and said, "Listen, there's a Polynesian Revue, a Vegas type thing in Waikiki, you should go and audition." I said, "I don't dance." He said, "You're the right type." So, I went, and I got it. The choreographer was from Los Angeles, and his assistant was this gorgeous, chiseled LA dancer. And LA dancers back then were different from New York dancers, they were more commercial. We were in rehearsals for a month in Honolulu and all the girls were all over him but we couldn't tell if he was gay or not. All these girls, these Polynesian beauties were after him. He used to ask me if I could drive him to certain places. I was so clueless. Then I brought him to a friend's house to visit one night and we were talking and he said, "You wanna … " We spent the night and fucked. Everybody was telling me, "You didn't know!? Everybody else knew that he was after you." He was the reason I moved to LA after doing the show. I was deeply in love. – Simeon Den

―――――∇―――――

Texas (USA)

I fell in love with J.P. J――― of Mesquite, Texas, when we were both actors at North Texas State University's summer theatre in 1975. He was playing Sheriff Will Masters in William Inge's *Bus Stop* and I was a big hit playing Ronnie Shaunessy in John Guare's *House of Blue Leaves*. I was 21 years old and a virgin. He invited me to his apartment, and I will never forget my first kiss with him. I was sitting on his sofa and he came up behind me, leaned over and kissed me as I had never been kissed before. I still remember the electric feeling throughout my body and I think it was at that moment that I began falling in love with him. We were together for 16 years, bought a house, and loved each other until that virus came and took him away. – David Cee

―――――∇―――――

St. Louis, MO (USA)

In college with a boy who lived on the same floor in the dorm. He was beautiful, masculine, kind. Unrequited. – Mark Zubro

―――――∇―――――

Sydney (Australia)

I believe that I've only truly experienced love once in my life, it took me about two years into my relationship with my partner to even begin to understand the concept of love. My upbringing was totally devoid of love, so I really didn't have an understanding of what it was or how it felt.

It was when we started having the usual relationship problems that everyone goes through that I started to understand what love really is. My partner understood my background and would not give up on me no matter how hard I pushed him away. His total devotion to me eventually wore down my emotional walls to let me show my feeling of love for him that I used to keep bottled up and secret. After more than 35 years together our love is stronger than ever. – Ian Davies

—————∇—————

North Carolina (USA)

My dad. My uncle Ken. My cousin Doug ... and someone new in every grade of school. Teachers, a principal or two ... and then pretty much every long-haired hippie I met through the late '60s ... – Gavin Geoffrey Dillard

—————∇—————

Cherry Hill, NJ (USA)

I was a sophomore in high school, he was a junior, I was cast in a bit part in the school play, he was cast as the romantic male lead. He was handsome and friendly and touched everyone he spoke with. I remember one time we were sitting in the auditorium during a rehearsal and as we chatted, he stroked an index finger along my forearm – talk about dying and going to heaven! He had a girlfriend and showed no special interest in me whatsoever, but my fantasies went crazy. I attended rehearsals even when I wasn't on call, just so I could sit in the auditorium and watch him. Between classes, I scanned hallway crowds in the hope of spotting him so I could call out his name and wave. After he graduated, I wrote him letters vowing eternal friendship. He never replied. – Daniel M. Jaffe

—————∇—————

Manhattan Beach, CA (USA)

That was my roller-derby crushes. I'm in straight Whitesville, where do I go to meet some gay women? So I started going to the games at the Olympic Auditorium by bus, not telling anybody. I ended up meeting a lot of them, but there was this one and her name was Tonette and she was from Manhattan Beach too. Being an artist, I drew a portrait. I did some real crazy whacky thing and gave it to her. Of course, that knocks people. I started going to the games, she would say hello to me. Then one night she said, "Do you have a ride home?" And I said, "No." She lived down the street, so she took me home. But she was with somebody then but when they broke up, we started dating and I was with her for maybe 6 or 7 years. I was in my early 20s, 1973, '74. That was Tonette. – Siouxzan Perry

Tell Us About the First Time You Fell in Love?

——————▽——————

Salzburg (Austria)

I think it was when I went for my first female partner that I ended up living with, that was E_____ . I just knew I had to be with her, even though she was not openly gay and had had a male partner. So it was quite a trial to get where I wanted to be, but I did. We ended up being together for 15 years. She works at the Mozarteum University of Arts and Music. I used to go to the Arts House, which had a bar and everything, and mingle with the artists there. She just walked in and she was beautiful. I just saw those big blue eyes and I knew. She was so lovely to me and the first thing she said was, "Oh my god we've got a little red-headed Brit here." So I knew I was in. That was it. – Helen Macfarlane

——————▽——————

Orlando, FL (USA)

I was about 18 and I was living with this older guy who was really more of a predator. He had a friend who was older, his age, who had a boyfriend that was my age. He thought getting the four of us together was a good idea. But what happened was that me and the younger one, we fell hard for each other. Oh my god, it was so passionate. At first, he would tease me, and I couldn't tell if he really liked me or he was a real asshole. But he was being safe because he wasn't sure if I liked him. So, one time, after some drinks, he went inside to use the bathroom, then I went inside. We didn't say anything, but we just went at it in the hallway. That was the most passionate kiss I've ever had in my life. – Bart

——————▽——————

Washington DC (USA)
Alexandria, VA (USA)

My friend and I were bar-hopping, Plus One, and also a bar called the Pier 9 where they had phones on the table, because at that time in Washington DC you could not stand with a drink in your hand. You had to be seated at a table. If you wanted to move, you had to get the waiter to carry your drink. You could not carry it by yourself. They had numbers on each table and if you saw a cute guy you dialed that number and you would say, "I want to speak to the one with ... whatever." So my friends and I were barhopping

and we went to a bar called the Hideaway which was across the street from the FBI building. There was this cute blond boy and my friends and I, they took me to their apartment in Alexandra and we had wild passionate sex. He was my first lover ever. I didn't know he was an alcoholic at the time. He would be dry for several months then go into a binge. My mother loved him.
– Marc

————————▽————————

Sydney (Australia)

His name was Greg. I was going to move in with him. He lived with his parents and they were much older, they probably had Greg in their 40s. And I don't know what happened. I can't remember what happened, but I loved him. His parents loved me and I lived in the suburbs and I'd go out to them or he would come and pick me up. I just fell madly in love with him. But I don't know what happened. I think I must have moved back to New Zealand.
– Gib Maudey

————————▽————————

Ventura, CA (USA)

The first time I fell in love was definitely when I met Charlie. We met in 1987. We met at the gym. We weren't really sure the other one was gay. It was an aerobics class, so everyone had their little shorts and socks. I'd just moved to Ventura not long before and the story is that Charlie and another guy who we became friends with named Don, they would both talk about me and they both wanted to ask me out. Charlie was encouraging Don to do so, but he never did. Charlie finally said, "Do you want to get something to eat or go to the movies?" So we started hanging out for about three months and I really liked Charlie because, 1) he was cute and Hispanic. I thought that was so different to anything I grew up with in Baltimore. And 2) He was incredibly punctual. Never wore a watch but he was always on time for whoever he was going to meet. We just hung out, then one night we went to a club in Ventura, a straight club called Club Bombay to listen to rock music and dance with girls, or whatever. We got back to my place, it was well after midnight and it was cold. It was November. The heater in my little apartment by the beach wasn't working. Charlie was drunk and I was pretty tipsy too. I said, "Why don't you just spend the night here." He said, "OK." He flops onto my bed and says, "It's cold in here, can you turn the heat on." I said, "I'm sorry, the heater's broken." Charlie says, "Well, let's create some body heat." My clothes were off like that. We spent the night together and I woke up the next morning thinking, "Fuck, what if he's straight and he was just drunk? And he wakes up and hits me." Well he woke up and didn't hit me. That was November 1987 and we've been together ever since. Charlie is my first true love. – Cody

————————▽————————

Milwaukee, WI (USA)

My first girlfriend and I moved into an apartment together – with twin beds – while she was still in a relationship with a guy. But she was blond and smart and funny so I did my best to be understanding about why she couldn't/wouldn't break it off with him. She finally did and we were together for several more years. She broke it off with me to start seeing other women. Shortly after that my mother died. I moved to California; there didn't seem to be anything left for me in Milwaukee. – Yvonne Zipter

————————▽————————

Oxford (UK)

I don't know. It's more that I get obsessed with people and then get upset when it falls apart. I'm not sure, I've never really got to grips with the concept of love. I guess I probably have but I don't know really. I don't think about it in those ways. I get confused when somebody really likes me, I think I love them. – Martin

————————▽————————

Chicago, IL (USA)

I'd go out Country & Western dancing and I'd see this guy. One time I asked him to dance. Sometimes I'd see him on the El platform. My heart always quickened when I saw him. I joined a square-dance club, a gay and lesbian square-dance club, to make friends but also because he was in it. I figured this would be a good way to know him better. But he was dating somebody. We went away for Christmas, came back and he said, "How was your Christmas?" I said, "Well, I got dumped. How was yours?" He says, "Well I was involved with somebody but I'm not." We were going to the square-dance – the group was sending people to the outskirts, the suburbs. That was called Traveling Squares. Although we were gay and lesbian square-dancers, we were part of the mainstream square-dance group. So I went to his place and had dinner, then we got in his little pick-up and drove to the suburbs and danced. Had a wonderful time. He drove me back and he said, "Do you mind if we stop at my place first because I'm a little tense from driving in the snow – there was a blizzard. I thought, "Well, that's a line." I said, "Sure, I wouldn't mind listening to some music and relaxing. As soon as we sat down, I threw myself at him. I found out later he just wanted to relax and take me home. That man was my husband. – Michael Wayne

———————▽———————

Berwyn, IL (USA)

The first time I fell in love was long after the first time I'd had actual sex. The first time I'd had sex, I felt more curious and exhilarated on a physical level with very little emotional connection. The first emotional attachment came in my late 40s. I was 48 years old and living in a suburb of Chicago with someone I care about deeply. I'd happened to reestablish contact with friends overseas, and I made new overseas friends as well. As it happens, I had long distance communication with a substantially younger guy in Prague. We connected and opened up in ways that I didn't expect. On many occasions, people will say that virtual life isn't as "real" as "real life" and yet the connection was deeper between myself and the guy in question. I was the other guy's first attempt at an intimate relationship. I felt a strange, unexpected connection that was almost purely emotional/spiritual and even the idea of physical intimacy had more to do with wordless, physical conversation than "fucking." For me, falling in love in that way was the first time that I felt something about myself that was as intoxicating as being with the "hot guy." I was happy to be me at that time, because he made me touch some aspect of myself that the other guy liked. Things didn't end well but I changed because of that, as did my life and my ambitions. Love changes your life and makes it impossible to revert to the person you were before love occurred. – Chip H

———————▽———————

New York, NY (USA)

The first time I fell in love was with a female. We were together for a long time, through junior high school, high school, and then college. The first male was my first lover, Franz, and that just happened by itself, and we lived together until he died from AIDS. He was Dutch, from Holland. – Juan-manuel Alonso

———————▽———————

Tell Us About the First Time You Fell in Love?

Florida (USA)

It wasn't real love. It's what I thought was real love. My marriage that I'm in now for seven years, I'm in love. It's totally different but that very first time with that one girl, I just thought that I'd met THE ONE and she turned out to be THE NOT. She is a federal sky marshal and I found myself – she was off working and I was ironing her clothes and playing the whole little housemaid, wifey type role. I'm telling my mother how much I'm in love with her. Three days later, I'm like, "You fucking bitch." I'm screaming at her, cursing her out. Yeah that was my first time. – Jade

————————▽————————

Santa Monica, CA (USA)

I was 12 and it was with my best friend. I was in love with her for years. I had dreams about her. Her name was Tricia and she was my everything. I told her everything and even though I moved away from Santa Monica we talked every day on line and text. I tried to visit her once a month. I would send her gift packages. Our favorite pastime in Santa Monica was to go to the promenade and we would go to Barnes and Noble, get a stack of Yaoi, so that's Japanese gay porn … stacks! And just read it for three or four hours. That was our thing, that's what we did. Then we would go back to her place and we would read it online because that's what normal friends do together, read explicit gay porn. In a very platonic manner, obviously. – Bambi

————————▽————————

Southern California (USA)

The first time I fell in love was just after I transitioned when I was living in a house with a bunch of LGBT people. I was having a hard time because I was losing touch with my family. I was up one night sitting in the living room crying. I was overwhelmed. My now ex-husband – but we're very, very close – happened to come into the room and said, "Do you need someone to talk to?" That night we sat in his room and talked from 10 p.m. until the sun was up. He said, "You should probably get some sleep." I had never talked to someone and felt so validated and understood. At that moment I realized I wanted to be with that man, and I loved him. – Hayley

————————▽————————

Tell Us About the First Time You Fell in Love?

Southern California (USA)

I fell in love in high school for the first time. I believe there's three kinds of love, your 1st, your 2nd, and your 3rd. This one was the first time. I became very infatuated because this was the first time someone gave me attention that I thought was a loving attention. I was literally at their beck and call every day. I had to call them, and I had to do this, and I had to do this. We were together for about three years and it was very intense. I couldn't see past her to anyone else, there was no-one else I could think of at the time. I was just totally smitten. I think a lot of it had to do with that she was very pretty, beautiful, strong. I was attracted to that as well as envious of it because I wasn't really able to express who I was then. I think it was partly that as well.
– Chloe DeCamp

———————▽———————

Westmont, IL (USA)

I was 12 years old. It was a boy from Chicago, who moved into the neighborhood and I stalked him. We were in 6th grade, he was a year younger than me, and when he played basketball after school, I would ride my bike there. He would go to the motorcycle trails, I would ride my bike over there. I can remember sitting and gawking at him. It's funny because here I am almost 60 and 48 years later we're still friends. As I became an adult we rekindled a love we had for each other, best sex, best mad sex I've ever had in my life. He and I have had this conversation. He used to consider himself bisexual but he thinks he's more gay than he is bisexual now. I felt free and uninhibited to be with him. I was 12 years old and I loved that boy. Now I think, 'Ugghhh!!" – Cathy Melton

———————▽———————

Boston, MA (USA)
Oakland, CA (USA)

I was working in a lesbian bar in Boston, taking IDs and as a bouncer. I got that job as an evening thing. I worked at a radio station during the day. I started going to this women's bar and the bouncer was a gay guy and he was so friendly and nice. I loved him, his name was Eric. So, I said, "I sit here with you all night long, just hanging out with you, why don't they pay me to stay here?" He said, "OK we will." That's how I got a job as a bouncer in a lesbian bar. So it was just me and Eric. There was a cute little girl named Donna _____ who came to the bar and she was my kind of gal. Then one night I had to throw her out because she was drunk and acting-out. I was escorting her out with some kindness and said, "Let me take you out sometime and we'll get a diet Coke or something." She came back and she was just completely cute and loveable, and she could play pool like nobody's business. I don't know exactly how it happened, but we went around the corner to a different women's bar and we ended up coming to my house. She never left for a week because it was a snowstorm ha ha! Then she said, "I really want to share my music with you." She was quite a gifted performer, songwriter and singer. We went to her place in east Boston and got her guitar and returned to my apartment and she serenaded me all night with her own music, some other people's music, but mostly her own. And it was absolutely captivating, mesmerizing, and other-wordly. If I hadn't been before that, I was completely in love with this woman and she was completely fucked-up. She was so far into her disease at that time. I had no clue because I had no experience with alcoholism or drug addiction. I tried to follow her through her disease. She left me, I chased her across country. She came out to Oakland, I chased her. I tried to tell her, "I'm the one, but you just don't know it yet." That was my first falling in love. – Leslie Tisdale

———————∇———————

Melbourne, Victoria (Australia)

It's 2004 and I'm 18. I'm cis female and I'm bisexual, so the first time I fell in love was with my first boyfriend. I remember walking upstairs one day complaining to him about being unattractive to boys. The next day he kissed me. He was a good boy and my parents approved of him. I was conflicted about having any sexuality at all, because of the no sex before marriage rule pushed by my Christian parents. I hadn't realised I was bisexual at that point. – Anita Morris

———————∇———————

Dallas, TX (USA)
Houston, TX (USA)

The first time it was the most like love was with the man who bought me out. I had already been married, I already had a kid, I'd already divorced. But all that was to meet family expectations – go to college, get a job, get a wife, get a kid. I fulfilled that, but then I met Patrick in a cruising area. He was so patient with me and so understanding. He taught me stuff like when you put the pate on the coffee table, you take it out of the can (laughs). I didn't know a lot about how to be gay. I had custody of my son. He did not agree with that. He had a son that he was not in contact with. He may have had some guilt attached to that. But he found another boyfriend and moved to Atlanta, then he moved back to Dallas. He then contracted AIDS and passed away. I had been travelling to Illinois on a trip and came back to Dallas. Somebody told me he was in hospital down in Baylor Scott & White, which is down by Austen. Immediately, I didn't even unpack, I went to see him. He was not far from death. That was my last contact with him. Then the family swished him off to Houston for burial, instead of honoring his request. I drove to Houston, found the cemetery, found the plot, plucked a rose from one of the arrangements, laid it on my dashboard and drove back. I loved him immensely. It was different expectations with a woman, and I tried to define it as love, but it never was. There was respect and companionship, but it wasn't the way I define love today. – Don Rockwell Coffee

—————▽—————

Albuquerque, NM (USA)

Not counting childhood, I assume (I had lots of girlfriends between diaper-age and nine years old, and they were a blend of friendship and romantic connection with hand-holding and secret note-passing and us-against-the-world promises and stuff) ... When I was 17, a family where the parents had known my parents when I was born came by to drop in a few days during their tour-of-the-west vacation; they had a daughter 14 years old and we were immediately interested in each other. The cool thing was that we could talk about anything including romantic aspirations and frustrations, sexual feelings, ambivalences, our annoyance at how we were perceived ... finally instead of playing stupid boy-girl courtship "games" (which totally didn't work for me. I don't fit the boy role at all), I was with someone I could bare my soul to and who was doing likewise in return. I remained obsessed with her for years even though she lived on the other side of the country; we kept writing letters etc. – Allan Hunter

—————▽—————

Detroit, MI (USA)

Oh that's easy, Menjo's white party. I was all in white. That's where I met Mitch. He was devastatingly handsome and looked like Gregory Peck. Black hair, black eyes, beard, tall, well dressed." – Jack Farquhar Halbert

—————▽—————

Tell Us About the First Time You Fell in Love?

Hartford, CT (USA)

It was a guy going to dental school. He was in one of those schools where they had a dental emergency room that you could call. I went there and he was really friendly and nice and wanted to meet me later. It turned out he was away from his boyfriend and he was lonely. But I thought he was paying attention to me. Oh my God, he's a dentist and really cute. A couple of times we met for coffee and I finally had to ask him, "How do you feel about me?" he said, "Oh dear." So that was the end of that. Never saw him again. – Paul

————∇————

Columbus, OH (USA)

His name was Fred and we came out to each other when I was 23 and he was 22. It was just such a different time and we were both so scared. The world got in the way of that one and I'll regret that for the rest of my life. That situation is quite painful for me to think about. – Mike Gifford

————∇————

London (UK)

That's a broad question. That period of limerence I remember most. When I met my first long-term partner, that's when I really fell in love with somebody. That all-consuming passion, always wanting to be in touch, always talking, phoning. We didn't have texting then, but I would have been texting if it had been available. It's just overwhelming and I'm glad it doesn't last very long because it was all so exhausting, that level of intimate communication. That constant, "Where is he? Can I phone him?" All that angst was just very, very, wearing. – Tess Tickles

————∇————

New York City, NY (USA)

Summer 1981. Right after I came out, I was hugely hung up on this guy from college. It never came together. He went off with someone else and I landed very hard. Years later, we ended up living in adjacent neighborhoods in New York and we got together and had a great time reminiscing about school. We promised ourselves another meeting, but we never had it. He died a few months later. – David Pratt

Tell Us About the First Time You Fell in Love?

————————▽————————

Milwaukee, WI (USA)

He was an architect and I was 18. I was so impressed by how worldly he was and his ultra-modern apartment. I told him that living there would take some getting used to. I'm sure the line terrified him. He broke up with me the next time I saw him. "One day you'll find the right person for you … " blah blah blah. I was devastated – for about a day. Falling in love is mighty easy when you're 18. – Anonymous

————————▽————————

Chicago, IL (USA)

It was my first trip to Chicago, and I saw a woman at Bulldog Road, then at Paradise. I went back to my college town and sent a classified to *Gay Chicago* or maybe it was *Gay Life* and she responded. Turns out she worked at Crazy Mary's – next to Bulldog Road. I made another trip and spent a weekend with her, nothing happened. I moved to Chicago and was a lovesick puppy. Nothing ever happened but I followed my heart and got to Chicago where I fell in love many times after. – Terry Gaskins

————————▽————————

Chicago, IL (USA)

It lasted about four months and then he broke my heart into little pieces that it took me about 10 years to get over. – Anonymous

————————▽————————

Orlando, FL (USA)

Jim was partnered with Scott. I met Jim bowling Thursday nights, and we had a three way. I lost contact with Scott and Jim. Many years passed until a Gay Pride in Chicago and Scott and I re-connected at Little Jim's, having an on and off relationship. Scott and Jim broke up but still owned their residence together. Sadly, Jim passed away from AIDS. I moved in their residence and finally Scott and I moved to Orlando, Florida. And we've been partnered over 27 years. Don't have me talk about the one's I thought I was in love with, but weeks, months passed and a BIG NO. – David Plambeck.

Tell Us About the First Time You Fell in Love?

———————∇———————

Bath (UK)

First true love was Sukie de la Croix. Funny, talented, kind, interesting. Few people "got" our relationship (which lasted six years), but essentially the trade-off was he taught me not to be afraid of using my imagination (for writing and other crafts), while I taught him the disciplines of writing (how to use an apostrophe, for example). It was a romantic relationship with lots of great sex, good friends, good music, good books, radical politics, a lot of laughs and a few tears too. We both grew as people in each other's presence. And, yes, it's true what they say – the first cut is the deepest. – Diesel Balaam

———————∇———————

Chicago, IL (USA)

I was freshly 21 and was invited to a Thanksgiving party at my upstairs neighbors. I walked into the kitchen to get a drink and instantly fell in love with a very handsome Latino man who was sitting atop the kitchen counter very animatedly holding court. He was wildly charismatic and captivating, and I was enthralled. I pursued him relentlessly and finally won him over. We were together for three tumultuous years. – Paul Mikos

———————∇———————

New York, NY (USA)

I clearly remember the first time I fell deeply in love. I was seeing this guy I had met one night on the D Train returning back home to Brighton Beach, Brooklyn, from the Village. He lived in a nearby neighborhood, walking distance from me. He came from a really religious family, was really handsome, and we had really wild wonderful sex. I was living in my own apartment and he'd come over pretty regularly, but when we weren't having sex, all we seemed to do was argue. EVERYTHING was an argument. We tried going out once or twice and while having a not so bad time, it wasn't so great either. He was still hung up on a guy that dumped him. He also let his family, and especially his brother, walk all over him. Whenever he told me about how they treated him, I would defend him, but then he would end up taking their side! I remember, one night he came over and was all happy. In bed, I asked him what was going on, and he actually said to me, "I realized today that I could never love you." But, still, we kept seeing each other because the sex and chemistry between us was the greatest either of us had experienced.

I arranged to meet him one night in the Village, after he was done with his classes at optometry school, and go back to my apartment together. We got to my apartment building, only for me to find out I had lost my keys. It was pouring out! We had to walk one mile in the rain to a friend who had a spare set of keys to my apartment. During the walk, drenched, I told him that we should probably not see each other because it wasn't going anyplace. On the one mile walk back to my apartment I went on with my spiel how this was probably for the best, and we would never get along anyway. He was silent, but agreed with me that we should end it.

We got up to my apartment, dried off and jumped into bed. I then suddenly told him that I was in love with him, and he confessed he was in love with me. He was one of the greatest loves of my life.

We broke up after about five years, and we both went our separate ways. We stayed in touch, spoke on the phone sometimes and occasionally saw each other. Then I received a note from his partner, that Stephen had passed away from AIDS. I still find myself missing him and wishing that just for a minute, I could talk to him. – Ian H

———————▽———————

Chicago, IL (USA)

It was with a man I saw on the subway as I was coming home from work. We were both married to women at the time, so it made it all terribly romantic. Turned out he was tricking all over town. – Rick Karlin

———————▽———————

Chicago, IL (USA)

1978. He was more mature than I, and had an excellent job with *Gay Life* newspaper, and I was totally bowled over by him. I met him working with the guys at Peeping Tom's. He lived just down the street on Wells St., I don't recall the address now, but I could find it if I went though some old things. He was handsome, and was great sex, my key criteria at the time, and a bit of a kinkster which was where I think I started to go down that path. He seemed quite infatuated with me, I thought. Well I had to go away to college, and I wrote him every day a note or a post card or something, and then he moved back to Indianapolis to help his mother, and we tried to keep it going but it seemed to fall apart, and he told me I needed to move on to others. It was funny 'cause he moved out to Redlands where I went to school, after I was there. I was told recently by a friend that he became a McDonald's franchise owner and now has several and a multimillion-dollar business. Not sure if it really is him or not but I am glad he found success and I am thankful for that time we had together as I remember it being so romantic in my mind and loving. – Dean Ogren

—————▽—————

(Venezuela)
Guadalajara (Mexico)

When I first met my husband. He's the only one that I have loved since I started dating men. He's the only one. I met him on a gay site Silver Daddies. He was here in Palm Springs and I was in Venezuela. That was back in 2006. A year passed and I lost track of him, then we met in Mexico City. Eight months later we were living together in Guadalajara. – Carlos

—————▽—————

Chicago, IL (USA)

I fell in love with a friend in the neighborhood and we were "Secret Lovers" (just like the Atlantic Starr song) for a number of years in the mid to late '80s. He couldn't be out because his family would either harm him, disown him or both. We had discussed moving in together, but he could never muster the courage to do so while I was more than ready to start a life together. We eventually broke up, though we remained friends and he ended up marrying a woman and leading a somewhat "normal" life and I ended up marrying a man and living, so far, an "extraordinary" life. – Robert Castillo

—————▽—————

Seattle, WA (USA)

With a man or with a woman? Let me do a two-parter then. With a woman because in retrospect that was what I was supposed to do. She was just a very, very, delightful, honest, sweet person. That was the woman I married. I had never been in love or infatuated with anybody until then. In retrospect I think it was love because it was the right fit for me, but not really the right fit. In terms of men, I had a total and complete fascination with a friend, but it was lust it wasn't love. Then when I met my partner of 28 years, that was love. – OT

—————▽—————

WHAT WAS THE MOST ROMANTIC THING ANYONE HAS EVER DONE FOR YOU?

Chicago, IL (USA)

A lover who very rarely smiled ... and chose to go back to Lima Peru ... Kissed me Hollywood style in the airport ... and left a picture of himself smiling under my pillow!!! – Don Strzepek

––––––––––∇––––––––––

Newport Beach, CA (USA)

I was never in a relationship long enough, I never dated anybody long enough. Whenever I got involved with somebody it was always a mess. A straight friend of mine once asked me, "Have you ever been in a relationship with a woman?" And I'd say, 'Every relationship I've been in has been a mistake." I just leave it at that. But there was one guy I dated for a couple of months, very cute, a furball of a little bear. He was bearded and furry, but he was too young, only 22 years old. We dated for a few months. We went out to Balboa Island, Newport Beach, the harbor there. I was sitting out there by the water and he disappeared. His name was Michael. Michael disappeared and came back with this envelope, just for buying one cookie. It was around Valentine's Day. I pulled the cookie out and it was heart-shaped, and it said, "You and Me." That was sweet. And then the first time I ever had a book-signing at A Different Light in West Hollywood, that was such a disaster. They scheduled me the same weekend when they had an AIDS bike ride. They blocked off Santa Monica Boulevard, and anyone that wanted to come to my book-signing couldn't get there. It was a disaster, when you're waiting

273

to sign people's books and the guy comes along and starts collecting the chairs before you sign anybody's book. I was wandering around the store and went to the magazines and there was Michael on the cover of a magazine. He was really cute. It wasn't *Bear* magazine but some Bear-oriented magazine. I remember leaning over to a guy who was looking at the magazines next to me, and I said, "It's a hell of a thing to pick up a porno magazine and see someone you used to date on the cover." – Tim Barela

———————▽———————

Chicago, IL (USA)

Okay. This is bleak. I can't think of a single romantic thing. – Thomas Bottoms

———————▽———————

Chicago, IL (USA)

Drove five hours to take me on a date to dinner and drinks. I was highly impressed, and it worked. – Jim

———————▽———————

New York, NY (USA)

We had dinner at the Russian Tea Room and *Kiss of the Spider Woman* tickets. – Thomas Autumn

———————▽———————

Bolinas, CA (USA)

Told me he loved me for who I was, not what I did for him. – Louis Flint Ceci

———————▽———————

St. Louis, MO (USA)

It was 1990, and I remember that because *Twin Peaks* was in its first year and I loved that show. One day I just luckily happened to be in my apartment when there was a knock at my door. A delivery guy was there with roses for me, and I was stunned. By reading the card I found it was a guy that I had played with a couple times and he wanted to thank me for spending time with him – he apparently didn't feel amazingly desirable to most guys and wanted to show his appreciation. He was sweet and I did get to see him several more times. I was once invited to an evening birthday get-together at his house which was a distance away across the Mississipi River. I made sure to set my VCR for *Twin Peaks* and drove to his place. His friends and some family were there, and he proudly slow-danced with me with them present. It was lovely. Distance kept us from seeing each other often, and I am a bit sad that we lost contact. I still think about him and it always makes me smile. – Todd Jaeger

———————▽———————

Seattle, WA (USA)

My husband and I have our birthdays two weeks apart. We were out of the country for my 40th. While in Italy, he planned out, invited the guests, and made all arrangements for a surprise party when we returned home – all without ever giving me the slightest hint or question. He threw MY 40th birthday surprise party on HIS birthday two weeks later. – Eric Andrews-Katz

———————▽———————

Elmhurst, IL (USA)

That would be Steve the "boy next door." The next day after our first meeting he walked next door to me with a bouquet of flowers and asked me out on a date. – Robert Hansen

———————▽———————

(USA)

My first partner constantly pursuing me, when I tried everything in the world to get rid of him. We met at a birthday party for a friend's English sheepdog. Wally wanted an excuse to throw a party and it was Duncan's birthday, so he held a party. I was there with a friend and Joe was there with his ex. We chatted across the table, there was interest, but he was there with somebody and I was there with somebody. It was the holiday season of 1987 and I was in a piano bar singing and he came in with another friend. He turned to her and said, "That man is going to date me." When I got ready to leave, he followed me to my car and asked if I wanted to go out afterwards. I said, "No, I've got to be up early." I was a church pastor at the time. So I said, "You can come to church tomorrow if you want to." I thought, "Best line to scare any man away." Who showed up in church the next morning, but him? Stayed for the after-Christmas party we were doing at the church. He said, "Would you like to come to dinner tonight?" I said, "I can't, I have to go to my company dinner party for my other job." He said, "Well, do you want to come over for a drink afterwards?" I thought, "This man is not going to give up." I got to his house, his entire family room was lit with candles, soft music playing, there was a bottle of chilled champagne, he had chocolate, he had strawberries. He said, "I have to get you into my house." That was December 1987 and we were together within about two weeks, until he passed away in 2013. So the romance worked. – Art Healey

———————∇———————

Tennessee (USA)

I'd love to say there was some big, over the top gesture that I could go into all sorts of details about but no. It was one small thing that has stuck with me for over 20 years. I was living in Tennessee near Short Mountain Sanctuary, a fairy community there. This guy Brandon L_____ came over with his partner for dinner. Being a commune, we always had people coming and going. I didn't know Brandon that well, he barely ever spoke. So shy, but so sweet. He was the most sincere person I've ever met, and I really wanted to get to know him. But I thought he didn't like me. I mean, I wasn't special or anything compared to all the people we each knew.

But that night, after dinner a bunch of folks wanted to make a bonfire, and I just wanted to work on some crazy art project alone in my room. Brandon stood at my door, so quietly and watched me just make a mess, trying to paint a mannequin. I was in the zone and didn't notice him there, until after about ten minutes he peeped out a twangy "Hey Raid." And I about lost it. He had the most beautiful smile on his face and as I stood up, he walked over and kissed me. We tried to get it on, but we ruined it by talking, and didn't stop talking. I miss him every day, he was my best friend. – Daniel Fisher aka Raid

———————∇———————

(USA)

I'm going to go with the first thought, which is, I had a partner who died about four years ago. He sought me out for four to five months before I would even go on a date with him. I wasn't interested, I didn't feel any chemistry with him. He wasn't handsome. I had this conversation with him when he was alive, so I'm not talking behind his back. I didn't think he was handsome, I didn't think he was my type, I didn't think he had anything to offer. He wore me down and I went to dinner with him. I liked him and thought he was entertaining and lovely. When he told me the story of who he was, I knew at that point that I loved him and could be his partner. Be somebody important to him. The first thing we did together was take a cruise. He was a cruiser, he loved to go on cruise ships. He was this little Scottish guy with red hair and blue eyes. He was hairy, furry, crazy, adorable little guy who was not the type that I went for. The most romantic thing ever was telling me on the first cruise we were on, standing on the deck of the ship, that "You make me happier and more full of life, full of love, full of happiness, than anyone has ever made me feel in my life. I will do anything you want so that you will continue to do that for me." I'd never heard anybody say anything like that. I remember crying." – Joseph S

———————▽———————

Chicago, IL (USA)

I was told to pack a bag for two weeks, he took me to NYC to see my friend on opening night of *The Color Purple*. The next morning, he said we are off the airport (I was a little upset because why would I pack for two weeks when it was an overnight trip). We got to the airport and caught a flight to Paris, France. – Dale

———————▽———————

Chicago, IL (USA)

Back before digital pix, my lover bought us a Polaroid camera and said, "Take all the pictures you want for yourself, but take one of your dick in my ass for me." I got hard just hearing those words. – R.M. Schultz

———————▽———————

Palm Springs, CA (USA)

John and I have this thing and I feel romantic with him all the time. I guess it would be the first time he took me to Mexico, to Puerto Vallarta. It was just the two of us and we had a blast. – Rory

What Was the Most Romantic Thing Anyone Has Ever Done for You?

—————▽—————

(USA)

Saved my life when I was totally down and out. He rescued me almost 15 years ago. I call him my husband now. – Driveshaft

—————▽—————

Chicago, IL (USA)

The most romantic thing I've experienced is yet to come. But in the past, just traveling the world with my husband. – Tripp

—————▽—————

Chicago, IL (USA)

When someone "sees" me. Rarely do I think people really "see" me, and my love of films and art, so when my boyfriend bought me an antique film projector, I cried. And every meal he has cooked for me. – Martin Mulcahy

—————▽—————

San Diego, CA (USA)

My ex-partner, we were together 22 years, and he was a good cook – which I'm not – and when we first met … you know that, "the way to a man's heart is through his stomach." I was very sick one winter, wondering if I had AIDS – it turned out to be a very bad case of the flu – and he took care of me. We had just met, and he decided this was a keeper and he cooked for me and he was a wonderful cook, and thereafter I got better and still he did the cooking. That has remained as the most endearing thing about him. My mother did not like to cook for the family, she resented having to cook. So here was a man who wanted to cook for me, cook good dinners, and that was amazing. – Bill

—————▽—————

Cathedral City, CA (USA)

When I asked my current husband to marry me and he said, "Yes." – Ron

What Was the Most Romantic Thing Anyone Has Ever Done for You?

—————————▽—————————

(USA)

I had a guy I dated take me to Las Vegas for my birthday. I also had another guy years ago send me flowers. – Greg R. Baird

—————————▽—————————

Los Angeles, CA (USA)

For my 50th birthday, Bob Robinson arranged for my sister and my best girlfriend to come from London to Los Angeles. He picked us up in a limousine and we go off to the Pantages Theatre to see *La Cage Aux Folles*. Then from there we went for dinner. Lovely and romantic, and it was all sad because he and I were no longer partners, but we were very good friends. That's what he did for my 50th. – Bob Brown

—————————▽—————————

San Francisco, CA (USA)

My present husband who was my interest, that's about it. We met online, then in person in San Francisco Folsom Street Fair in 1998. He wasn't answering his cell phone, so I called the hotel. He was there but his phone didn't work in the hotel in San Francisco because it was too earthquake reinforced. I got to the hotel, went up to his room. We were supposed to meet at 5:30 p.m., got there at 4:45 pm. The most romantic thing he ever did for me, that same night about 1:30 a.m., he said, "Are you hungry yet?" – Hal

—————————▽—————————

Palm Springs, CA (USA)

Romanticism is left up to a person's own mind. Everyone sees it differently. For some people receiving flowers is romantic. For me being romantic is more a look in the eye, rather than what somebody does. The reason I put it that way is when I look into a person's eye and I know that we're on the same wavelength, the same page, on the same energy level, that's transferred between us, to me that's the most romantic. It's beyond words. It's not an act that they're doing, it's their meaning. – David Vega aka Lucifers Axe

What Was the Most Romantic Thing Anyone Has Ever Done for You?

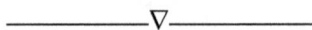

————————▽————————

Chicago, IL (USA)

I had a lover for 10 years and a boyfriend for 12 and I can't think of ever getting flowers, I can't think of anything. – Laurie Cowall

————————▽————————

New York, NY (USA)

This is going to sound really strange, and I'm sure you haven't got answers like this. Having your husband do things like change mother's diaper, selfless, caring, it shows such a love-bond. That type of selfless giving … I don't know how to elaborate on it without getting into tears. – Keith Kollinicos aka Missa Distic

————————▽————————

New York, NY (USA)

I would meet these guys who were rice queens and they would always say. "I can put the world at your feet." I would say, "But I can put the world at my feet myself." Or I would go home with them and rice queens would go, "Can you put this kimono on?" I'm like, "No, you put on the kimono." I don't care less about shit like that. Then this one guy, he was really into me and he was so sweet and nice, but I wasn't into him at all. On my birthday, I was walking down the street, on Broadway in New York, and I bumped into him. He said, "Come in here, let me buy you something for your birthday. Anything you want." I said, "Anything?" He could afford it. I just thought, "How sweet of him." Of course, I was looking at the cheap things, and he said, "Oh no, no, no, ANYTHING!" I got a really good gift that year. – Simeon Den

————————▽————————

West Hollywood, CA (USA)

Funny … this is the only question that stumps me. But I'd say it was when a trans girlfriend showed up and physically carried me away after a lover had almost killed me. – Gavin Geoffrey Dillard

What Was the Most Romantic Thing Anyone Has Ever Done for You?

———————∇———————

Chicago, IL (USA)

I've never had a great romance. I think that is important to note – especially for younger people in the LGBTQIA community who may be struggling. Being single is a very viable option. Therefore, the most loving thing that has been done for me was by one of my best friends, Kirsten. She knew that I was feeling a bit vulnerable about turning 50. I was actually thrilled to achieve that age – I've known so many who haven't had that privilege and I treated the whole year as a celebration. But she knew that I was just a bit worried that, because I live alone, there would be no one to make a big deal out of the milestone. Therefore, she was a triple treat: buying me lunch one day, arranging an outing with some mutual friends, and presenting me with a goodie bag of very specifically "me" gifts and then, as we are both film fans, she made a very public announcement and got an audience of movie goers to sing to me and presented me with cupcakes that I passed out to everyone in the theater. It was truly a beautiful thing for her to do and something that I will never forget. – Brian Kirst

———————∇———————

Sydney (Australia)

I was attending a tertiary education class a few years ago and it was an anniversary of my relationship with my partner. During the class there was a delivery of an enormous basket of fragrant flowers, all the women in the class were so excited hoping they were for them. Their jaws dropped when they realized they were for me and the stir it created made me feel like the Prom Queen. – Ian Davies

———————∇———————

Santa Barbara, CA (USA)

In 2013, after both California and Federal law changed to allow same-sex marriage, my partner of twenty years by then, Leo, and I eloped, marrying at the County Courthouse without having told anyone we knew. As the clerk performed the marriage ceremony, Leo held my hands and looked into my eyes with tears dripping down his cheeks. His gaze, that gaze, that gaze of love and adoration, was the most romantic gift anyone has ever given me. – Daniel M. Jaffe

What Was the Most Romantic Thing Anyone Has Ever Done for You?

——————▽——————

Los Angeles, CA (USA)

Actually, this last weekend when we went to see Hanna Gadsby in LA. That was a really big thing to do as we hadn't been away for a while and Siouxzan arranged it for a surprise. It was a beautiful, fantastic evening with champagne. That was romantic. – Helen Macfarlane

——————▽——————

(New Zealand)

The most romantic thing was when he got me residency in New Zealand. Because he was here on a work visa and couldn't stay. So, he said, "Why don't we see if we can get residency in New Zealand." It was easy. New Zealand had at that time what they called de facto relationships. It had nothing to do with gender or sexual orientation. As long as you were together and could prove it. I ended up getting New Zealand citizenship as well. – Marc

——————▽——————

North Hollywood, CA (USA)

That's a funny thing. Years ago, I lost my sight and it took a long time for it to come back. But initially when they released me from the hospital, I had hand motion and light. That's all I could see. I was in the hospital for so long that I missed the holidays. When I got out in the middle of January my friend, who picked me up from the hospital, took me to his house, and he had set back up his Christmas tree for me. That's probably the most romantic. I thought that was really kind, because I couldn't see but I could see the lights, so I knew. – Bart

——————▽——————

Ventura, CA (USA)

It's funny, neither of us are heavily romantic. I think the most romantic thing Charlie did was cry when we got legally married. We both had tears of joy. The court clerk saying, "I now pronounce you married," I thought that was incredibly romantic. – Cody

What Was the Most Romantic Thing Anyone Has Ever Done for You?

———————∇———————

Chicago, IL (USA)

That's a tough one. My wife does romantic things for me on a regular basis. Just today, she bought me flowers because she was proud that I'd had a good pitch session with a literary agent. – Yvonne Zipter

———————∇———————

Chicago, IL (USA)

I was having a 50th birthday party and I knew that my dad and his wife were going to be there for the occasion. So we were out and about running errands the day before, getting ready for the party. When we came back my sister and my nephew were there by surprise. I thought, "Oh wow, wonderful." Then we went out to do a little tourist thing with my dad and his wife. When we came back my brother and his wife were there. The day went on and my brother and his wife were going to see a play downtown and we were all going to a restaurant, have dinner together, they were going to see the show and we were going home. We got to the restaurant and there was an aunt and a cousin sitting at the table. And what had happened was that Tim had paid for their airfare, any member of my family that wanted to celebrate my birthday. – Michael Wayne

———————∇———————

Prague (Czech Republic)

I was returning to Chicago, from the Czech Republic, friends took me to the airport (after getting me totally snockered) to say a "proper goodbye." After a while of not talking, my best Czech friend and I were given time together and I received the biggest, longest (most crushing bear hug) I'd ever gotten from anyone. The kiss that accompanied it was unexpectedly deep and passionate. As the hug went on, on, and on, I felt his lips brush my ear as he whispered, "Hurry up and come back home." I haven't gotten back there yet, but I have somewhere to go.

2: Prague (Czech Republic)

On a day shortly after my birthday, I was working at a hostel and a friend visited. He learned (through someone else) that my birthday had come and gone. He took it upon himself to take me to lunch and to show me a good

283

time. We spent a nice afternoon at a restaurant named "Trilobit" (Trilobite) and afterward, walked around taking photos of insects. During our walk/talk, he learned of my love of insects and said that he hopes that whenever I saw firebugs that they'd remind me of him. (They do.) I guess the way to my heart is through an insect. – Chip H

—————∇—————

Chicago, IL (USA)

The glib part of my personality wants to say it was when my boyfriend Roberto would bring me flowers after one of our customary violent fights. But that pales in comparison to what my ex-boyfriend Chip did after I had open heart surgery, with complications, in 2010. For the first week afterward, I was pretty much incapacitated. While all my other so-called friends paid lip service, Chip jumped into the breech – while working a full time job – and handled everything. He got me through a very difficult time. It's not exactly hearts and flowers, but anyone who's willing to deal with all the unpleasant things that happen with a person after major surgery, has proved how strong their love is. – Xavier Bathsheba-Negron

—————∇—————

Palm Springs, CA (USA)

My wife. Just recently for my birthday. I'm pretty close to my mother-in-law, and she's afraid to fly, and afraid to travel by train. She only lives in Sonoma so she's not far away. On my 50th birthday in January, I got real sick, I was almost hospitalized. It was a Saturday night and I was sitting on the couch. I wanted to go to bed because I was feeling bad. My wife kept saying, "A package is being delivered for your birthday. You have to stay awake until the package gets here. It's coming between 6 and 7." Around 6:30 I'm on the couch and I'm crying. I'm just exhausted and I want to go to bed. She goes out front, she comes in and she says, "Did you call somebody about some groceries?" I'm like, "What!" I lean up on the couch and there's my mother-in-law standing there. Between those two she had hired a driver and she and my wife together brought her down for my 50th birthday. My own mother isn't going to celebrate shit with me. It may not sound romantic, but it was just lovely. I cried tears of joy, not tears of sorrow. To me that's the most romantic thing that's ever been done." – Jade

—————∇—————

What Was the Most Romantic Thing Anyone Has Ever Done for You?

Southern California (USA)

This was not my ex-fiancé, this was someone after. We were chilling at his house and they drew me – I've had several people paint me – but he did this full-scale portrait of me. He gave it to me. When he first met me, he made it, then four years later he gave it to me. He said, "I've always had an attraction to you, I've admired you and I think you're wonderful." I said, "Thank you." That night we were in his pool and the sun was setting. He picked me up and twirled me around in the pool and a bunch of bats flew out. It was amazing because I love bats. He said, "I couldn't have planned that any better." It was really tender and very sweet. It was just a nice moment. – Bambi

—————▽—————

Palm Springs, CA (USA)

This might sound funny but I would tell you at this age, it was when Leslie asked me to marry her. She said to me, "Do you have health insurance?" I said, "Not anymore." And she says, "We need to get married." And I thought, "That is the weirdest proposal ever, ever." But then I thought, "We've known each other a long time and she doesn't want me to get sick, she wants to take care of me." If I was younger, I would not have said that was romantic but as an almost-60 years-old woman, I would tell you that was the most romantic thing ever. – Cathy Melton

—————▽—————

(USA)

My old husband would buy me things, like a watch. He would just come home with it and if I liked it, he would buy another. He died seven years ago. – Jack Farquhar Halbert

—————▽—————

Glenview, IL (USA)

My partner was always romantic. He knew from day one that I was the one he wanted to live with. He always gave me roses for our anniversary. His cards were fancy deluxe cards with flowering verses that stated how he felt about me. The one romantic thing that sticks out in my mind happened under a sad circumstance. While shopping, I felt a pressure in my chest, and assuming something was wrong, I dropped my food and rushed home. My partner drove me to the emergency room. I did have a slight heart attack and the next day I had a stent inserted. I was in the recovery room when I saw my partner as I awoke. He was crying and said, "You can't leave me now. You are the light of my life." – Yehuda Jacobi

————————▽————————

(USA)

I can't think of deliberate romantic gestures so much as romantic moments that just crop up. Often when traveling. My husband is different. He thinks it's romantic if I remember to buy laundry detergent. – David Pratt

————————▽————————

Chicago, IL (USA)

Bought me a condo. – Anonymous

————————▽————————

(USA)

He took me to Hawaii. – David

————————▽————————

Chicago, IL (USA)

Given me a pedicure in the bathtub. –Rick Karlin

————————▽————————

New York City, NY (USA)

In the late '90's I moved with my job to NYC. I was dating a beautiful male model who single handedly painted my entire apartment in his Calvin Klein briefs, while singing along to Dusty Springfield. I couldn't help because I had broken my arm roller blading and was in a cast and in pain. It was charming, sexy and wildly romantic to me. –Paul Mikos

————————▽————————

What Was the Most Romantic Thing Anyone Has Ever Done for You?

Milwaukee, WI (USA)

What comes to mind is the day that my boyfriend and I spent the entire day in bed reading the ridiculous novel *Our Hearts Were Young and Gay* to one another – having sex, drinking coffee, getting drunk, having sex. The sweetness and the closeness I felt with him that day still makes me sigh. We were young and penniless and so in love. – Anonymous

——————▽——————

Bath (UK)
(Wales)

Written me a poem – yes, that'll be Sukie de la Croix, again. Although my current partner did rent a castle in remote rural Wales to celebrate my last birthday, which maybe topped the poem. – Diesel Balaam

——————▽——————

Seattle, WA (USA)

I can't say it was one single moment. I guess it's things like cuddling when you're down. When you're feeling very vulnerable. Or you are so sad, you don't know where you're going or what you're doing. The arms around you, the embrace, that much more than giving a physical thing. – OT

——————▽——————

Chicago, IL (USA)

My late husband John married me; that was pretty romantic and we had a great life together, sharing 20 years of great memories. He was a caring, loving compassionate man and I miss the little things like holding hands at the movies or the smile and Hey! when he got home from work. He was also never shy about expressing affection and that was very romantic. – Robert Castillo

——————▽——————

Chicago, IL (USA)

I think the most romantic thing that anyone ever did for me was just recently for Christmas 2017. I was kind of in a down sort of mood and my boyfriend gave me an amazing Christmas gift of a trip to Amsterdam that would happen in the spring of 2018. The delivery of the gift was what made it so special as it was delivered in a windmill cookie jar. But as I look back on that I recall an even more romantic thing that he had done shortly after our first anniversary of meeting. I made him a nice dinner at home just the two of us, and he gave me an ID bracelet with the date engraved on it. I had always wanted an ID bracelet with the link chain around the wrist. It was so the thing when I went to school, so that gift was also a special romantic moment. He did not even know or ask me, he just made an excellent choice. – Dean Ogren

———————∇———————

Chicago, IL (USA)

One boyfriend insisted on giving me head until I came no matter how long it took. And he swallowed. Man was a saint. – Mark Zubro

———————∇———————

Chicago, IL (USA)

Not sure it classifies as romantic, but it was extremely touching and I still remember it. It was my 40th birthday and he bought me a Lego Pirate Ship. I was touched because it was both expensive and he could ill afford it, and meant he knew me better than anyone else in the world. – Ian H

———————∇———————

IF YOU COULD GIVE ONE PIECE OF ADVICE TO YOUR YOUNGER SELF, WHAT WOULD IT BE?

Manchester, IA (USA)

Stay in the moment. None of this is permanent and it can all disappear in a heartbeat. I hold no regrets and at age 58, feel like I've not really wasted a second. But when my partner, Jeff, died in 2011, after 21 years together, I experienced grief and loss like I'd never known before. Had it not been for my own awareness of my emotions, my ability to express my feelings in words and poetry, and a very close friend always urging me to "keep in the moment," I don't know that eight years later, I would be the fully integrated person I am now. – Timothy Juhl

———————▽———————

Chicago, IL (USA)

Just ... BE YOU!!!! – Don Strzepek

———————▽———————

Temecula, CA (USA)

Just be patient because good things will come eventually. Things always seem to work out with my career as a cartoonist and author. I always seem to have success in spite of my worst expectations. – Tim Barela

—————▽—————

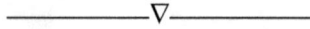

Chicago, IL (USA)

I do a joke about this. I talk about a support group and we are given this exercise. People instantly start crying; "Cherish your loved ones." … "Pursue your dreams." I look down at my younger self and say, "End it now, honey, it don't get no better." The support group is offended. Security is called to remove me. I make a motion towards my wrist and shout to my younger self, "It's down the road, not across the street! Down the road, not across the street!"

In all seriousness, I would tell my younger self, "You don't deserve the abuse you receive. If the voices in your head tell you to run, head towards the door, don't pass go, and leave immediately. People may hate your bluntness, but honesty is a strength. Own it. Being single isn't a curse and marriage isn't a goal. Be the person you need to be for yourself. Pet the cats more." – Thomas Bottoms

—————▽—————

Chicago, IL (USA)

Everything will be alright. It will take some time for you to figure out why things happen and what it all means but it will make sense soon. Be kinder to yourself and fully appreciate those people who are there for you. – Jim

—————▽—————

Chicago, IL (USA)

Pay attention and keep a journal. – Vincent Rideout

—————▽—————

Portland, OR (USA)

Don't give up on yourself and listen to your heart, and not to anyone's advice. There will be people who will tell you that something can't be done or in the case of wanting to move to San Francisco, it's too expensive and you'll never make it. Just tell them that they're not paying the bills and airplanes fly in more than one direction. You do what your heart and brain tell you to do, trust in God and be yourself." – Jerry S

—————▽—————

Gainesville, FL (USA)

If you stay in the closet, keep your mouth shut, keep yourself guarded and don't give away your heart – you will probably have a much easier time in life; but the views, experiences, friendships, challenges and benefits would not be nearly as rewarding.

(Oh yeah, when you get set up with R_____ – DON'T GO! TURN AROUND, AND RUN FAR AWAY!) – Eric Andrews-Katz

—————▽—————

Nevada City, CA (USA)

Pay attention to your body. It knows what it likes. – Louis Flint Ceci

—————▽—————

Greenwich, CT (USA)

Fight back! – Thomas Autumn

—————▽—————

Rancho Mirage, CA (USA)

Don't worry so much. It takes too much out of you over the years. Also, seek out Reiki (wish I had learned it YEARS ago). By not worrying so much it has helped me realize that things have a way of working out for me. The Reiki sessions I give to people, patients at a hospital, and animals, help them and yourself CHILL. I'm not a religious person and "thoughts & prayers" are not the answer. Taking ACTION is, which is what I do with the energy work. I am doing something to help others and myself and it doesn't require having faith in something you can't really know for sure is there. While some folks might doubt what I do, well I can for sure say I've seen very good results in others' health and well-being, and for them and myself felt physical things happen during sessions whether it be warmth, sensations, colors, etc. Even for those that were skeptical have still found relaxation, and in many cases, just fallen asleep. You can't lose when you have time to not worry and catch up with yourself. – Todd Jaeger

————————∇————————

California (USA)

Be true to yourself or stand your ground. Be true to yourself, it might not have an immediate dividend but a long-term dividend to bear. – Dave

————————∇————————

Cathedral City, CA (USA)

Don't pretend and don't do what people expect you to do. I got married because I was told that it would make things different. All it did was make a whole lot of problems. – Art Healey

————————∇————————

Palm Springs, CA (USA)

Always value yourself because you are the most valuable thing there is. No-one can be you and no-one can take you away. – Joseph S

————————∇————————

Chicago, IL (USA)

"You are bisexual and can only be understood by other bisexuals! You might think that a queer boyfriend or straight girlfriend understands you, but only other bisexuals do!" Told this to my bisexual son and daughter, but they seem to think that "things are different now." They aren't! Bisexuals are their own thing and we should only have marriages with each other. – R.M. Schultz

————————∇————————

If You Could Give One Piece of Advice to Your Younger Self?

(USA)

One piece of advice? That's a tough one... I guess I'd tell my younger self, "How you carry yourself matters." (My not so subtle way of offering more than one thing) Life can be rough but take a few little lessons and you'll be alright. Listen more and talk less. Don't be a gossip and don't say things that aren't true. Stand by your convictions, follow through and don't worry if people like you as long as you like AND respect yourself. Dignity no matter the adversity, comes from inside. It can't be metered out by others. Be there for the people who are there for you, because they won't always be around. Loss and pain are a part of life, not the end of it. Mostly, a lesson I believe in with all my soul is that: Laughter is a powerful weapon. It's easy to break a person physically, but if someone can stare death in the face and laugh about it, no power on earth can break their will. – Daniel Fisher (Raid)

———————∇———————

Chicago, IL (USA)

Be yourself! – Gary Chichester

———————∇———————

Palm Springs, CA (USA)

Just have fun and don't take life seriously. It could be gone tomorrow. Be yourself and don't be ashamed of who you are. – Rory

———————∇———————

Jacksonville, FL (USA)

At 53 years old and living in Jacksonville, FL., I would have to say, "Don't be afraid to be who you are." – Driveshaft

———————∇———————

Chicago, IL (USA)

Oh God! I have so many. Don't be such a dick! – Tripp

(USA)

Rise up and ignore the bad energy being presented to you in your life. Value education more and work to be more financially secure. Take care of your body and know food is not a comfort blanket to fill your void but for sustenance. Embrace your beautiful gift of love for people and know that you are indeed a healer. – Greg R. Baird

San Diego, CA (USA)

Masturbation is a path to God. – Bill

Chicago, IL (USA)

DO NOT BE AFRAID OF WHAT PEOPLE THINK OF ME? Be true to yourself, rather than trying to be what others want you to be. – Martin Mulcahy

Chicago IL (USA)

Take your time, it all works out in the end. Study early so you can rest later. – Dale

Rancho Mirage, CA (USA)

Have patience and don't believe everything you hear. – Kalvin

Cathedral City, CA (USA)

Like yourself. – Ron

―――――――∇―――――――

Cathedral City, CA ((USA)

I would advise myself not to be so distracted from your career by the gay life, as a youngster. I think that if I'd really concentrated on my theater and my work, and less of the gay sleeping with and looking for the next one, for the parties and things. Had I concentrated more I think I would have made a fairly good actor. I think that's why I ended up making wigs. – Bob Brown

―――――――∇―――――――

Cathedral City, CA (USA)

Go for quality over quantity and take all your other experiences when you need them, tricks, whatever, in the bushes and the bathhouses, don't take them seriously. I didn't. It still boils down to its not necessarily a bad thing to live alone and make it on your own. You don't have to have someone, but when it's time, quality over quantity. – Hal

―――――――∇―――――――

Palm Springs, CA (USA)

I always wished I had learned morals. I think parents teach their daughters' morals, I don't think they teach their gay sons morals. I grew up in a time when everyone was promiscuous, and I thought that every time you went out you were supposed to have sex every night. I wished that I had known better. – Laurie Cowell

―――――――∇―――――――

Palm Springs, CA (USA)

Live out your fantasies. It doesn't matter what anybody else has to say because their opinion doesn't matter. Live your life on your own terms the way you want and do as much as you can. – Keith Kollinicos aka Missa Distic

If You Could Give One Piece of Advice to Your Younger Self?

—————∇—————

Palm Springs, CA (USA)

If I could go back in time and talk to myself, it would be a long conversation, but the main point I would have to get across to my younger self would be life is too short and you have to do as much as you possibly can. I would have to say, "Don't worry about what's happening over there, because those people, they don't matter in the long run." I grew up being too worried about what other people thought but that's how I was raised. So, I would try to change that part of myself and not have to worry about what those people are thinking. I've wasted too many years of my life, I would have come-out sooner. I waited until I was 24 to have sex with another man. Full-blown sex, not just fooling around touching, that's not sex. I waited too long to come out and start living my life, to make me happy. I should have done it so much sooner. I would have been a much happier kid. – David Vega aka Lucifers Axe

—————∇—————

Cathedral City, CA (USA)

I have no regrets. If I had to verbalize, I'd just say, "Be fearless." – Simeon Den

—————∇—————

Palm Springs, CA (USA)

Follow your heart and don't care what other people think. – Helen Macfarlane

—————∇—————

Mokena, IL (USA)

Two pieces: It's okay to be gay. You're going to be all right. – Mark Zubro

—————∇—————

Chicago, IL

I guess like the Liza Minnelli song ... that it truly is a quiet thing. I always thought that there would be one great event or some classic moment, that I'd reach this certain age ... and boom! ... I'd feel whole – have a true and complete sense of myself. But really, it's just time and experience. We step forward and then step back ... we react with confidence one moment and fear and worry the next. It's ever changing, always a fight of some sort – the journey to self-acceptance never really ends. It definitely gets easier as age takes hold and less fucks are given on a daily basis, but it's never perfect. If I would have known that a bit sooner, I think it would have been a bit easier for me – maybe I would have relaxed and just "let it be" a bit more. It would have been nice to have felt a little more contentment in my younger days, less of a struggle. – Brian Kirst

—————∇—————

The Entrance, NSW (Australia)

The best piece of advise I would have given to myself (in hindsight) would be, to not be so quick to "come out" until you have an understanding of homophobia, religious beliefs and how badly people can respond. I doubt the advise would have changed the outcome, but it might have made it less devastating and hurtful for me to know what to possibly expect. Unfortunately, that was a very harsh lesson I got all in one day. – Ian Davies

—————∇—————

North Carolina (USA)

NEVER EVER EVER say No when you mean Yes! – Gavin Geoffrey Dillard

—————∇—————

Palm Springs, CA (USA)

Just do it. Go with your gut, don't be afraid of people pointing at you or making fun of you. I wish I could have been more out in the beginning. It was easier to say, "I'm bisexual." More accepted. Men would always say,

"What a waste." A waste for who? Coming out in the 1960s there weren't a lot of people who supported us, except our little groups, now the world is supporting us. – Siouxzan Perry

———————▽———————

Chicago, IL (USA)

I'd say: "Expose yourself to the world and find your tribe as soon as you can. As soon as you graduate from college, GO TEACH ENGLISH OVERSEAS … STAY THERE and forget your parasitic family and fucked up country! But don't live anywhere where people think "white" is a race!" – Chip H

———————▽———————

Chicago, IL (USA)

Don't try so hard; just be you. I always worried I wasn't good enough, attractive enough, talented enough, etc. But in the end, it's all worked out just fine. I'm happier in my life than I ever thought possible. – Yvonne Zipter

———————▽———————

Palm Springs, CA (USA)

Be yourself, don't be afraid. Don't worry about what other people say. – Marc

———————▽———————

Palm Springs, CA (USA)

Observe and listen. Be true to yourself. – Gib Maudey

———————▽———————

Cathedral City, CA (USA)

Be easier on yourself. Let things happen as they happen. Don't fight it. – Cody

If You Could Give One Piece of Advice to Your Younger Self?

————▽————

Cathedral City, CA (USA)

Love yourself. – Bart

————▽————

Abingdon-on-Thames (UK)

I came out quite late. I feel I should have come out about 10 years before I did and not be scared. I didn't know any other gay people. I was the only gay person I knew. It was only when I started meeting other people that I realized that I could come out. But I would have liked to come out earlier but then I would have been at greater risk from HIV because there was less knowledge at that time. My coming out was at the knowledge time of that – when they knew how it was transmitted and what to avoid, condoms and all that sort of thing. Ten years before that, that wasn't known at all. – Martin

————▽————

Cathedral City, CA (USA)

Buy Apple. – Michael Wayne

————▽————

Fort Lauderdale, FL (USA)

The "it gets better" line comes to mind. Yes, it gets better, but it can take a long time. Be patient, be kind to others, and don't forget to be kind to yourself. – Gregg Shapiro

————▽————

Palm Springs, CA (USA)

Do not waste time thinking whether you should or not. Just do it, because life is too short and a couple of blinks and you're 70. I'm 67, but it's gone fast. Some time I have wasted my life thinking if I should do something or not. Now I realize it's not about that, it's about who you are and how you approach anything that comes into your path. – Juan-manuel Alonso

————▽————

Palm Springs, CA USA)

Live out loud and live proud, earlier and sooner. Live out loud, be who you are, and don't let others get you down. If you feel queer, then you are queer. That's it. I'm gonna go with it the next time I come around. If I happen to be a gay that time, I'm coming out soon. Come out of the womb with my little top hat and stick ... who knows? – Jade

————▽————

Chicago, IL (USA)

Take more chances. Learn a trade you can actually make a living at, and don't settle for less than you're worth. That, and get as far away from your family as humanly possible. – Xavier Bathsheba-Negron

————▽————

Cathedral City, CA (USA)

Stop thinking you're going to die this year. – Bambi

————▽————

Cathedral City, CA (USA)

Just keep moving forward and not to let the bad things weigh you down. Not lose hope, but I lost hope quite a bit throughout my transition. That would probably be the biggest thing, not to lose hope. – Hayley

————▽————

Cathedral City, CA (USA)

Have the courage to accept who you are and not be afraid of what people are

going to think. At the end of the day you're always living with your own self. To make yourself happy, to be who you are was more meaningful in my life than anything I ever tried to pursue before that. – Chloe DeCamp

————————▽————————

Palm Springs, CA (USA)

Be yourself. Don't be intimidated by your parents, don't be intimidated by your friends. If you love somebody, love somebody. You can't help who you fall in love with – risk it all! Risk it all! I was willing to live a life that did not have love in it, if my children – I have three children, and four grandchildren – if my children didn't accept the fact that I was openly gay, and accept my girlfriend, I would have lead a life that was loveless. I would tell myself be true to your heart because I think that I probably would have had a woman a lot sooner in my life. I can remember being in a shelter for battered women and it was run by lesbians. I remember this woman, a tall drink of water. I remember helping her move, and I fell on a mattress and she went to kiss me, and I said, "Oh! No! No! Strictly dickly here." I look back and think, "Wow, she liked me." So I would tell people be true to yourself. I would rather have one moment of happiness than a lifetime of being unhappy. I spent a lot of years unhappy because I thought that I was supposed to love a man. – Cathy Melton

————————▽————————

Palm Springs, CA (USA)

Listen to your heart and don't be affected by outside noise and outside "rules." I did try to conform for some time, but I'm just not a conformer. I'm OK with that. Being a butch lesbian, being a gender non-conforming lesbian, being a lesbian who has worked in blue collar work most of her life, I have found it most genuine when I have followed my own heart. Being a woman loving woman first. Being clean and sober. Having a career working with animals. Something else that has been near and dear to my heart, always since I could remember. Ever since I was a little kid I've had a sixth sense with animals. The natural world is my thing. It took me a long loopy way to get back to my center and I lost my center when I was drinking and using but sobriety certainly gave that back to me. I reclaimed what was my spiritual center. Because my spiritual center means so much to me. Not everybody knows what their center is. Not everyone knows what they want to do for a living. I think if I could talk to my younger self I would say, "Trust yourself and don't be influenced by pressures. Maybe you can avoid the drugs and alcohol." – Leslie Tisdale

——————▽——————

Cathedral City, CA (USA)

Don't wait. I waited. Explore your emotions, explore your desires. Find somebody who will help you with that. – Paul

——————▽——————

Glenview, IL (USA)

If I could give advice to my younger self, it would be to never give up. If you allow yourself to be immersed in self-pity, you will have nothing but darkness. Pull back momentarily and get out of yourself (or to put it more directly, get yourself out of your head). Go to a movie, attend social events, see a play, exercise. The answers to your question will come, if you are patient and allow the world to direct you where to go. Simply notice where you are in the world and you will see the signs that will give you a direction. It's simpler than it looks. It's easier than it feels. The mind can create so many scenarios of darkness, but that darkness originates from fear, loneliness, and isolation.

I would dearly love to hug my younger self and show him what I became. I turned out alright and I became who I am because my younger self, in spite of his desire for suicide, never did kill himself. That night, on an impulse, he drove to the Metropolitan Community Church in Chicago. That's when his new life began and how he met his first partner. – Yehuda Jacobi

——————▽——————

Palm Springs, CA (USA)

I don't think I'd suggest a career change or anything like that. At school I was studying for a medical degree, but I switched to art and that was a wise choice. I think I should have paid more attention to who was liking me. – Jack Farquhar Halbert

——————▽——————

If You Could Give One Piece of Advice to Your Younger Self?

Palm Springs, CA (USA)

Be a little more health conscious, and don't start smoking. – James S

—————▽—————

Milwaukee, WI

Quit being so self-conscious. Nobody cares. I spent so many years worrying what other people thought. The only critic that really matters in the long run is me and I was much tougher on myself for doing nothing than for doing something poorly. – Anonymous.

—————▽—————

(USA)

I don't think there is anything substantial I could say that he would be able to hear. – David Pratt

—————▽—————

London (UK)

If you can be brave enough and not get beaten up, come out. I was way too nervous for far too long to actually acknowledge my own sexuality and so I spent my twenties alone because I couldn't deal with that. I also started to develop a drinking problem because that was my refuge. If I could go back to my college days, I'd say, "When you meet that guy, don't run away from a drink with him. Go home with him." – Tess Tickles

—————▽—————

Chicago, IL (USA)

Practice patience and forgiveness with yourself and EVERYONE. And save money now for your retirement! – Paul Mikos

—————▽—————

If You Could Give One Piece of Advice to Your Younger Self?

(UK)

Lighten up and don't worry. It'll work out. – Diesel Balaam

—————∇—————

New Orleans, LA (USA)

Be strong and be proud. – Terry Gaskins

—————∇—————

(USA)

Don't be in so much of a hurry to fall in love. – David

—————∇—————

Chicago, IL (USA)

Relax! – Anonymous

—————∇—————

Cathedral City, CA (USA)

Pay attention to the clues. The little things that you dismiss are a part of you. Try and put the puzzle together. But aren't we always doing that? Aren't we always trying to put the puzzle together with everything that happens in our lives? So, I would have said to myself in high school, "To thine own self be true. Look inside yourself." And I'd say, "You don't think it's possible to have a meaningful, loving gay relationship but you can." – OT

—————∇—————

Palm Springs, CA (USA)

Pay attention to what's going on around you, especially when it came to AIDS. – Felix

If You Could Give One Piece of Advice to Your Younger Self?

—————▽—————

Fort Lauderdale, FL (USA)

You're actually pretty cute, and you've got a killer ass! Don't be afraid to approach people. If they say no, there's someone else around the next corner. So much of my insecurity was tied up in the fact that I wasn't as good looking as the rest of my family. – Rick Karlin

—————▽—————

Palm Springs, CA (USA)

Not to pay attention to what other people say because it makes you vulnerable. – Carlos

—————▽—————

Chicago, IL (USA)

Be kind to all, and don't let what people say or do to you make you think that you are less than you are. Everyone has reason to be and to be here, and to live their life their way. Live your life to its fullest and be kind, and helpful, to others and it will all come full circle to reward you. – Dean Ogren

—————▽—————

Palm Springs, CA (USA)

Funny, I have been thinking about this a lot lately because I have come across the journal I kept from 1973 to 1985. I've begun to transcribe them and see how insecure I was and just how much energy I invested in fretting and worrying.

If there's one thing I wish I could tell my younger self, or rather slap him up the side of his head and scream in his ear is, "Why are you wasting time worrying about small insignificant stuff. Just relax and enjoy the moment. Enjoy being with the guy you're with and stop fretting. Enjoy your time with him. Enjoy hanging out and goofing around. Enjoy the sight, smell and feel of him, because before you know it, this moment will be gone and beyond your reach forever." – Ian H

OTHER BOOKS BY ...

ST SUKIE DE LA CROIX

Chicago Whispers: The History of LGBT Chicago Before Stonewall
The Blue Spong and the Flight from Mediocrity
The Memoir of a Groucho Marxist: A Very British Fairy Tale
Gay Press, Gay Power – contributor
Out of the Underground: Homosexuals, the Radical Press, and the Rise
     and Fall of the Gay Liberation Front
St Sukie's Strange Garden of Woodland Creatures – with Roy Alton Wald
Tell Me About It – with Owen Keehnen

OWEN KEEHNEN

Tell Me About It – with St Sukie de la Croix
The LGBTQ Book of Days: Revised 2019 Edition
Dugan's Bistro and the Legend of the Bearded Lady
Night Visitors
Love Underground
The Matinee Idol
Young Digby Swank
Vernita Gray: From Woodstock to the White House – with Tracy Baim
The LGBT Book of Days
Gay Press, Gay Power – contributor
The Sand Bar
We're Here, We're Queer
Jim Flint: The Boy From Peoria – with Tracy Baim
Leatherman: The Legend of Chuck Renslow – with Tracy Baim
Doorway Unto Darkness
Nothing Personal:
Chronicles of Chicago's LGBTQ Community 1977-1997 – co-editor
Rising Starz
Ultimate Starz
Out and Proud in Chicago – contributor
More Starz
Starz

www.ingramcontent.com/pod-product-compliance
Lightning Source LLC
Chambersburg PA
CBHW052031090426

42739CB00010B/1858